20/90/80

Mobilizing for Peace

MOBILIZING FOR PEACE

Conflict Resolution in Northern Ireland, Israel/Palestine, and South Africa

Edited by
BENJAMIN GIDRON
STANLEY N. KATZ
YEHESKEL HASENFELD

UNIVERSITY PRESS

2002

Oxford   New York
Auckland   Bangkok   Buenos Aires   Cape Town   Chennai
Dar es Salaam   Delhi   Hong Kong   Istanbul   Karachi   Kolkata
Kuala Lumpur   Madrid   Melbourne   Mexico City   Mumbai   Nairobi
São Paulo   Shanghai   Singapore   Taipei   Tokyo   Toronto

and an associated company in Berlin

Copyright © 2002 by Oxford University Press, Inc.

Published by Oxford University Press, Inc.
198 Madison Avenue, New York, New York 10016

www.oup.com

Oxford is a registered trademark of Oxford University Press

Library of Congress Cataloging-in-Publication Data

Mobilizing for peace : conflict resolution in Northern Ireland, Israel/Palestine, and
South Africa / edited by Benjamin Gidron, Stanley N. Katz, Yeheskel Hasenfeld.
p.   cm.
Includes bibliographical references and index.
ISBN 0-19-512592-4
1. Diplomatic negotiations in international disputes.   2. Non-governmental
organizations.   3. South Africa—Politics and government—1989–1994.   4. Arab-Israeli
conflict—1973–1993.   5. Northern Ireland—Politics and government—1969–1994.   I.
Gidron, Benjamin.   II. Katz, Stanley Nider.   III. Hasenfeld, Yeheskel.
JZ6045 .R47   2002
303.6'9—dc21   2001050017

9 8 7 6 5 4 3 2 1

Printed in the United States of America
on acid-free paper

To the activists, members, and volunteers of the peace/conflict-resolution organizations we studied. Through their courage and determination to "swim against the tide" during dire times, they have demonstrated the importance of organized citizens' action in changing the course of history from war to peace.

PREFACE

This book is a culmination of a large comparative research project entitled "Peace/Conflict-Resolution Organizations in Northern Ireland, South Africa, and Israel/Palestine." The academic interest in international conflicts, in general, and in these three specific conflicts, in particular, has resulted in hundreds of publications, only a few of which deal with all three conflicts from a comparative perspective.[1] The interest in these conflicts—and the temptation to compare them—stems in part from the fact that during the early 1990s the conflicting parties in all three of these regions appeared to be progressing toward a resolution, or at least toward a negotiated rather than a violent mode of operation. This was part of our rationale in choosing these conflicts for our comparative study.

There were several additional factors that motivated us to initiate this project. In addition to our own personal interests in and commitments to world peace and the resolution of violent conflicts, we are academically involved in third/nonprofit-sector study at the international level—in fact, we actually met through our involvement in the International Society for Third Sector Research (ISTR). Thus, this book (and the project leading up to it) combines many of our interests: it examines citizens' groups and associations within the third sector that were organized in order to promote peace and/or resolve conflict by means other than violence. At a fairly early point in the project, we recruited Professor Yeheskel Hasenfeld to assist us in refining the methodology of the project, and he soon became our full partner in helping us to complete the book.

In this project, we have intersected two traditionally separate fields of study—namely, the third sector, and peace processes and conflict resolution—leading us to explore new and uncharted paths. In terms of the third sector,

1. See, for example, H. Giliomee and J. Gagiano, eds., *The Elusive Search for Peace* (Cape Town, South Africa: Oxford University Press, 1990), and C. Knox and P. Quirk, *Peace Building in Northern Ireland, Israel and South Africa* (New York: St. Martin's, 2000).

we opted to focus on a specific category of organizations in a substantive area of social action (in this case, the peaceful resolution of conflict). With regard to peace processes, we emphasized peace and conflict-resolution organizations and their roles in facilitating a change in the resolution of a violent conflict. Later in the project, we also included insights from the literature on social movements. In addition, we had to formulate a comparative framework that would guide our data collection and enable us to analyze the similarities and differences among the organizations in the three regions without eroding their distinct contexts.

Thus, we were faced with the challenge of finding creative solutions to complex substantive and methodological problems without the benefit of prior studies dealing with similar projects. In particular, we needed, on the one hand, to spell out a conceptual model and a set of variables that could be used to compare and explain the organizational attributes and behavior of these peace- and conflict-resolution organizations. On the other hand, we wanted to make sure that this conceptual model would not mute the distinct narratives of these organizations within the unique national contexts in which they existed. In the chapters that follow, we detail the various strategies and specific methods we employed to respond to these challenges. The balance we tried to achieve is manifest in both the comparative chapters and each country chapter.

This study involved many individuals, who provided their own unique contributions without which this book would not have been possible. Local teams in each region carried out the empirical aspects of the study. We chose these teams through an international "call for proposals" at the outset of the study. Each team was headed by a leader: Seamus Dunn in Northern Ireland, Manuel Hassassian in Palestine, Tamar Hermann in Israel, and Rupert Taylor in South Africa. We are greatly indebted to them and their respective team members for their deeply informed insight and careful research into the local realities surrounding the three conflicts. These local perspectives were absolutely crucial in formulating the research tools used in the study and providing the data necessary for an international comparison. We are also grateful to both the leaders and the entire country teams for helping us to develop and refine the intellectual structure of the project. Most of all, we want to thank the leaders and staff of the numerous organizations included in this study. Their willingness to give us access to their organizations and records, and to provide us with the necessary data, made this study possible.

We also recruited a distinguished International Advisory Board whose wisdom benefited the project tremendously. The Board members included: Helmut Anheier (Germany/U.S.A.), Mussa Budeiri (Palestine), Galia Golan (Israel), Adrian Guelke (Northern Ireland/South Africa), Virginia Hodgkinson (U.S.A.), Wilmot James (South Africa), Quintin Oliver (Northern Ireland), and Dirk Rumberg. Individually, each member offered expertise in one or more areas of the study—that is, in one of the three conflicts, the third/nonprofit sector, or the processes of conflict resolution; collectively, they helped us conceptualize and smooth many of the rough edges of the study.

We are especially indebted to The Atlantic Philanthropies, the funder of this study, which showed vision and courage in supporting us in this project. The funds were channeled through the Nonprofit Research Fund of the Aspen Institute, which acted as much more than a fiscal agent. Under the leadership of both Elizabeth Boris and Alan Abramson, the Institute showed a keen interest in the study throughout its duration.

We also were blessed with excellent research support staff who helped us carry out different aspects of the project and book; these included Jonathan Crane, Megan Meyer, Raviv Schwartz, and Simon Stacey. Megan's systematic and comparative content analysis of the case studies and her dissertation greatly enhanced our comparative analysis. Last but definitely not least we want to thank our editor, Rena Hasenfeld, who made a tremendous contribution by turning the different chapters, written by various individuals, into one coherent whole.

Benjamin Gidron
Stanley N. Katz

CONTENTS

CONTRIBUTORS

Feargal Cochrane
   Department of Politics and International Relations, Lancaster University,
   Lancaster, United Kingdom
Seamus Dunn
   Centre for the Study of Conflict, University of Coleraine, Northern Ireland,
   United Kingdom
Benjamin Gidron
   Israeli Center for Third Sector Research, Ben Gurion University of the
   Negev, Beer-Sheva, Israel
Yeheskel Hasenfeld
   Department of Social Welfare, School of Public Policy and Social Research,
   University of California, Los Angeles, Los Angeles, California
Manuel Hassassian
   Bethlehem University, Bethlehem, Palestine
Tamar Hermann
   Tami Steinmetz Center for Peace Research, Tel Aviv University, Ramat
   Aviv, Israel
Stanley N. Katz
   Woodrow Wilson School of Public and International Affairs, Princeton
   University, Princeton, New Jersey
Megan Meyer
   School of Social Work, University of Maryland
Rupert Taylor
   Department of Political Studies, University of Witwatersrand, Johannes-
   burg, South Africa

Part I

Introduction, Theoretical Approach, and Methodology

1

INTRODUCTION

The place and role of nongovernmental organizations (NGOs) dedicated to the promotion of peace and the resolution of intractable social conflicts is a newly emerging field of study to which we aim to make a contribution with this book. We hope to add to existing empirical studies—especially those from a comparative perspective—that inform us about the nature of these organizations, their accomplishments, and how the various social systems in which they operate influence their functions and structures.

We chose to study organizations that were trying to promote peace, reconciliation, and coexistence between peoples in societies that have known fighting and bloodshed for many years. The impetus for the study arose when significant breakthroughs in three major violent international conflicts occurred: the first cease-fire between the Protestant and Catholic paramilitaries in Northern Ireland (1993), the unbanning of the ANC that led to the first democratic elections in South Africa (1994), and the Oslo Accords between Israel and the Palestine Liberation Organization (PLO; 1993). In all three regions these historic agreements were preceded by intense activity from nongovernmental/civil society groups and organizations, which advocated for peace, reconciliation, and resolution of the conflicts through nonviolent means, primarily during the 1980s. Some of these groups, such as Peace Now in Israel, Black Sash in South Africa, and The Peace People in Northern Ireland, often gained the attention of the international press; the founders of The Peace People, Mairead Corrigan and Betty Williams, won the Nobel Peace Prize in 1976. In all three locations, we quickly discovered that these more famous organizations were at the forefront of a broader phenomenon that included a wide range of groups, which we termed "peace and conflict-resolution organizations" (P/CROs). These third sector/civil society organizations, many of which were initiated and managed by concerned citizens, shared the same general goal of promoting peace and an end to the violence but found different organizational means to express this objective.

It did not take long for us, working with our in-country research partners, to discover that we were on to something. In each of the three regions, we discovered evidence of what one P/CRO leader called "magic moments." Syl

3

Slabbert, one of the founders of Idasa in South Africa, noted that "For an NGO to be successful [it] needs a magic moment, otherwise it just dies." Slabbert went on to observe that "the Dakar meeting was our magic moment." He was referring to the fact that the Dakar Conference (held in Dakar, Senegal, in July 1987) organized by Idasa, brought together for the first time leading "white" intellectuals and politicians (mainly Afrikaner), and key African National Congress members "to begin the process of demystifying an organization which by the nature of its considerable support . . . was destined to play a major role in negotiations towards a non-racial, democratic South Africa."

A similar magic moment occurred in Israel with the origins of the important P/CRO, Peace Now. The specific event that encouraged the emergence of Peace Now was the impending journey of Prime Minister Menachim Begin to Washington to present President Jimmy Carter with a plan for future negotiations, which Begin considered to be potentially acceptable to the Egyptians. The trip came after several months in which no progress in the negotiations was achieved. A letter of protest to the Israeli Prime Minister was written by a group of 348 young Israeli IDF reserve officers. The letter indicated their dissatisfaction with his policies, mainly with his positions on the question of a territorial compromise in return for peace with Egypt. They hoped that the letter would reflect their apprehension that this policy and the ongoing occupation of the Territories might severely damage the Israeli national interest and the democratic nature of the country. The letter, later known as the Officers Letter, implied that if the prime minister did not respond to their demands the signers would "question the justification of Israel's way." The letter received unexpected public and media attention and support, and served as the basis for the establishment of Peace Now and the new peace movement.

Something similar came about in Northern Island with the creation of a P/CRO named Peace Train. The idea to operate a Peace Train was in direct response to persistent and sustained attacks on the cross-border rails service by terrorist groups and in particular the IRA. These attacks were having a significant detrimental impact not only on railway operations but also on the whole economic and social fabric of the province, and were costing jobs. At its worst, in one year alone (1988) cross-border rail services were disrupted on 172 days during which time passengers had to be conveyed by bus for all or part of their journey. There was a gut feeling that destroying one of the major cultural, social, and economic links between Dublin and Belfast, the two capitals of the island, was wrong. There was something inherently appalling about that, and the issue needed to be addressed. The group which was regularly blowing up the line and putting passengers' lives at risk was the IRA, so it was necessary to confront them.

The Peace Train concept was initially an idea developed by a group of individuals who regularly used the Belfast-to-Dublin rail service. This group comprised prominent business people, politicians, academics, and trades-union officials from both sides of the border. A Peace Train committee was established in 1989. Mr. Sam McAughtry, a well-known broadcaster from a Protestant unionist background, chaired the committee. Sam, who is currently an Irish Senator, was chosen because he was regarded as someone who worked extensively in both the north and south of Ireland and having no party affiliations was considered to be without "political baggage."

Some of the full range of P/CROs we studied were advocacy organizations that attempted to influence public opinion—and policymakers indirectly—in order to change policies regarding the conflict. For example, the End Conscription Campaign (ECC) in South Africa engaged in a national campaign against drafting South African whites into the military, and the Council on Peace and Security in Israel, which was composed of high-ranking veteran officers, engaged in lobbying and public speaking. Other P/CROs were professionally based organizations, such as Lawyers for Human Rights in South Africa, Physicians for Human Rights in Israel, or the Northern Ireland Council for Integrated Education. These groups approached the conflict and its toll from their professional perspectives, raising awareness of its costs (in terms of human rights, public health, education, etc.) but also providing services to those who were denied them because of the conflict. Some of the P/CROs focused on reaching out to the "enemy," such as Women Together in Northern Ireland, Bridge to Peace in Israel, the Jerusalem Center for Women in Palestine, and the South African Institute of Race Relations. Such organizations created opportunities for human dialogue and joint ventures on an equal basis, thus demonstrating that a different paradigm for relations with the "other side" was possible. Still other organizations were engaged in consciousness-raising, focusing on changing attitudes regarding the conflict. These included organizations such as the South African Catholic Bishops' Conference, the Justice and Peace Commission in South Africa, the Peace Train in Northern Ireland, and Rabbis for Human Rights in Israel. Finally, other P/CROs were research institutions or "think tanks" that produced studies on various parameters of the conflict. These included organizations such as the Institute for a Democratic Alternative for South Africa (Idasa), the Tami Steinmetz Center for Peace Research in Israel, and the Centre for the Study of the Conflict in Northern Ireland.

We could not overlook the possibility that a relationship existed between the breakthroughs in the three conflicts and the P/CRO activity that preceded them. It was very intriguing to us that these groups and organizations, which at the time represented a dissenting view from the national consensus on how to deal with the "other side," might have played a role—even if modest—in the three historic breakthroughs. Also of interest was the nature of these organizations in the different locales and the question of whether they shared certain common features, across countries and conflicts. In studying these organizations, could we learn any lessons that could be applied to other countries beset by protracted conflicts?

In selecting the regions for our study we were mindful of similar conflicts in other parts of the world. Rwanda, Bosnia, Chechnya, and Afghanistan stand out as sites where violent conflicts have taken a terrible toll in terms of human lives and misery. In addition, the unresolved conflicts in Cyprus and Kashmir are potential powder kegs ready to explode at any time. Nonetheless, we recognized early in our research that P/CROs require at least a rudimentary foundation of democratic institutional and legal infrastructures, which were absent in many of these other regions. Moreover, this infrastructure must include an institutional capacity to promote civil society through the formation of voluntary associations. Given these criteria, we chose Israel/Palestine, Northern Ireland, and South Africa for our study.

In approaching a comparative study of P/CROs, we identified three different levels on which to base our analysis: substance, form, and a comparison of the P/CROs. Concerning *substance*, recent literature on international conflict resolution emphasizes "Track II Diplomacy," which focuses on the roles actors outside of the government play in resolving conflicts. Thus, in all three regions we were concerned with the possible contribution these groups had made to the historic decisions to "change courses" in terms of dealing with the conflict, preferring peace and reconciliation to military force. With regard to *form*, these groups and organizations operated at a time when the third sector/civil society was experiencing tremendous expansion and growth in most societies and in practically all fields of activity. Since the P/CROs were part of that sector, we were interested in the unique characteristics that enabled them to participate in this expansion. Finally, we were interested in *comparing* these groups since they operated to further the same general goals during the same approximate time period, but nevertheless were involved in different conflicts and existed within different social and political contexts. Thus, we were interested in determining factors that could explain both the similarities and the differences in their characteristics.

Specifically, in this book, we (1) portray the organizational characteristics of peace/conflict-resolution organizations; (2) explore the methods they used to achieve their goals within the political and societal contexts in which they existed; (3) compare the organizations across regions and conflicts; and (4) assess the P/CROs' contributions to society and to peace (and/or the resolution of conflict) in their respective regions, and specifically to the historical breakthroughs in the three conflicts.

Protracted Conflict and War

The second half of the twentieth century can be characterized as one of conflict and war. Since 1945, over 150 armed conflicts have claimed an estimated 25 to 30 million human lives, not including the effects of famine and disease, and humanity has experienced only twenty-six days without war.[1] Social conflicts, whether based on ethnicity, religion, economics, or territorial differences, are endemic to human life[2] and range from disputes between individuals, organizations, and groups to international warfare and genocide. In some ways, social conflicts are necessary for the stability of a democratic society.[3] Oppressed groups create situations of conflict to spark social change.[4] Yet, social conflict can be dangerous in that when it turns violent, there is a chance that a cycle of violence will persist, sometimes for generations and even centuries, resulting in many victims, including innocent people who are not party to the actual conflict, and causing irreparable damage to society.

This is especially true in societies that experience *intractable* conflicts, where the price that both individuals and society pay is very high. Bar-Tal has summarized the nature of such conflicts as: (1) protracted—they last a long time; the parties to the conflict accumulate hatred and prejudice; (2) perceived as irreconcilable—the parties involved view their goals as radically opposite; neither side sees the possibility of making concessions; they expect the conflict to last indefinitely; (3) continual—the parties to the conflict have an interest in its continuation and make vast military, economic, and psychological investments that later impede its resolution; having vested interests in the conflict makes it difficult to change beliefs and behaviors; (4) violent—wars and terrorist attacks wound or kill soldiers and civilians, property is destroyed; they often create refugee problems and atrocities; (5) zero-sum in nature—the parties involved perceive any loss suffered by the other side as their gain and vice versa; (6) total—they are perceived as being about needs or values that are absolutely essential for the parties' existence and/or survival; (7) central—members of a society involved in such conflicts are preoccupied constantly and continuously with it; this centrality is reflected by the fact that the conflict preoccupies the cognitive repertoire of individuals, as well as by its saliency on the public agenda.[5] As is shown in later chapters, all three regions examined in this study experienced such consequences from the intractable/protracted conflicts in which they were engaged.

The Role of Peace/Conflict-Resolution Organizations in Ending Violent Conflicts

The need for effective conflict-resolution strategies has increased since the end of the cold war with the emergence of numerous regional and subregional conflicts around the world. Scholars expect that the number of conflicts will increase along with rapid population growth, expanding environmental degradation, increasing income discrepancies between countries, immigration and migration processes, and the proliferation of conventional, nuclear, and chemical weapons.[6]

The transition from violent conflict to negotiation and the creation of a new type of relationship are complex and occur on several levels and in different phases. First, the political leadership must decide to pursue an alternative path to the existing violent one. Such a decision is rarely made without the support of important political constituencies, which often express themselves through public opinion favoring a resolution of the conflict. This support does not happen instantly but usually comes after the issue has been brought up, fought for, and deliberated in various forums, including NGOs dedicated to the cause of peace and conflict resolution. After the political decision to "change course" has been made and implemented, actual arrangements have to be created to accommodate the changes resulting from the new reality. For example, after the decision was made in 1994 to hold democratic elections in South Africa, the population needed to be prepared to vote since it never had participated in such elections. This also was true for the referendum in Northern Ireland that followed the Good Friday Agreement (1998) and the elections for the Palestinian legislature (1995)—mechanisms unknown to the populations involved. It also is the case for other institutions that are now being created. Finally, a peace agreement can endure only if a new type of relationship is developed between the conflicting parties and new social and economic institutions—based on values that reflect the new reality—are created.

Galtung uses the concepts of "peace-building," "peace-making," and "peace-keeping" to depict these different phases and levels.[7] In pursuing peace—which includes all of these elements—institutions in the public sector, headed by the official leadership of the country, typically play certain roles; the business sector can and often does play other roles; and organizations belonging to the nongovernmental/nonprofit/third sectors play yet other roles. This division of labor is based on the sectors' differential characteristics and mandates, yet it is important to stress that all three types of organizations can be involved in all three phases or levels of the conflict-resolution process. Thus, for example, while peace-making usually is considered to be within the public sector domain, both the business and the third sectors can have a role in pressuring the official leadership to make the appropriate political decisions. A case in point is the resolution of the conflict in South Africa, where economic boycotts of the country in the 1980s led the business community to withdraw its support from the political leadership advocating apartheid and in turn to support de Klerk's policy of ending the racist regime. Furthermore, the Institute for a Democratic Alternative for South Africa (Idasa), a nonprofit organization, initiated and organized the 1987 Dakar meeting that brought together for the first time leading "white" intellectuals and politicians (mainly Afrikaner), and key ANC officials.

Scholars and policymakers increasingly recognize the importance of the third sector, especially in peace-building and peace-keeping. The Carnegie Commission on Preventing Deadly Conflict states:

Three broad categories of NGOs offer especially important potential contributions to the prevention of deadly conflict: human rights and other advocacy groups; humanitarian and development organizations; and the small but growing number of "Track Two" groups that help open the way to more formal internal or international peace processes. Human rights, Track Two, and grassroots development organizations all provide early warning of rising local tension and help open or protect the necessary political space between groups and the government that can allow local leaders to settle differences peacefully. . . . Some NGOs have an explicit focus on conflict prevention and resolution. They may: monitor conflicts and provide early warning and insight into a particular conflict; convene the adversarial parties (providing a neutral forum); pave the way for mediation and undertake mediation; carry out education and training for conflict resolution, building an indigenous capacity for coping with ongoing conflicts; help to strengthen institutions for conflict resolution; foster development of the rule of law; help to establish a free press with responsible reporting on conflict; assist in planning and implementing elections; and provide technical assistance on democratic arrangements that reduce the likelihood of violence in divided societies.[8]

Similarly, there is a growing body of research—mostly from a social-movement perspective—on these types of organizations, especially regarding how they arise, organize, and the strategies they use to promote peace and institutionalize democratic institutions.[9] More generally, Seymour Lipset has argued that NGOs, which constitute civil society, are fundamental to a stable democracy.[10] As he puts it, "Organizations stimulate interests and activities in the larger polity; they can be consulted by political institutions about projects that affect them and their members, and they can transfer this information to the citizenry. Civil organizations reduce resistance to unanticipated changes because they prevent the isolation of political institutions from the polity and can smooth over, or at least recognize, interest differences early on."[11] As we shall see, the P/CROs in this study did indeed fulfill such a role.

In all three regions, third-sector organizations did not become involved in the promotion of peace during the 1980s or even during the preceding decade; rather, they had a history that in some cases dated back to the 1920s. For example, the South African Institute of Race Relations (SAIRR) was founded in 1929 and Black Sash in 1955. In Israel, the first peace organization—the Peace Covenant (Brit Shalom)—was founded in Jerusalem in the mid-1920s. Only in Northern Ireland and Palestine did peace organizations specifically dedicated to bridging the two communities emerge primarily during the 1970s. Furthermore, individuals and organizations dedicated to peace in other parts of the world and around different conflicts (e.g., Gandhi, Martin Luther King Jr.) served as examples for and inspired many of these organizations.

In all three regions, the initial efforts to mobilize for peace and conflict resolution had humble beginnings, usually precipitated by a critical political event. In Israel, the Movement for Peace and Security was organized shortly after the 1967 War to warn about the threat the occupation posed to Israeli democratic institutions, a theme that later peace organizations utilized. A similar organization, Strength and Peace (Oz Ve'Shalom), offered a religious rationale for the need for peace. In Palestine, several peace organizations, such as the Alternative Information Center, rose in tandem with the Israeli peace movement. In Northern Ireland, the outbreak of violence in the late 1960s served as an impetus for the rise of such organizations as the Northern Ireland Civil Rights Association and the Peace People. Likewise, in South Africa, the increasing repression of the apartheid regime provided the impetus for the formation of peace organizations: Black Sash was formed in reaction to the 1956 Senate Act, and the End Conscription Campaign emerged in response to the increasing use of the military to repress dissent.

These initial and very modest attempts at changing the reality and course of the conflict through mobilization for peace were carried out by a very small number of individuals and groups in all three regions; their work was sporadic and isolated so that few people were even aware of or affected by it. This reality changed during the 1980s and 1990s. First, as has been mentioned previously, there was a multitude of groups and organizations—reflecting a variety of ideologies and strategies—that advocated an end to the violent conflicts. Second, at times (mostly during demonstrations) some of these organizations were able to mobilize tens and even hundreds of thousands of supporters, receiving ample media coverage. Third, some of them were able to attract significant funds to carry out their mission. Indeed, as noted in subsequent chapters, many of the key organizations became professionalized, developing permanent and stable organizational features to accomplish their work. Moreover, over time an identifiable network of peace/conflict-resolution organizations emerged in each region. In this book we focus on these networks and the key organizations within them.

Peace and Conflict-Resolution Organizations and Civil Society

The development of a network of peace and conflict-resolution organizations must be viewed in the broader growth of the development and expansion of civil society in the three regions. Indeed, it is fair to say that the maturation of civil society was a prerequisite for the institutionalization of the peace and conflict-resolution organizations. One of the important characteristics of democratic societies is the existence of organizations that are neither public (created by law or official regulation) nor commercial (with a profit orientation). These organizations, which have different names in different countries (i.e., voluntary organizations, NGOs, nonprofit organizations) reflect a fundamental freedom in democratic societies—the freedom of association. The number and roles of these organizations vary in different countries, but for the last two decades their numbers have increased dramatically in practically all countries of the world. Furthermore, they have become active in new fields of activity and thus have taken on new roles and responsibilities; hence their importance has increased significantly, as well.

The expansion of civil society, or the third sector, and its constituent organizations has spawned considerable research both within and between countries. The comparative perspective has been particularly instrumental in identifying and understanding the common features of civil society across countries.[12] Most important, it also has shown how societal factors—such as the role of the central government, the attributes of the legal system, and the class structure—influence the formation, size, and characteristics of civil society. Still, most of the research on civil society has focused on service organizations in such fields as health, culture and education, and the environment. Organizations dedicated to the resolution of intractable societal conflicts have received less attention. By undertaking a comparative study of peace and conflict-resolution organizations, we aim to broaden the intellectual boundaries of the field, both by studying this particular set of organizations, which typically has not been included in studies of civil society, and by doing so from a comparative perspective.

Although "peace and conflict-resolution organizations" is admittedly a social construct (as are other third-sector categories), it is important to recognize that the term signifies actual organizations that have expended considerable resources—human, fiscal, social, and political—to advance the cause of peace. In all three regions, many of the organizations we categorized as P/CROs did in fact view themselves as part of the peace "camp" or "network"; there were directories that listed them, and often they coordinated activities around issues of mutual concern. This does not imply that these organizations had only cooperative interrelationships; in fact, as we show, some of them were in stiff competition with each other. While the category of P/CRO was essential to the organization of this study, we believe that it also has important theoretical and empirical implications beyond the actual organizations we studied. The category stands for an important class of voluntary associations that are committed to addressing and resolving intractable social conflicts, whether ethnic, religious, geographic, or class. As noted in our study, we believe that this class of organizations shares some common characteristics. Moreover, an analytic model can be developed to explain their development, goals, structure, and strategies across societies, as we have done in our own study. Therefore, this category of organizations merits closer attention as an essential feature of civil society.

An international comparative study always presents difficult methodological problems for the researcher. The ways in which we dealt with these are outlined in the next chapter. However, a comparative study of third-sector organizations engaged in the peace and conflict-resolution work differs from studies of other organizations that deal with mental retardation or cancer, for example. For these latter organizations, the substantive issue around which they are formed—whether they are service provision or advocacy organizations—has a clear and accepted definition.

This is not the case for peace and conflict-resolution organizations because "peace" is differentially defined in different conflicts and sometimes by those on differing sides of the conflict, as well. The history and nature of the specific conflicts created different definitions of "peace" in the three regions we studied. Thus, for example, in South Africa, where a racial regime was in power, the goal of the organizations was not only to end the violence but also to achieve *peace with justice* or end the apartheid regime. These organizations differed from the ANC guerillas, who fought for the same end but used violence as a tactic. In Israel/Palestine, where two peoples claimed the same piece of land, but where one occupied the land leaving the other without any political rights, the P/CROs' goal was to create a situation of *mutual recognition* that could lead to practical peaceful solutions. In Northern Ireland, where two ethnic/religious groups claimed that the same piece of land belonged to different sovereign states, the P/CROs aimed to find a creative solution that would enable the two communities to end the violence and coexist and the society as a whole to develop.

In studying this complex phenomenon, it soon became clear that certain characteristics of the P/CROs would be lost if we maintained only an international comparative focus. On the other hand, using a comparative approach enabled us to focus on certain distinct dimensions of the phenomenon, which elicited some surprising and important findings. Therefore, we decided to structure the study around a dual focus: local in-depth analysis of the P/CROs and an international comparison of the P/CROs across regions (see chapter 2).

Structure of This Book

This book consists of five parts. Part I includes two chapters that provide an introduction to the International Study of Peace/Conflict-Resolution Organizations, review existing literature, and outline the study's conceptual and methodological framework. Part II comprises one chapter that discusses the histories of the three conflicts and suggests some similarities and differences among them. Part III has four chapters that summarize the data from the individual team studies in South Africa, Northern Ireland, Israel, and Palestine. Part IV contains two chapters that present a comparative analysis. The book concludes with an appraisal of the study.

Notes

1. H. Miall, *The Peacemakers* (New York: St. Martin's, 1992), p. 9.

2. Ibid.; T. Saaty and J. Alexander, *Conflict Resolution* (New York: Praeger, 1989); A. Oberschall, "Theories of Social Conflict," *Annual Review of Sociology* 4 (1978): 291–315.

3. H. Bash, "Social Movements and Social Problems: Toward a Conceptual Rapprochement," *Research in Social Movements, Conflict and Change* 17 (1994): 247–284; R. Pong, "Social Problems as a Conflict Process," *Perspectives on Social Problems* 1 (1989): 59–76.

4. C. Grosser and J. Mondros, "Pluralism and Participation: The Political Action Approach," in *Theory and Practice of Community Social Work*, ed. S. Taylor and R. Roberts (New York: Columbia University Press, 1985), pp. 154–178; L. Schaller, "Conflict over Conflict," in *Strategies of Community Organization: A Book of Readings*, ed. F. Cox, J. Erlich, J. Rothman, and J. Tropman (Itasca, Ill.: Peacock Publishers, 1970), pp. 171–198.

5. D. Bar-Tal, "Societal Beliefs in Times of Intractable Conflict: The Israeli Case," *International Journal of Conflict Management* 9 (1998): 22–50.

6. Miall, *The Peacemakers.*

7. Johan Galtung, *Peace by Peaceful Means* (London: Sage, 1996).

8. Carnegie Commission on Preventing Deadly Conflict, *Preventing Deadly Conflicts: Final Report* (New York: Carnegie Corporation of New York, 1997).

9. Marco Giugni, Doug McAdam, and Charles Tilly, eds., *How Social Movements Matter* (Minneapolis: University of Minnesota Press, 1999).

10. Seymour Martin Lipset, "The Social Requisites of Democracy Revisited," *American Sociological Review* 59 (February 1994): 1–22.

11. Ibid., pp. 12–13.

12. L. Salamon and H. K. Anheier, *Defining the Non-Profit Sector: A Cross National Analysis* (Manchester: Manchester University Press, 1997).

2
THEORY AND METHODOLOGY

Theory

Undertaking a comparative study of peace and conflict-resolution organizations (P/CROs) presented several theoretical and methodological challenges. The first was conceptualizing the P/CROs as a class of organizations. The second was formulating a theoretical framework that captured the distinct nature of these organizations while specifying the societal and organizational factors that could explain their commonalities and differences across the regions. The third was enabling the research teams to emphasize those aspects of the framework that were particularly salient to their region. In other words, each research team had its own theoretical perspective on both the nature of the conflict and the role the P/CROs had played in it, and this was useful in studying the P/CROs within the distinct context of their respective regions (see the "Methodology" section below). The fourth was operationalizing the critical variables about the P/CROs that would inform the data collection. The final challenge was developing a set of data-collection instruments and protocols that would enable each team to characterize the P/CROs in its region while preserving a common methodology for the comparative analysis.

Conceptualizing P/CROs

We approached our study by focusing on P/CROs primarily as organizations. As such, the P/CROs shared certain basic characteristics and imperatives: they set goals, used resources (e.g., human, financial), made decisions, etc.—all of which usually fall into distinct patterns. As organizations, the P/CROs also belonged to several specific categories. In the larger context, the P/CROs were part of the third sector, as opposed to the public or business sectors. In terms of the substance of their work, they belonged to the peace and conflict-resolution domain, which includes a diverse set of organizations ranging from grassroots protest groups to highly professional lobby organizations to cross-community dialogue groups to organizations engaged in mediation. The P/CROs also were part of the broader civil society—which includes the many political, social, religious, and ideological associations that mediate between individuals and families, and the state. Finally, since they made moral claims that were in opposition to those of the dominant political elite and they actively challenged and sought to change the forces that perpetuate violent conflict or prevent peace, the P/CROs also could be categorized as social-movement organizations (SMOs).

In order to capture these dimensions, we defined P/CROs as follows for the purposes of this study:

> Citizens' voluntary/nongovernmental organizations advocating peace/
> reconciliation/coexistence between the major contenders to the conflict
> in the three countries/regions, on the basis of mutual recognition and/or
> use of dispute resolution strategies as a means of addressing conflict.

This definition includes three major conditions: (1) The nature of the organizations included in the study had to be *citizen-initiated* and *voluntary*. That is, we required that they be formally organized (in contrast to informal or sporadic associations) and clearly part of the country's civil society.[1] (2) The major goal of the organizations had to be the promotion of peace/reconciliation/coexistence between the major parties involved in the conflict—specifically, between the Protestants and Catholics in Northern Ireland, the proponents and opponents of the apartheid regime in South Africa, and Israelis and Palestinians in the Middle East. We also recognized that the organizations might have been pursuing other goals, such as social justice and the development of democratic institutions. (3) The type of peace the organizations advocated and the methods they used to achieve it had to include the mutual recognition of the rights of each side and/or the utilization of dispute resolution strategies, such as negotiation and dialogue, rather than confrontation and violence.

The research questions we posed for this study clustered around three major issues: (1) *What were the organizational attributes of the P/CROs across countries and conflicts?* How were they formed? Who joined them? What activities did they engage in? How were they led? How did they make decisions? How did they obtain their resources (e.g., financial, human)? What ideologies did they espouse? What strategies and tactics did they use? What kinds of relationships did they form with other organizational entities and individuals supporting or opposing them? Finally, how did all of these factors change over time and in light of the fluctuating conditions and dynamics of the conflict? (2) *How did these dynamics compare across regions and conflicts?* What were the similarities and differences among the P/CROs across countries and conflicts? How could they be explained? (3) *What roles did the P/CROs play in the transition to peace and the resolution of the three conflicts?* Did they have a role at all? If so, what was their contribution? Were specific P/CROs prominent in this regard? How did they play this role?

The P/CRO definition we used and the research questions we posed reflect three levels of analysis—societal, associational or organizational, and programmatic. At the societal level, we viewed the P/CROs as vital elements of a civil society and were interested in exploring the ways in which social forces, such as the structure of the regime, affected the formation of these organizations. At the associational level, the P/CROs could be viewed as social-movement organizations, and we wanted to examine the ways in which they became organized and institutionalized. Finally, at the programmatic level, we recognized that the substance of the P/CROs' work was peace promotion and conflict resolution, and we wanted to investigate the various strategies they employed.

P/CROS and Civil Society

As constituent elements of civil society, P/CROs operate in an arena in which voluntary and nongovernmental associations mediate between individuals and the state. In representing the people's interests, these organizations may challenge the state's power through various means, such as offering alternative services that compete with, supplant, or supplement those the government provides,[2] and/or by challenging and protesting state policies through advocacy and constituency mobilization. Through the power of association and network building, nongovernmental organizations (NGOs) create social and cultural capital to advance their causes. Social capital is manifested in the form of networks that enable effective mobilization for political action. Cultural capital—that is, the institutionalization (i.e., public acceptance and legitimacy) of values, norms, and cognitive schemes as alternatives to those the state espouses—is generated through the belief systems the associations adopt and their efforts to influence the public to accept them. Diamond, for example, proposes that these associations promote democratic institutions by (1) containing the power of the state through public scrutiny; (2) encouraging citizen participation; (3) promoting norms of tolerance and compromise; (4) creating new ways to articulate, aggregate, and represent interests outside the existing political parties; (5) mitigating conflict through cross-cutting associations; (6) recruiting and training political leaders; and (7) disseminating information.[3] As we shall see, the P/CROs we studied engaged in all of these activities to promote peace and conflict resolution.

Within the civil society framework, a key question is the relationship between the nature of the regime, the societal capacity to form associations, and the attributes such associations are able to assume.[4] That is, the political context is a major determinant of citizens' abilities to form associations and the role these associations can assume in relation to the state. States clearly differ in the degree of inclusiveness and openness that they will tolerate and in their capacity to respond to diverse social needs.[5] These variations, in turn, influence the size and scope of civil society and its capacity to generate social and cultural capital. The issues, for example, were particularly paramount in Northern Ireland and Palestine, where a tradition of civil society was lacking. Likewise, in South Africa, the repressive regime impacted the P/CROs' attributes, and in Israel the rapid growth of civil society during the 1970s and 1980s stimulated the formation of P/CROs. This theme also is evident in the social-movement literature, which provided the second theoretical component of this study.

P/CROs as Social-Movement Organizations

In many respects, P/CROs are social-movement organizations par excellence. They make moral claims that are in opposition to those of the dominant political elite, and they most actively challenge and seek to change the forces that fuel and maintain conflicts and prevent peace. As such, these organizations are at greater risk for antagonism (from the state, the public, and other opposing organizations) than most other voluntary associations. In addition, P/CROs commonly identify themselves as part of a larger network or movement of peace and reconciliation organizations—an important feature of SMOs.[6]

Three interrelated issues regarding social movements were relevant to our study: (1) their evolution and genesis, (2) their survival and continued development, and (3) their methods of retaining members.[7] In the addressing of these issues, recent formulations have combined three theoretical strands—political opportunity structure, resource mobilization, and framing.[8] Since this three-tiered approach offers the most comprehensive, complex, and thus powerful conceptual framework for analyzing social movements, we adopted it for our comparative research.

Political opportunity structures (POS) explain how movements ascend and decline as a function of opportunities available in the political environment, especially the role that state structure and elite alignments play in a group's ability to mobilize resources.[9] Four dimensions of the POS have been identified: (1) the openness of the political system; (2) the state and/or nonstate's capacity and propensity for repression; (3) the stability of that broad set of elite alignments that typically undergird a polity; and (4) the presence of elite allies with the movement.[10]

The state may limit certain types of civil society organizations or the particular roles they may play in society (e.g., advocacy), thus restricting their repertoire of strategies, organizational forms, resources, leadership, and expertise. Therefore, for our study, the *openness of a political system* was crucial for the existence, and even legality, of P/CROs. The *state's propensity toward repressive behavior* affects civil society organizations' choice of strategies, and in our study, reflected the states' attitudes toward P/CRO activity, especially controversial activity, as was clearly apparent in South Africa. The *stability or instability of elite alignments* is an important factor in whether opportunities exist for political action. In all three regions, instability in the elite alignments created a window of opportunity for the P/CROs to mobilize for action. Finally, the *presence of elite allies* that supported the P/CROs was a major factor in their capacity to influence political processes.

Mobilizing structures (MS) influence the capacity of social movement organizations to mobilize for action and sustain themselves. Crucial to these are the existence of individual and organizational networks, which provide legitimacy and financial and membership resources to SMOs.[11] Incorporating mobilizing structures into our research framework prompted us to consider the manner in which P/CROs acquired, maintained, and utilized their resources. These included both financial and human resources needed to sustain the organizations and help them achieve their goals. In particular, we considered the P/CROs' capacity to recruit members, as well as their links with other organizations that provided financial resources, legitimacy, and expertise.

Closely related to MS is the issue of how social movement organizations institutionalize over time and create structures that enhance their survival. To address these questions, we augmented MS with *institutional theory*, which maintains that organizations seek to attain legitimacy from the environment in which they operate by adopting culturally sanctioned organizational forms and by conforming to socially acceptable values, ideologies, and norms—a process that has been termed *institutionalization*.[12] In other words, through coercive, mimetic, and normative forces, organizations adopt the structural features of other successful organizations, resulting in structural isomorphism.[13] Hence, institutionalization poses a major challenge to P/CROs. On the one hand, they are established to challenge existing political organizations. On the other hand, in order to survive, they have to adopt some important structural features of the organizations they challenge, such as formalization and professionalization, leadership recruitment and succession, decision-making processes, and interorganizational relations. How the P/CROs resolved these issues was an important theme of this study.

Finally, *framing* explores the cognitive processes that influence movement mobilization.[14] Framing refers to the process by which social movement actors "assign meaning to and interpret relevant events and conditions in ways that are intended to mobilize potential adherents and constituents, to garner by-stander support, and to demobilize antagonists."[15] This perspective enabled us to understand how the P/CROs in each region framed the nature of the conflict, viewed its etiology, and formulated a solution. It drew attention to the cultural symbols and language these organizations used to address the conflict, and the degree to which these symbols offered an alternative discourse about the conflict that could facilitate the processes of peace and conflict resolution. For example, the Israeli peace movement embraced the Palestinians' right to self-determination. In Northern Ireland, several P/CROs framed the conflict as emanating from interpersonal prejudices. In South Africa, the P/CROs spoke of social justice and democracy as key alternative symbols to apartheid. In all of these instances, the P/CROs offered alternative frames to define the conflict and its solution in ways that differed significantly from those of the political elite. Understanding these frames and how they influenced the organization and strategies of the P/CROs was a major facet of our study.

P/CROs and Theories of Peace-Making/Conflict Resolution

A distinctive feature of P/CROs is the choice of strategies and the tactics they employ to promote the idea of peace and the resolution of conflict within the societies in which they operate.[16] In fact, these activities represent the substance of their work. In our study, the P/CROs selected activities that were either explicitly or implicitly informed by a theory of peace-making and conflict resolution. Therefore, we used theories on peace-making and conflict resolution to understand how the P/CROs made such choices.

All P/CROs must decide how to frame the conflict and its solution in a way that avoids the appearance of using sacrosanct values that are not negotiable.[17] In other words, the organizations need to define their interests in a manner that can appeal to contesting parties. In South Africa, for example, the P/CROs chose to emphasize democracy and social justice, and in Israel the P/CROs focused on the mutual recognition of the legitimate rights of both Israelis and Palestinians. In the same vein, P/CROs also need to identify and articulate some mutual interests that are common among the contesting parties. The literature on conflict resolution refers to such shared interests as the "superordinate goal."[18] For instance, in Northern Ireland the P/CROs stressed the need for local community economic development that cut across the Protestant and Catholic communities. In South Africa the P/CROs underscored the shared desire to strengthen democratic institutions.

An important concept in the field of peace-making is the "readiness to negotiate," which arises when the contesting parties become interdependent and must engage each other.[19] P/CROs can play a significant role in promoting such readiness by developing "bridging" projects, such as community development in Northern Ireland, or by providing an opportunity for the contesting parties to interact, such as the Institute for a Democratic Alternative for South Africa's (Idasa) initiative for the Dakar meeting between Afrikaner and black intellectuals. In addition, successful negotiations require the development of effective means of communication between the contesting parties. These include the use of language, terms, and cultural symbols that are acceptable to both parties, and the cultivation of interpersonal skills that can bridge the long, and often state-sponsored, antagonism between them. A key element of these communication patterns is the conveyance of mutual respect and trust that fosters a perception of parity between the contesting parties.[20]

The importance of developing tools for effective dialogue between the contesting parties cannot be underestimated. One of the most difficult aspects of peace-making is the need to replace the arsenal of cultural tools (e.g., language, images, symbols) that the contesting parties have institutionalized over time to define their opponents. These tools often are connected to events that are rooted in the historical ethos of each opponent's collective identity (e.g., the Protestant marches in Northern Ireland). Because of the manner in which they frame the opponents and define the conflict, these tools become major impediments to the peace-making or conflict-resolution process. As noted earlier, one of P/CROs' major contributions is providing alternative cultural tools that redefine both the contesting parties and the nature of the conflict in a manner that enables dialogue and negotiation. In our study, we paid particular attention to this issue.

Finally, the role of third parties in facilitating dialogue and negotiation between the contesting parties has long been recognized as an indispensable tool in the peace-making and conflict-resolution process.[21] P/CROs can play a major role in serving as neutral third parties. Such examples abound in our study: Quaker House in Northern Ireland, Idasa in South Africa, and Rapprochement in Israel are but a few. In our study, we explored the characteristics of such organizations, particularly the belief systems they adopted that enabled them to assume this role.

Use of Theory in a Comparative Study: A Cautionary Note

One of the challenges we encountered in undertaking a comparative study that involved both an in-depth analysis of the P/CROs in each region and comparisons across countries and organizations was the application of a theory that both preserved the comparative perspective and, at the same time, enabled each research team to focus on the theoretical framework that was most relevant to its respective region. Throughout the study, there were two unifying theoretical themes that the research teams adopted for both the national and comparative analyses. The first involved understanding the P/CROs as elements of civil society. Hence, at both levels of analysis, we examined the relationship between the state and civil society and its impact on the P/CROs' development. We also explored the P/CROs' place in civil society and how it influenced the formation and survival of these organizations. The second theme entailed viewing the P/CROs as social-movement organizations and examining in detail the organizational issues that they encountered and the solutions they devised in the particular political and social contexts in which they operated.

However, each research team was at liberty to emphasize that perspective that was most suitable to its context. The Northern Ireland team, for example, based its work on theories of peace-making and conflict resolution. It was particularly concerned with the P/CROs' role in establishing intergroup community-development enterprises, as well as the P/CROs' mediating functions. In contrast, the Israeli team embraced the social-movement perspective to explain the P/CROs' development. Understandably, the Palestinian team focused on the emerging civil society, its complex relationships with the Palestinian Authority, and the impact of these relations on the P/CROs. The South African team, while anchored in a civil-society perspective, was more eclectic, using all three theoretical perspectives to analyze and explain various facets of the P/CROs. Finally, studies of social-movement organizations particularly informed the comparative analysis itself.

Methodology

The design of an international comparative study in the social sciences is always complex and difficult, regardless of the specific subject matter that is being studied. However, our study was complicated further by the fact that the theoretical frameworks and literature, and therefore the concepts, we used were drawn from different theories. Moreover, although individual P/CROs had been studied in the past, the phenomenon as we defined it had not and therefore we could not draw upon prior experience. Finally, these complexities were compounded by the fact that we were interested in obtaining current empirical data on the P/CROs (rather than historical or interpretative), which meant that the bulk of the information had to be obtained from the organizations themselves.

All of these difficulties made it practically impossible to clearly lay out the methodology of the study at the outset. It called for an evolving and iterative process that not only necessitated a creative approach but also required the active participation and cooperation of all those involved. Thus, we did not plan the study in detail at the beginning, but decided to follow certain principles to guide us in dealing with the methodological issues we faced. These included the use of (1) a local base, (2) an inductive and phased study, (3) coordinating mechanisms, (4) a comparative and local focus, and (5) different research methodologies.

First, we determined that the study should have a *local base* wherein local research teams would collect and interpret the data, but even more important, actively participate in the design of the comparative dimensions of the study based on their knowledge of the local environment. We used an international competition to choose the research teams in each region, which had to include researchers from both sides of the conflict (e.g., Protestants and Catholics in Northern Ireland). For a variety of contextual reasons not related to the researchers themselves, this turned out to be impossible to do in the case of the Israeli/Palestinian conflict. Thus, while we studied P/CROs in three conflicts, we actually had four research teams.

Second, we chose to organize our work as an *inductive and phased study* because some of the major parameters of the phenomenon in which we were interested were unknown to us in the specific regions at the outset, and also because this was not a hypothesis-testing study. Thus, we started from a general description of the phenomenon as a whole, based on the entire population of P/CROs, and gradually moved to an in-depth analysis based on a structured selection of these organizations.

Third, we used several *coordinating mechanisms* to ensure the comparative nature of the study. The most important of these were three meetings, one in each region studied, where all issues pertaining to the study were discussed in detail. We also employed an International Advisory Board consisting of prominent international researchers in the field, as well as leading researchers of the three specific conflicts.

Fourth, as the study had both a *comparative and local focus* and was empirical, its design called for a strict social scientific protocol. This entailed a common definition of P/CROs, common research tools, and common data-collection and analysis methods that all of the research teams agreed upon, used, and later analyzed comparatively. In addition, based on the data collected, each team was expected to write a report on the P/CROs in its own region. Thus, in order to retain conflict-specific information, each research team was able to make additions to the comparative protocol. For example, the research teams could add to the selection of P/CROs studied some that did not fit the international definition but were considered P/CROs in the local context, or include a few interview questions that were important in the local context. This ensured that both the comparative and local data would be collected and used.

Finally, since we were interested in both the P/CROs' structural properties and the specific dynamics of their operations, it was necessary to use *different research methodologies* to address these various aspects. Specifically, we used quantitative (used primarily in survey analyses) and qualitative (used principally in case studies) methods to measure the different parameters. This variegated approach enabled us to be sensitive to the integrity of the unit of analysis (i.e., the P/CRO) within its contextual dynamics—that is, we were able to examine the P/CRO's response to the changes in and dynamics of the conflict and the society in which it existed. Early in the process, we chose to use the comparative case study approach in the final phase of the study.

The Comparative Approach

The comparative method has been used extensively in studies of organizational entities. For example, scholars have used this approach to examine the public approval of social movement goals,[22] as well as the organizational viability,[23] protest methods and political strategies,[24] and identity formation[25] of social movement organizations. The comparative method also has been used in third-sector research.[26] Skocpol and Somers suggest that different forms of comparative inquiry facilitate the discovery of similarities among various contexts.[27] One type of comparative inquiry stresses parallels for the purpose of testing theories or hypotheses. Another form identifies and analyzes contrasts between two or more different historical or social contexts that share a common origin or point of departure. Finally, a third approach, recognizing both similarities and contrasts at the macro level, focuses on particular problems or phenomena common to the societies in question, rather than a presumed commonality among the societies themselves.

Our study most resembles this latter method in that it is not a comparative analysis of the three conflicts, their respective dynamics, or the attempts to resolve them, but, without ascribing any inherent similarities to the three societies or conflicts, our study calls attention to the fact that in each circumstance, citizens' organizations emerged that challenged, to varying degrees, the inevitability of the conflicts. We therefore targeted these organizational forms—i.e., P/CROs—as the locus of our analysis and the basis of our comparative inquiry.

Thus, we did not assume that the conflicts we chose to study were comparable—while they shared certain common characteristics, as outlined below, they also were very different in nature,[28] as were the processes of conflict resolution in each region. It is, however, important to stress that the study, and the comparisons presented in this book, focused solely on peace and conflict-resolution *organizations*, not the conflicts or even the processes of conflict resolution. We made the assumption that the P/CROs were comparable across countries and cultures based on the mere fact that as organizations they shared specific features and had to address certain imperatives. In addition, since they were active in the domain of war and peace, the P/CROs encountered similar issues and conditions.[29]

Therefore, we used the individual organization as the unit of analysis and treated it like a single case study using qualitative data methodology and an open-ended interview protocol. However, the qualitative data were collected along a number of key variables, which enabled comparisons with other organizations, at least along certain parameters. These case studies were then analyzed individually, as aggregates within the same region and comparatively across regions.

Research Setting

In undertaking a cross-country, cross-conflict comparison, it was important that the contexts of the phenomenon studied be both similar and different in certain respects. The similarities accentuated the fact that the phenomenon studied was the same across countries and conflicts; the differences enabled the researchers to distinguish universal traits from particular ones. In these regards, the conflicts we chose for this study provided an excellent context for a cross-country comparison of P/CROs. While the conflicts differed in their histories, duration, dynamics, and central points of contention (see the chapter 3 for more details), the P/CROs in all three regions engaged in significant activities during the 1980s, and during the 1990s breakthroughs in the violent and protracted conflicts occurred in all three regions.

Yet, in a study of this kind, it also was important to consider similarities and differences in the nature and characteristics of the society and the country, especially its polity, in which the P/CROs functioned. In terms of similarities, all three regions (1) were basically democratic, with major democratic institutions (although political rights was the very issue around which the conflicts evolved in South Africa and Israel/Palestine); (2) had experienced colonial British rule, currently or in the past; and (3) had a thriving third sector.

But these societies also differed along certain dimensions, the most important of which were size and demographic composition. Geographically, Northern Ireland and Israel/Palestine were very small compared to South Africa. The same was true regarding population size—1.5 million in Northern Ireland, 6 million in Israel, and 2 million in Palestine, versus 40 million in South Africa. Finally, whereas the populations in Northern Ireland and Israel/Palestine consisted primarily of two major religious/ethnic groups, which also were the parties involved in the conflict, South Africa was a multi-ethnic and multireligious society and the conflict was focused on the nature of the regime.

Although these differences and similarities provided an excellent *conceptual* context for the comparative study, some of the differences created major *methodological* problems. The different nature of the conflicts meant that the terms "peace" and "conflict resolution" had different meanings in the various contexts. In Northern Ireland, peace for the most part meant a cessation of physical violence; in South Africa, terms pertained more to the protection of rights or the cessation of political violence; in Israel, they meant reaching an agreement with the Palestinians that would end the conflict; and in Palestine, it meant an end to the Israeli occupation. Also, in designing the actual data-collection process, we had to consider differences in the geography and populations of each region. For example, in South Africa, the team had to cover a massive geographic region and thus had to employ a large number of researchers who belonged to different ethnic groups to facilitate the data-collection process. In contrast, one field researcher covered the small region of Northern Ireland. Finally, while English was the official language in Northern Ireland and South Africa, it was not so in Israel and Palestine, where the research tools had to be translated into the local languages and the findings translated back into English.

Based on the definition of P/CROs as enunciated in the "Theory" section of this chapter, we studied the following types of organizations in the three regions: (1) in South Africa, we studied organizations that objected to apartheid, advocated a system of government that treated all people equally and democratically, and called for negotiations as a means of achieving these changes; (2) in the Israeli/Palestinian conflict, we examined organizations that advocated an end to the Israeli occupation of the West Bank and Gaza and a parallel cessation of the Palestinian armed struggle, and also included organizations composed of Israelis and Palestinians advocating coexistence; (3) in Northern Ireland, we investigated Catholic, Protestant, and joint organizations, as well as other associations, such as labor unions, that advocated reconciliation between the two communities and a negotiated agreement.

Based on the research teams' prior knowledge of the field, we determined that the organizations that met this definition usually performed one or more of the following functions: (1) *Service delivery*—these were primarily organizations composed of professionals who provided medical, legal, social, educational, and other services to populations that were denied such services because of the conflict. These organizations also stressed the price (in professional terms—i.e., human rights, public health, etc.) society paid for the continuation of the violent conflict. (2) *Advocacy*—these were primarily organizations that engaged in various forms of political pressure with the aim of changing the official policy from confrontation to negotiation and reconciliation. (3) *Dialogue*—these organizations and groups engaged in face-to-face dialogues and worked on joint projects with the other side aiming to create a better understanding and awareness. (4) *Consciousness-raising*—these organizations sought to educate or sensitize individuals and the public about the negative implications of continuing the conflict and the possibilities its peaceful resolution offered.

In order to facilitate a meaningful international comparison in the category of NGOs called P/CROs, it became necessary at the final phase of the study to establish additional selection criteria that conformed to the agreed-upon definition and were logical within the study of organizations, in general, and third-sector organizations, in particular. Thus, we determined to study organizations whose activities (as opposed to rhetoric) reflected the notion of peace/conflict resolution and embodied one or both of the following: (1) *advocacy*—namely, the organization's actions attempted to change the policies or practices of governments or other forces toward peace/reconciliation/coexistence, etc.; and (2) *ongoing contacts* with individuals or groups from the other side of the conflict, through either dialogue, joint projects, or the provision of services.

INTERPRETATIONS OF THE JOINT DEFINITION.   In light of the data from the scan of organizations during the first phase of the study, a few of the research teams stressed the need to refine the P/CRO definition to portray their local context more accurately. Accordingly, the definition of P/CROs in Israel was adapted to denote:

> Any voluntary/nongovernmental body or group of people residing in Israel or the occupied territories . . . that has promoted mutual recognition of [the right to] national self-determination as a necessary but not sufficient condition for achieving peace between Jews and Palestinians . . . and that [has] been involved with consciousness-raising, dialogue, advocacy, and the provision of professional services directed to assuage the injustice and grievances caused by this conflict in the social, economic, legal, religious, and cultural realms.[30]

This revised definition made more explicit the precondition that only those Israeli P/CROs that recognized the Palestinians' right to self-determination were included in the study. The South African team reframed the P/CRO definition to include any "voluntary nongovernmental organized body . . . concerned to promote justice and freedom from the violence and disorder generated by apartheid and which in some way has contributed to the building of a nonracial and democratic South Africa."[31] In this case, "peace" was contextualized by making the rejection of apartheid and a commitment to nonracialism prerequisites.

PALESTINIAN DEFINITION OF P/CROs.   While these slight deviations from and reinterpretations of the P/CRO definition to reflect local contexts did not constitute a major challenge to the international and comparative nature of the study, the Palestinian context did. In the context of the occupation during the 1980s and early 1990s, the first goal of Palestinian civil society organizations was to end the occupation and its evils, not necessarily to promote "peace." Thus, the P/CRO definition a priori was problematic. In addition, Palestinian society, which for a whole set of reasons had few opportunities to develop its own civil society, had a comparatively smaller and less independent third sector than the other regions. Furthermore, the whole categorization of P/CROs we developed (i.e., advocacy, service, dialogue, consciousness-raising) was irrelevant in that context. This situation, however, did not mean that individuals and groups within Palestinian society were not interested in the promotion of peace, especially after the Oslo Accords of 1993. Some joined Israelis to form joint Israeli/Palestinian P/CROs, most of which were dialogue and service organizations, and others operated within Palestinian society. Thus, in the Palestinian context, the definition of P/CROs included NGOs that, after the institutionalization of the Palestinian Authority, opposed the continuation of an armed struggle and promoted a democratic society (see the chapter 5).

Obviously, this description did not conform to the agreed-upon P/CRO definition for the study. In light of this, it might have been logical to exclude the Palestinian organizations from the study altogether. However, we decided to include them for the following three reasons: (1) the analysis of the roles and characteristics of P/CROs active in the Israeli/Palestinian conflict would not have been complete without studying Palestinian activity in this domain, regardless of the precise definition of such activity; (2) there were joint Palestinian/Israeli organizations that needed to be studied from both angles; and (3) since the study had both an international and a local focus, it was important to fulfill this aspect of the study, even if we could not systematically compare the findings at the international level. Thus, we allowed the Palestinian team to formulate its own P/CRO definition and to present its findings solely within the local analysis of the study. However, we did examine the joint Israeli/Palestinian organizations from both angles and present the findings from the international analysis within the Israeli context.

In the remainder of this chapter, we outline the methods we used for the different phases of the study—namely, sampling, research tools, data collection, and analysis. This methodology was aimed at obtaining data on various aspects of the organizational life of a structured selection of P/CROs and using this information to understand the P/CRO phenomenon in the conflicts studied. It is important to note that this information pertains to the organizational analysis aspect of this study only. The methodology used to study the efficacy of P/CROs is outlined in chapter 9, where this question is addressed.

Research Questions

In studying P/CROs, we were interested primarily in understanding the forces that shaped their organizational behavior. We used the literature on this subject (see chapter 1) to help us formulate the major research questions. Like other organizations, P/CROs have certain goals that are based on belief systems or *ideology*(*ies*) regarding the conflict—ranging from those P/CROs that consider the system to be the source of the conflict to those that target individuals and attitudes—and these give the organizations their direction. P/CROs also have *structures*, both formal and informal, that ensure their continuity and stability. These include a certain form of leadership and a pattern of decision making. In addition, these organizations need both *human resources* (e.g., members, workers) and *financial resources* in order to survive and function. All these components form the internal aspects of the organization.

In order to achieve their goals, organizations also interact with their environments according to certain patterns. They may have *cooperative, competitive,* or *conflictual* relations with certain organizations or individuals. All of these form the external aspects of the organizations. Beyond the immediate environment, there are also the national and international contexts in which the organizations operate. Within these environments, a variety of events may occur, which the organizations aim to influence (e.g., negotiations, peace agreements) or prevent (e.g., violent attacks, terror, incarcerations). In both instances, these events impact the organizations. All of these interacting elements (i.e., internal, external, and contextual) help determine the strategy an organization chooses, which is then translated into tactics and activities. Finally, organizations change over time, mostly in reaction to changes in their immediate (e.g., specific funders, politicians, the media) and more distant (e.g., political or ideological changes) environments.

While P/CROs share most of these organizational components, they also have a unique characteristic that rarely is observed in other third-sector organizations—namely the element of *risk*. Being at the forefront of controversial political struggles, P/CROs are opposed by both government authorities, who see them as a threat, and countermovements, which oppose them ideologically. Thus, some P/CROs face a dilemma: in order to convey their message, they must employ certain attention-getting tactics; however, these strategies often result in clashes with police and countermovements, and create risky situations. Some organizations are more amenable than others to using these tactics.

A Phased Selection Procedure

The selection procedure for the P/CROs included in the study was divided into three phases (see table 2.1). The first phase (Phase I) entailed a scan of all of the organizations that fit the P/CRO definition we used in each of the locales. Each research team compiled a list of these organizations based on information gathered from foundation offices, networks, and personal contacts. The goal was not only to identify P/CROs but also to categorize them. The categories included function (advocacy, service, dialogue, consciousness-raising), membership-based (yes/no), size (small, medium, large), gender-specific (yes/no), ethnic-specific (yes/no), religious orientation (yes/no), existing/defunct, and presence (local/national) (see appendix D for a list of all of the organizations scanned). Obtaining most of these data did not necessitate site visits but was achieved through telephone conversations and by reading brochures and other literature these organizations produced. This process provided a general picture of

TABLE 2.1. Phased Research Design

	Phase I	Phase II	Phase III P/CRO reports
Rationale	Gain a coarse view of the diversity and complexity of local P/CROs; guide the selection of P/CROs for Phase II	Gain a rough but systematic depiction of P/CRO form and behavior; refine the research strategy for Phase III	Provide detailed organizational profiles sensitive to the local context yet structured to allow for an international comparison
Selection	All P/CROs that fit the definition used in each locale	Structured selection	Subset of structured selection
Research tool	Organizational scan	Preliminary questionnaire	Comprehensive questionnaire
Data collection	Prior knowledge and literature review	Survey of P/CRO leaders/directors	Series of semistructured interviews and observation of P/CRO activities
Data analysis	Impressionistic	*Local*: Descriptive *International*: Quantitative	*Local and international*: Comparative case-study analysis

the size and nature of the P/CRO phenomenon in each society. The process used to scan the P/CROs is explained in more detail in chapters 4 through 7.

In the second phase (Phase II), a subset of the initial scan of P/CROs was selected and examined—approximately thirty organizations from each region—using structured questionnaires to obtain basic and primarily quantitative data on the P/CROs' structure, budget, number of members and employees, etc. (see the section on "Research Tools" below). This phase also entailed a meeting with the organizations' representatives. The goal in this process of sampling was to assure that, based on the organizations and categories identified in the first phase, the P/CRO phenomenon in each locale was represented adequately, particularly given the variability among the P/CROs. The idea was to include organizations that represented the categories we had identified in the first phase. Since these categories reflected various dimensions of the organizations, each P/CRO fit into several different categories. For example, one P/CRO could be ethnic-specific, small, local, and defunct. The selection process for this phase yielded an international sample of 111 P/CROs—thirty-six South African, thirty-six Northern Irish, twenty-five Israeli, and fourteen Palestinian (see table 2.2). This phase also served as a test for the next and final phase of the study by giving us an idea of the type of data that were available and accessible, and the organizations' willingness to cooperate with our research teams.

TABLE 2.2.   Selection of P/CROs

	Phase I	Phase II	Phase III
Number of P/CROs			
Northern Ireland	70	36	8
South Africa	72	36	10
Israel	77	25	9
Palestine	14	314	6
Selection criteria	Census of P/CRO sector	Representing phenomenon	Structured selection
Research tool	Organizational scan	Preliminary structured questionnaire	Comprehensive semistructured interview outline
Type of data collected	Classification	Basic descriptive data	Comprehensive qualitative data

Finally, in the third phase (Phase III). a limited number of organizations (up to ten) from each region were studied comprehensively as case studies, which formed the basis for the international analysis. The ten P/CROs chosen for further study in each region represented the local P/CRO phenomenon based on the research team's judgment and included all of the categories of organizations identified in the previous phase. Six new P/CROs, which were not among the original fourteen in the second phase of the study, were included in the Palestinian sample during this phase since they better fit the study criteria. Three of these organizations were joint Israeli-Palestinian P/CROs that the Israeli team investigated, as well. For a list of all of the organizations chosen at each phase of the study see appendix D.

Research Tools, Data Collection, and Analysis

Whereas the initial organizational scan in Phase I of the study included very general, factual organizational parameters of the P/CROs—that is, composition, size, and primary function—the research tool developed for Phase II was a structured "preliminary questionnaire" designed to provide a crude profile of the organizations surveyed. It included questions on formation patterns, leadership, participation, decision making, budgets, and so on, as well as those pertaining to the nature and frequency of relations with various actors in the organization's environment (see appendix A). In most cases, this survey was conducted in person with an organization's director or chairperson, though in some instances it was conveyed via mail. Generally speaking, the research teams encountered little difficulty gaining access to the organizations and their members/officeholders. Frequently, the researchers were personally familiar with the organizations and/or their leaders. The South African team, in particular, successfully exploited the diversity of its staff in accessing certain organizations that appeared more inclined to share information with researchers of a particular racial or ethnic background. In addition, in South Africa (and in Israel to a lesser degree) some of the organizations were circumspect about divulging financial information. Both the Israeli and Palestinian research teams experienced difficulties translating the questionnaire from English to Hebrew and Arabic, respectively, in order to distribute it, and then translating the responses into English.

Since one of the goals for this second phase was to ascertain the availability and accessibility of data, we used both the data-collection process and the findings from Phase II to structure the research tool used in the third phase of the study. Thus, for example, based on our findings from the preliminary questionnaire, we focused on the centrality of foreign funding in explaining P/CRO behavior, the importance of "charismatic" leaders, and the large number of P/CROs that were established during the peak years of the conflicts—key findings in our study.

At the same time, the data received during this phase underscored certain limitations that hampered the data-collection process. We discovered, for example, that certain questions pertaining to the conflict were so subjective that in many cases the answers could not be put into simple categories. Indeed, the highly subjective dimensions of each conflict—such as the particular discourse and underlying interpretations of the conflict's history—seemed impossible to scrutinize effectively with a structured questionnaire. Furthermore, while one team was able to furnish complete and consistent responses to questions for a particular topic, others sometimes received only crude and partial data. This made the prospects for a systematic comparison of these data across countries rather difficult.

Compounding these problems was the fact that after conducting its initial scan of P/CROs, the Palestinian team realized that the organizations appeared to be oriented more toward community development and capacity building than toward peace. Moreover, they maintained that the P/CROs were subject to the high degree of politicization that characterized contemporary Palestinian society, in general. More specifically, the emerging Palestinian public sector, in the form of the Palestinian Authority, exerted considerable influence (if not outright hegemony) over the P/CROs, a factor that might have called into question their conformity to the generally accepted criteria of third-sector organizations.

Ultimately, the first two phases of the study were useful—as the research teams affirmed themselves—in providing an overview of the peace movement in each of the regions and in establishing both an entree and a set of preliminary insights into the organizations being studied. More specifically, the preliminary questionnaires and the methodological challenges they posed served to guide and refine the strategy for the subsequent phase of the study—comprehensive data collection—which yielded detailed reports on each of the P/CROs included in the final selection.

The primary objective for Phase III of the study was to elaborate upon what was gleaned from the previous phases in a more comprehensive way using a different methodology (see appendix B). The substantive areas examined were similar to those explored in Phase II; however, the investigators used several research mechanisms that enabled them to obtain more detailed and in-depth information. The researchers conducted open-ended, semi-structured interviews with up to three different types of individuals within each organization—leaders, core members, and outer-core members. This allowed for considerably more depth, reflection, and interpretation from the respondents. To assess changes over time, the questions were related to three distinct time periods: formative years, critical years (i.e., the peak of the conflict, as determined by each research team), and the present (or in the case of defunct P/CROs, the period of organizational demise). Furthermore, the researchers were instructed to solicit some specific examples regarding the genesis, development, and implementation of a particular activity or episode within the organization. To gauge the effects of external events on the P/CROs, respondents also were presented with a list (compiled by each research team during Phase I) of significant events with direct or indirect bearing on the conflict and asked to relate these to activities within their organizations. Finally, the research teams reviewed the organizations' documents whenever possible and appropriate.

As mentioned previously, we chose a comparative case study approach for our project. Unlike the "classical" case study approach, in which the researcher depicts in great detail an organization's profile along dimensions chosen (and therefore deemed important) by the unit studied, the comparative case study approach calls for a more guided process in which detailed, qualitative data are collected along specific dimensions in a semi-structured interview. These data, collected from several individuals, are then compared and integrated into one case study, and the case studies are later compared across organizations. Such a comparison would not have been possible had we used the "classical" case study approach since the various organizations would have chosen to present different aspects of their work and a common basis for comparison would not have been found. Thus, the research teams compiled individual comprehensive case studies—written along specific parameters using numerous examples to illustrate specific points and principles—for each of the organizations studied during Phase III. The researchers produced approximately thirty of these rich case studies, which constituted the most important part of the data used for our analysis.

The process of data analysis consisted of devising a system of subcategories and codes for each of the various parameters studied. This process of categorization was based on both the data and theory. We used software designed for the analysis of qualitative data (i.e., Atlas) for these purposes. Thus, for example, if a case study described a certain form of behavior that a leader exhibited, it could have been categorized as fitting into a "charismatic" or a "democratic" pattern. This process enabled us to appraise the basic attributes of the phenomenon using qualitative data-collection methods and then partially transform the data into quantitative measures without losing their original qualities since specific examples from individual cases were presented, as well.

The organization of the case studies along the parameters we studied enabled us to analyze the findings on four different levels, by (1) the individual P/CRO, as a case study in and of itself; (2) P/CROs active in a specific conflict or region; (3) an international comparison of the entire sample; and (4) an international comparison by category of organization (i.e., religious, women, etc.). In this book, we present the results from the second and third levels of analysis only, and these too can be considered initial analyses since the rich data obtained from the study can be further analyzed in many additional directions.

Conclusion

Through the synergistic interaction among investigators within and across the research teams, a strategy evolved that gradually assumed a form consistent with the qualitative comparative case study advanced by Charles Ragin.[32] Such an analysis, striving for a degree of data reduction (i.e., simplifying complexity in a theoretically guided manner), on the one hand, and a holistic investigation of the object of analysis, on the other, ideally steers a course "between generality and complexity . . . between a radically analytic variable-oriented strategy and the highly personalized case-oriented strategy."[33] Our study, in terms of both its desired outputs and the processes adopted to achieve them, faithfully reflects this tension or dialectic.

Notes

1. This condition raised the issue of whether some research and mediation centers within universities (particularly in South Africa) should be included. We decided to include these organizations based on the nature of their activities and alignments.

2. B. A. Weisbrod, *The Voluntary Nonprofit Sector: An Economic Analysis* (Lexington: Heath, 1977); H. Hansmann, "Economic Theories of Nonprofit Organization," in *The Nonprofit Sector: A Research Handbook*, ed. W. W. Powell (New Haven: Yale University Press, 1987), pp. 27–42.

3. L. Diamond, "Toward Democratic Consolidation," *Journal of Democracy* 5 (1994): 4–17.

4. G. Hyden, "Civil Society, Social Capital, and Development: Dissection of a Complex Discourse," *Studies in Comparative International Development* 32 (1997): 3–30.

5. J. Dryzek, "Political Inclusion and the Dynamics of Democratization," *American Political Science Review* 90 (1993): 475–487.

6. M. N. Zald and J. D. McCarthy, "Social Movement Industries: Competition and Cooperation among Movement Organizations," in *Research in Social Movements, Conflicts and Change*, ed. L. Kriesberg (Greenwich, Conn.: JAI Press, 1980), pp. 1–20.

7. D. McAdam, J. D. McCarthy, and M. N. Zald, *Comparative Perspectives on Social Movements* (New York: Cambridge University Press, 1996).

8. Ibid.

9. P. Eisinger, "The Conditions of Protest Behavior in American Cities," *American Political Science Review* 67 (1973): 11–28.

10. See, for example, D. Della Porta, "Social Movements and the State: Thoughts on the Policing of Protest," in *Comparative Perspectives on Social Movements*, ed. Doug McAdam, John D. McCarthy, and Mayer N. Zald (Cambridge: Cambridge University Press, 1996); D. McAdam, "Conceptual Origins, Current Problems, Future Directions," in *Comparative Perspectives on Social Movements*; E. Zdravomyslova, "Opportunities and Framing in Transition to Democracy: The Case of Russia," in *Comparative Perspectives on Social Movements*; H. Kriesi, "The Political Opportunity Structure of New Social Movements: Its Impact on Their Mobilization," in *The Politics of Social Protest*, ed. Craig J. Jenkins and Bert Klandermans (Minneapolis: University of Minnesota Press, 1995); S. Tarrow, "Struggle, Politics, and Reform: Collective Action, Social Movements, and Cycles of Protest," Center for International Studies of Cornell University, Ithaca, N.Y., 1989.

11. D. McAdam, "Micromobilization Contexts and Recruitment to Activism," *International Social Movement Research* 1 (1988): 125–154; J. D. McCarthy, "Constraints and Opportunities in Adopting, Adapting, and Inventing," in *Comparative Perspectives on Social Movements: Political Opportunities, Mobilizing Structures, and Cultural Framing*, ed. D. McAdam, J. D. McCarthy, and M. N. Zald (New York: Cambridge University Press, 1996), pp. 141–151; E. S. Clemens, *The People's Lobby* (Chicago: University of Chicago Press, 1997); M. N. Zald, "Culture, Ideology and Strategic Framing," in *Comparative Perspectives on Social Movements*, pp. 261–274.

12. J. W. Meyer and B. Rowan, "Institutionalized Organizations: Formal Structure as Myth and Ceremony," *American Journal of Sociology* 83 (1977): 340–363.

13. P. DiMaggio and W. Powell, "The Iron Cage Revisited: Institutional Isomorphism and Collective Rationality in Organizational Fields," in *The New Institutionalism in Organizational Analysis*, ed. P. DiMaggio and W. Powell (Chicago: University of Chicago Press, 1991), pp. 63–82.

14. McAdam, McCarthy, and Zald, *Comparative Perspectives on Social Movements*; A. D. Morris and C. Mueller, *Frontiers in Social Movement Theory* (New Haven: Yale University Press, 1992).

15. D. Snow and R. Benford, "Ideology, Frame Resonance, and Participant Mobilization," *International Social Movement Research* 1 (1988): 197–217.

16. We are indebted to Mark Chesler for many of the ideas developed in this section.

17. L. Susskind and J. Cruikshank, *Breaking the Impasse: Consensual Approaches to Resolving Public Disputes* (New York: Basic Books, 1987); R. Fisher and W. Ury, *Getting to Yes: Negotiating Agreement Without Giving In* (Boston: Houghton-Mifflin, 1981).

18. J. Rubin, D. Pruitt, and S. Kim, *Social Conflict: Escalation, Stalemate and Suppression* (New York: McGraw-Hill, 1994).

19. Fisher and Ury, *Getting to Yes.*

20. B. Mayer, "The Dynamics of Power in Mediation and Negotiations," *Mediation Quarterly* 6 (1987): 75–86.

21. Rubin, Pruitt, and Kim, *Social Conflict.*

22. A. G. Mertig and R. E. Dunlap, "Public Approval of Environmental Protection and Other New Social Movement Goals in Western Europe and the United States," *International Journal of Public Opinion Research* 7 (1995): 145–156.

23. D. Cress and D. Snow, "Mobilization at the Margins: Resources, Benefactors and the Viability of Homeless Social Movement Organizations," *American Sociological Review* 61 (1996): 1089–1109.

24. G. Sussman and B. Steel, "Support for Protest Methods and Political Strategies among Peace Movement Activists: Comparing the US, Great Britain, and the Federal Republic of Germany," *Western Political Quarterly* 44 (1991): 519–540.

25. G. Sarup, "A Reference Group Theory of Social Movements and Identity," *Social Science* 50 (1975): 219–226.

26. L. Salamon and H. K. Anheier, *Defining the Non-Profit Sector: A Cross-National Analysis* (Manchester: Manchester University Press, 1997), pp. 29–100; W. Seibel, "Government/Third Sector Relations in a Comparative Perspective: The Cases of France and West Germany," *Voluntas* 5 (1990): 42–61.

27. T. Skocpol and M. Somers, "The Uses of Comparative History in Macrosocial Inquiry," *Comparative Studies in Society and History* 22 (1980): 147–197.

28. H. Giliomee, "Introduction," in *The Elusive Search for Peace*, ed. H. Giliomee and J. Gagiano (South Africa: Oxford University Press, 1990).

29. P. Van den Dungen, ed., *West European Pacifism and the Strategy for Peace* (New York: St. Martin's, 1985).

30. T. Hermann and P. Lemish, Cultivating the Ground: Israeli NGOs and the Peace Process, Interim Report B, Israel, ISPO, December 1996.

31. R. Taylor, Final Country Report, South Africa, 1998.

32. C. Ragin, *The Comparative Method* (Berkeley: University of California Press, 1987).

33. Ibid.

Part II

Histories of the Three Conflicts

3

CONTEXTUALIZING PEACE AND CONFLICT-RESOLUTION ORGANIZATIONS IN SOUTH AFRICA, NORTHERN IRELAND, AND ISRAEL/PALESTINE

This chapter provides a brief overview of the conflicts in South Africa, Northern Ireland, and Israel/Palestine that the peace and conflict-resolution organizations (P/CROs) described in this book were—and in some instances still are—attempting to resolve. The chapter is intended to provide only enough context to assist readers in locating the more detailed and specific discussions found in later chapters of the book and therefore is highly selective. It describes the origin and evolution of the conflict in each country, provides a sketch of the major parties to the conflict, and gives some background about the P/CROs, their genesis, and their fortunes. Rather than providing a historical review, this chapter traces developments until very recently and so in part is a record of current affairs and complements the later chapters of the book, which focus primarily on the last several decades. More comprehensive accounts of these countries and their conflicts can be found in many of the works referred to in the notes section of this chapter.

South Africa

When apartheid became official government policy in 1948, South Africa was already a racially structured society. Since the beginning of the twentieth century, South African governments—in league with organized mining, industrial capital, and increasingly white labor—had been committed to providing cheap, unskilled black labor for white-run businesses. By the 1940s the legislation designed to achieve this goal had severely disrupted established social and economic relations, and had begun to create a migratory population of black industrial workers. Furthermore, these workers were subject to a highly discriminatory set of labor practices and occupied the lowest rungs on the socioeconomic ladder. Blacks were excluded from political power, had limited freedom of movement, and according to the Native Land Act of 1913, had only limited access to agricultural land. The result of these restrictions was extensive poverty among blacks, both rural and urban.

Whites in general were far better off, although English-speaking whites had greater influence and access to education, jobs, skills, and capital than did Afrikaans-speaking whites. This longstanding class—and language—division within the white community had been deepened by events such as the 1922 Rand Revolt, when the centrist and assimilationist South African Party (SAP) ruthlessly suppressed striking Afrikaner miners, and by the Great Depression, which forced many Afrikaner farmers off of their land and into the cities, and caused immiseration and further disaffection with the SAP. Simultaneously, Afrikaner self-help networks began to develop, promoting both Afrikaner business interests and a program of "Christian nationalism," an eclectic, indigenous combination of Afrikaner patriotism and Calvinism.[1] By the late 1930s there was sufficient political variety among white South Africans so that responses to the outbreak of World War II ranged from support for the Allies, to nonalignment, to pro-Axis activities. In the 1943 general election, the National Party (NP)—the party of this new Afrikaner nationalism and later of apartheid—captured 43 seats against the governing SAP's 103 to become the official opposition; the NP went on to win the election of 1948, although historians of South Africa still struggle to explain how and why it fared quite as well as it did.

Apartheid's first decade codified and extended the policies of racial segregation that already existed. Marriage and even sexual contact between whites and other South Africans was prohibited; the classification of South Africans by racial categories was instituted; residential segregation was enforced; separate educational systems were established for different race groups (education for black students was designed to prepare them for little more than manual labor); and the Suppression of Communism Act granted the Minister of Justice almost unlimited powers to proscribe persons and organizations that represented a threat to the apartheid system. However, during the 1950s the practical needs of business stymied attempts to regulate the movements of black workers, so that the policy of "influx control" was ultimately applied pragmatically, which really meant fairly sporadically.[2] Black resistance to the imposition of apartheid was widespread during the 1950s, and although it sometimes took innovative forms, on the whole it was ineffective.[3] The principal resistance organization, the African National Congress (ANC), failed to unify protesters because its administrative and financial resources were limited, there was a large gap between the interests of its mainly bourgeois leaders and the concerns of working-class blacks, and competitor resistance movements offered alternative visions.

Indeed, one such competitor, the Pan Africanist Congress (PAC), organized an event that led to the Sharpeville shootings of December 1959 in which seventy people died when police panicked over the size of a peacefully protesting crowd and opened fire. Massive strikes and worker stayaways ensued, international condemnation of South Africa reached unprecedented levels, and, with nonviolence largely discredited as a means of struggle against apartheid, the ANC's armed wing, Umkhonto we Sizwe (Spear of the Nation), was formed. The government's response was to declare a state-of-emergency, detain black resistance leaders, and ban the ANC, PAC, and South African Communist Party (SACP). When apartheid drew serious criticism at a Commonwealth conference in 1961, South Africa withdrew from the organization and proclaimed itself an independent republic.

Internationally isolated and confident of a stable electoral majority after 1960, the NP began to extend and entrench apartheid. The security apparatus was equipped with wide-ranging discretionary powers to combat political dissent (these powers were used increasingly during the 1960s),[4] and "influx control" was more rigorously enforced. This latter tactic was consistent with the "broader plan of political and social engineering" that developed at this point.[5] "Separate development," as it was called, entailed the establishment of ten "Bantu homelands," in South Africa's most unviable and undesirable areas, to which South Africa's blacks were assigned (and denied South Africa citizenship) on the basis of their supposed ethnicity. Essentially, the homelands system was an attempt to "retribalize African consciousness,"[6] foment competing ethnonationalisms, divide black political energies and actors, and prevent organization and direction against the apartheid state, although blacks were still to provide a cheap source of labor for white industry.[7] Despite these developments, however, the 1960s were fairly calm compared to the preceding and following decades. Several factors contributed to this relative tranquillity: the banning of anti-apartheid organizations and the difficulty of operating from exile, the increased repressive powers of police and censors, the resistance-sapping effects of the forcible removal of urban blacks to the homelands, the ineffective homeland bureaucracies, and a buoyant economy.

In the early 1970s, however, the combination of falling gold prices and rising oil prices introduced a period of recession that upset South Africa's prosperity. Between 1973 and 1976 strikes occurred throughout the country, including those in Soweto in which fifteen thousand black students took massively and spontaneously (and now famously) to the streets during June 1976. Some commentators link the events in Soweto to these countrywide developments, but the more immediate reasons for the student protests had to do with schooling conditions: Afrikaans was being imposed as the medium of instruction in black schools; funding levels and equipment provisions had dramatically failed to match the increased number of blacks attending school since 1970; and most graduates were having difficulty finding employment by 1976. Police fired on and killed several of the marching schoolchildren, and conflict and violence escalated in the following months, with an official death toll of almost six hundred by the end of the year.[8]

Although the state was caught unawares, it managed to weather the storm. But the uprising was a sign of things to come, heralding a burgeoning anti-apartheid resistance. The origins of this growing resistance were many and complex, including the simple availability of leadership from a newly resurgent—although still banned and covertly operating—ANC; the continuing economic hardships of black industrial workers; the emergence of the radical, politicizing activism of the Black Consciousness Movement; and the encouraging examples of ongoing or successful anticolonial struggles in neighboring Mozambique and Zimbabwe, and in other African countries. After a relatively untroubled reign of almost thirty years, this suddenly more hostile environment generated a crisis of confidence in the NP, and provoked an enduring and wide-ranging debate among its members about how best to continue to secure the interests of white South Africans. One camp advocated preserving the apartheid system in its then-current form by significantly increasing repression, if necessary (a "more-of-the-same" strategy). A second camp recommended overhauling and modernizing the system, and maintaining it through more nuanced and sophisticated means.

The faction advocating for a rejuvenated apartheid system gained momentum throughout the late 1970s and achieved a decisive victory in 1982, when some of its members left the NP to form the Conservative Party. Two closely related factors led to this success. First, after the 1976 Soweto uprising, Umkhonto we Sizwe gained thousands of new recruits, making it a force with which to be reckoned for the first time since the state destroyed its internal organization in the early 1960s. Second, a widespread conviction arose among influential state—especially military—agencies that the USSR had targeted South Africa for a "total onslaught." This was supported in part by the fact that revolutionary movements with USSR backing were campaigning for liberation in neighboring countries. For the NP, mobilization against this "total onslaught" was critical because it threatened everything for which the NP and white South Africa stood.

In response to the "total onslaught" and the new strength of Umkhonto we Sizwe, the NP developed what it termed "total strategy," a diverse but systematically coordinated package of both repressive and reformist measures designed to induce black acquiescence to the apartheid regime by either "force or fraud." For the NP, with its political philosophy that racial and ethnic identities and differences were essential and ineradicable, "total strategy" was the most effective way to avoid losing what it perceived as a brute and zero-sum "racial war" that could not be mediated. The package of reforms was intended to either crush or mitigate the growing opposition and hostility to the apartheid state and the structures it had created. It involved both a significant centralization (and arguably militarization) of the South African state and a partial, state-led liberalization of some aspects of the polity. The centralization component of the strategy involved the establishment of the powerful National Security Management System (NSMS), which was charged with managing the many issues affecting national security. Staffed mainly by military personnel, the NSMS effectively determined most state policy, either through official channels and statutory authority or by informal influence and the co-option of key actors from other state agencies.

It is crucial to recognize that the state did not intend the liberalization component of "total strategy" to serve as a prelude to the dismantling of apartheid. Rather, without fundamentally altering the system, the object was to soften its impact and make it less objectionable, while ensuring continued white supremacy. The liberalization reforms involved three changes, the least important and least effective of which was a restructuring of the organs of government in an effort to enhance their legitimacy. The Tricameral Parliament of 1983 allowed for colored and Indian political representation (blacks were still excluded), but it was only ostensibly democratic. Agenda-setting remained with the office of the presidency (which the NP controlled); white representatives outnumbered all of the other representatives by four to three; and the independent jurisdiction of colored and Indian representatives was limited to matters that fell within the ambit of their "own affairs." The Tricameral Parliament was really just a way of "sharing power without losing control,"[9] and most Indian and colored voters boycotted it.

The second element of the liberalization program attempted to create a black middle class that would be interested in maintaining the apartheid status quo. After 1978 blacks were allowed to buy leaseholds in urban areas, regulations were relaxed that had restricted black-owned firms to African townships and the homelands, and the state and the private sector collaborated to establish a credit and training facility to support entrepreneurship among all race groups. In some respects, however, the more liberal macroeconomic policy that the NP adopted actually worsened the apartheid burden blacks bore. Among other things, it cut taxes, thereby reducing the state's role in providing a variety of social services, particularly to poorer black communities.

The third and most important element of the liberalization process was the relaxation of prohibitions on civil society organizations. Some apartheid legislation was repealed, the urban labor market was restructured, and social movements were permitted to organize (although no organizations were unbanned at this stage). For instance, during the 1980s, measures were abolished that prohibited common amenities for blacks and whites, along with laws that disallowed mixed marriages and sexual relations between races. The state abandoned its attempt to regulate the movements of black South Africans and instead adopted a policy of "orderly urbanization." This reform, too, was a mixed blessing: while the number of blacks living near their places of work in and around urban areas increased, the state did little to provide additional essential services; indeed, consistent with its turn to the free market and monetarism, the state reduced service provision levels in some instances. The state also legalized and recognized for the first time black trade unions, which had existed illegally. However, this legalization took place primarily because the NP hoped to benefit from it: legalization was expected to institutionalize and bureaucratize trade unions, to inculcate in their members a sense of loyalty to the capitalist system, and to make it easier for the government to monitor and regulate union activities.

The mobilization of civil society organizations resulted in both an enormous proliferation of new nongovernmental organizations (NGOs) and an expansion of the activities of those that had existed already. Simultaneously there developed opposition journals and newspapers, student organizations, and grassroots political organizations, such as the multiracial, ANC-aligned United Democratic Front (UDF) and the smaller Black Consciousness Movement–aligned National Forum. While some NGOs supported the apartheid order (indeed, some advocated positions to the right of the NP's stance), the majority of the NGOs formed at this time opposed it. These NGOs came in all shapes and sizes. They ranged from small, informal, unregistered groups to much bigger ones, with large budgets, professional memberships, complex organizational structures, regional or national headquarters, multiple constituencies, constitutions, and regular publications.

These NGOs were not simply taking advantage of the organizational opportunities that the newly relaxed climate presented; they also were responding to new needs. First, as has been noted, the state did not provide many of the new communities of urban black workers with social services, and most rural black communities had been dramatically underserved for decades. NGOs emerged to organize and serve many of these disenfranchised and marginalized populations. Second, to function effectively the newly legalized trade unions, and to a smaller extent the recently formed political parties, needed support from the NGO sector, including technical and legal advice, administrative and logistical training, and data, analysis, and research from independent sources. The liberal, English-speaking whites who overwhelmingly staffed professional and research-oriented NGOs were the primary sources of such assistance. Indeed, NGO work represented one of the first opportunities for whites to oppose apartheid outside the frustrating constraints of the political system, and this may explain their positive response to establishing NGOs.

For all of their diversity and variety, many of the NGOs showed marked similarities, as the following three examples illustrate. First, it bears repeating that "total strategy" was *not* intended to prepare South Africa for the abolition of apartheid. Accordingly, the state did not allow NGOs to organize its demise—the amelioration of the apartheid system's evils did not imply abandonment of the system. Therefore, when NGOs or other political actors threatened the state, it reacted decisively. For example, it banned the Catholic Institute (a group that mounted scriptural and theological attacks on apartheid) as early as 1977 and the End Conscription Campaign as late as 1988. Thus, many NGOs that opposed apartheid, especially prominent ones, developed organizational structures that allowed them to survive intensive surveillance—and sometimes more aggressive action—from the NSMS and its agencies. NGOs of the "total strategy" era tended to be highly formalized, to encourage centralized decision making (or, when cells existed, to encourage centralized decision making within them, but to give these cells considerable latitude in arranging their own affairs), and sometimes to expediently sacrifice organizational democracy for security concerns. NGO leaders during this period were often high-profile persons with strong personalities, and this also may account for such authoritarian tendencies.

Second, virtually all of the NGOs depended almost entirely on funding from foreign sources. The NGOs sought international funders largely because South Africa's corporate sector had virtually no tradition of philanthropy and social responsibility. In addition, supporting NGOs financially was unattractive to corporations owing to specific legislation, as well as the general law of taxation. Finally, the private foundations that supported domestic NGO work in many countries were almost totally absent in South Africa. On the other hand, it appears that the international funders did not attempt to overly influence their grantees' work during the 1970s and 1980s, and many NGOs enjoyed considerable latitude and freedom from rigorous reporting procedures during these years.

Third, despite differences of philosophy and policy, almost all of the NGOs considered apartheid to be the root cause of South Africa's problems and were in agreement about what needed to be changed. For instance, it was generally accepted that the state's pernicious story that South Africa was involved in a zero-sum racial war had to be countered with a more sophisticated and less pessimistic account of the conflict. In addition, most NGOs promoted the assertion that it was possible to settle the conflict through dialogue and negotiation rather than military force. There was also consensus that the NGOs needed to debunk the government's claim that both blacks and whites would lose everything if apartheid South Africa ended. Finally, there developed a widespread determination among the NGOs that only "peace with justice" would suffice as a solution to the conflict.

"Total strategy" was intended to prevent protests of the kind seen in the 1970s and to stabilize apartheid South Africa, but it achieved quite the opposite. Despite adverse economic circumstances, blacks took advantage of relaxed pass controls and flooded into the cities, and trade unions became more active and grew in size, political sophistication, and radicalism.[10] Throughout the mid-1980s, protests (some of which were coordinated) took place regarding such diverse issues as the deployment of army members as teachers in black schools, the pointlessness of homeland citizenship, and increases in township rents and service charges. Heavy-handed government repression (for example, there was a state of emergency for most of the period from 1984 to 1990 and the state showed rather obvious support for vigilante attacks on antistate forces) often fueled further resistance. By 1987, the army and police had quelled the protests; but there was still massive support for the UDF inside the country and for the ANC outside of it.[11]

With the failure of "total strategy," the apartheid state was bereft of ideas and relied on brute force for its continued survival. This approach did not eliminate the resistance forces and furthermore drew mounting international condemnation. The economy continued to suffer[12] and the government began to lose crucial support from the business community. When in 1985 the president of South Africa, P. W. Botha, vetoed the meaningful reforms his foreign minister promised and publicly rejected any suggestion that majority rule lay in South Africa's future, foreign banks called in loans they had made in 1982, the rate of disinvestment increased, and additional economic sanctions were imposed—all of which resulted in the collapse of the South African currency. Within a month, progressive members of the alienated business community made contact with ANC leaders in exile.[13]

A new frenzy of international outrage occurred when the South African army attacked supposed ANC bases in neighboring countries in 1986, and in the late 1980s the trade unions—in careful concert with the UDF—mounted a campaign of civil disobedience. Nevertheless, despite some tentative reforms from the Botha government, the destructive stalemate between the government and the resistance movement continued. But in August 1989, after months of intraparty wrangling, Botha, who had suffered a stroke earlier in the year and had already resigned as leader of the NP, was forced by his Cabinet to step down as president, and was replaced by his moderate minister of education, F. W. de Klerk.

In February 1990, without even informing his own party of his plans, de Klerk unbanned the ANC, PAC, and SACP, and soon after released dozens of political prisoners, including Nelson Mandela. The following year, key apartheid legislation was repealed and negotiations with resistance movements were initiated to inaugurate a democratic, unitary South Africa. A number of factors led to this abrupt change. Most importantly, South Africa simply could not afford to remain an economic pariah, whose economic interactions with the world consisted of exporting capital and repaying debts.[14] In addition, the collapse of the USSR assuaged fears about the "total onslaught." Furthermore, de Klerk's security advisers had informed him that the ANC was sufficiently weak by 1989 that it would be controllable if it was unbanned.[15]

There also seemed to be a fair chance of reconfiguring the NP and making tactical alliances so as to secure an electoral place for the party in a postapartheid South Africa. Finally, behind-the-scenes discussions between the ANC and prominent Afrikaner intellectuals (as well as de Klerk's own secret talks with Mandela) suggested that the ANC was open to negotiations.

The process of negotiation that ensued, however, was difficult and fraught. In addition to major disagreements about substantive provisions and a PAC boycott, the process was halted in 1992 as evidence surfaced of the apartheid state's involvement in assassinations and "dirty tricks," and as political violence increased—especially in Natal between the ANC and the Zulu nationalist Inkatha Freedom Party (IFP). The ANC continued to employ techniques of "rolling mass action" while it negotiated, and radical right-wingers began to threaten war if majority rule was implemented. Caught up in the world recession of the early 1990s, the economy continued to stagnate and the flood of investment many had optimistically anticipated did not occur. However, negotiations were resumed in 1993 with a new urgency in the face of increasing violence, and as a result, April 27, 1994, was set as an election date. Opposition to the election on a variety of fronts began to fade as the date neared, although the IFP waited until the election was just a week off before agreeing to participate. Twenty-two million South Africans cast their ballots in the first democratic election in South Africa's history during three remarkably violence-free days, and the ANC garnered almost two-thirds of the vote.

Northern Ireland

The roots of Northern Ireland's conflicted history lie very deep. As early as 1170, Henry II of England tried to incorporate the island into his kingdom. The small beachhead he founded around Dublin was not significantly expanded until the sixteenth century, however, and was not fully secured until 1609, when the last resisters of English rule in Ireland, the clans in the northern province of Ulster, were defeated. Their land was confiscated, and—in what became known as the Plantation of Ulster—the province was seeded with English colonists.

Thus, a foreign community, representing an alien culture and way of life, was established on expropriated land while the original inhabitants were relegated to the margins of their former holdings. Furthermore, the new settlers were mainly Protestant, while the defeated native Irish were predominantly Catholic. Within fifty years of the Plantation, the broad lines were established of a conflict that has endured for almost four centuries. Two rival factions, often living in close proximity, nurtured mutually incompatible ambitions and harbored deep suspicions about one another, with the Protestant camp feeling that it was under constant threat of expulsion, and the Catholic faction believing that its country had been usurped.[16]

The following two centuries cemented this antagonism. In response to regular rebellions, a series of penal laws against Catholics was enacted, and in 1801 England dissolved the Irish parliament through an Act of Union, and Westminster assumed administrative control of the island. Resistance to the union during the 1800s, sometimes violent and sometimes parliamentary, was widespread, especially toward the end of the century. The failed Easter Rising of 1916, the execution of the Easter Rising's nationalist leaders, and the subsequent surge in Catholic support for the Irish Republican Army (IRA) and its political wing—the Irish nationalist party, Sinn Féin—dashed any possibilities of home rule (that is, limited self-government within the British Empire). In 1918, Sinn Féin defeated the Irish Parliamentary Party (the long-time advocate of home rule) to win the first postwar election, despite having had little success in Ulster. Subsequently, Sinn Féin refused to take its seats at Westminster, established its own Irish parliament in Dublin, and began the War of Independence, the first incarnation of "the troubles."

The 1920 Government of Ireland Act ended the war; however, this compromise piece of legislation ultimately satisfied neither the Catholic nationalists, who demanded a wholly independent Ireland, nor the Ulster Protestants, who refused to be included in such an arrangement. Two subordinate administrations were established—one for the six northern counties of Ulster and another for the remaining twenty-six counties of the Irish Free State—and each was given a number of devolved powers, but ultimate sovereignty was reserved for the Westminster parliament. Although the population of the six northern counties was two-thirds Protestant and therefore the Unionist Party could expect an enduring electoral majority, a parliament in Belfast was not the triumph for the Protestants—whose ambition had never been any kind of home rule at all but rather unity with the United Kingdom—that a parliament in Dublin was for the nationalists in the Irish Free State. The Protestants realized, however, that there was little sympathy and affection for them in Britain, and accepted the partition of Ireland as a better alternative than Westminster's forcing them to be governed by Dublin.

The partition had many and varied consequences for Northern Ireland, but while generally it "restricted opportunities for regional development, in one crucial and ultimately fatal respect it allowed too much freedom: the working-out of sectarian rivalries."[17] The 1920 Act did not take into account historical differences in the North, its more recent struggles over home rule/independence, and its divided society in which a large proportion of the population identified with their co-religionists in the Irish Free State. The government relied on force merely to survive, and during the early 1920s a civil war nearly developed in Northern Ireland, resulting in hardened religious divisions.

The violent nationalism that arose in Northern Ireland aimed to destroy anything that symbolized the British administration, claimed to represent all of Northern Ireland, and often used the civilian population as a shield. It was so pervasive that almost all Catholics, even those who opposed violence but supported the tradition of constitutional nationalism, came to be identified with the IRA. The "Irish dimension," as evidenced by an independent state to the South that claimed sovereignty over the entire island and evinced an irredentist commitment to Irish unity, further contributed to the fear and bitterness in Protestant-Catholic relations. Long-standing emergency legislation that the predominantly Protestant government introduced (in effect martial law),[18] unsympathetic courts, and a justifiable perception of economic discrimination and second-class citizenship[19] suggested to Catholics that they were not living in a neutral liberal-democratic state. As a result, they opted out of public political life, in general, and the state's representative structures, in particular. Accordingly, a variety of Catholic voluntary organizations developed, some of which were highly exclusive or exhibited a strong religious bent.[20]

Intermittent economic difficulties, which afflicted the Catholic inhabitants of the southern and western areas disproportionately, compounded the problems of the new state during the interwar years. Although these years were relatively peaceful (with some notable exceptions, such as the 1935 riots in Belfast that erupted after protestors were fired upon in a Protestant march), the opportunity to consolidate a harmonious Northern Irish nation-state was not seized. Rather, "the divisive pattern of government and politics sketched out in the angry early months was confirmed and became even more deeply entrenched."[21]

Few shifts in the ossified politics of Northern Ireland occurred during the two decades after World War II—indeed, one study describes the 1950s as a period of "cold war"[22]—however, tensions relaxed slightly, largely because this was a prosperous period. Catholics continued to participate little in party political life, and the Nationalist Party (at that point the second largest party in the Irish parliament) was unable to offer a policy that went beyond general opposition to partition. Radical republicanism waned, and there was little support for the IRA campaign of 1956–1962. Accordingly, those who supported unionism became complacent, and generally politics were "stable to the point of sterility."[23]

However, some complex and cross-cutting socioeconomic developments occurred during this period. In the late 1940s, a welfare state was established, the consequences of which were wide-ranging. Some welfare provisions reinforced the division that characterized community relations in the North. For example, while the Education Act of 1947 provided for increased access to secondary and further education, such education still took place along predominantly sectarian lines, and so "continued, and arguably increased, socio-religious segregation."[24] Although an ambitious housing program was launched,[25] allocation often took place along denominational lines as politicians used housing as a means to maintain their electoral majorities. When Westminster guaranteed Northern Ireland's constitutional status in 1949, this bred a sense of security among Protestants and allayed a need to make concessions to the Catholic minority.

But welfarism also had countervailing effects. The good things the system provided depended on subsidies from the British state; this helped to cement bonds between Britain and the Protestants and perhaps even reconciled Catholics to the constitutional situation. Relatedly, the province's level of prosperity increased at a rate significantly higher than that of the Republic of Ireland,[26] and this economic divergence tended to weaken the links between northern and southern Catholics. As a result, "Catholic aspirations [slowly] began to focus on Northern rather than a united Ireland,"[27] a significant shift from the two decades after the partition. These events do not necessarily suggest any sort of reconciliation with Britain, but rather an increasing distance from the South and the parochialization of Catholic aspirations.

Once again, however, the benefits of the 1950s were not shared equally. While the Catholic professional and managerial class began to expand and to develop the skills and confidence that enabled it to put its case eloquently to the state in the late 1960s, a contracting agricultural sector pushed many Catholic workers into unskilled manual labor. Protestant workers, on the other hand, often were able to obtain semi-skilled, nonmanual employment. The straitened circumstances of many working-class Catholics meant that the volunteer and charitable organizations continued to be necessary to service their needs. On the whole, Northern Ireland in the 1950s was a "stable but deeply divided"[28] society that nonetheless held the future promise of reducing the depth of the division.

During most of the 1960s it appeared that this possibility would be realized, and there was little that anticipated the conflagration that engulfed Northern Ireland at the end of the decade. Later, many Catholics would look back on this period as a time when "things would have got better for us—or anyway for our children."[29] In almost every respect, the positive and promising features of the 1950s developed further in the following decade. While Protestants still enjoyed the lion's share of employment, housing, and social services, and property qualifications still disenfranchised Catholics at the local level, surveys from the late 1960s show that both camps believed community relations had improved and they looked forward to further progress.[30] The large majority of Catholics (81 percent) had come to expect fair treatment from their local authority,[31] and a still increasing GDP per head allayed many economic grievances.

When Terence O'Neill was appointed prime minister in 1963, it quickly became evident that he envisioned a Unionist Party officially committed to community reconciliation, as well as greater economic and social equality in Northern Ireland. Though he made little headway against the longstanding antagonism between Northern Ireland's communities, he nevertheless engen-

dered some Catholic trust in unionist government for the first time in Northern Ireland's history.[32] However, the newly confident and assertive burgeoning Catholic middle class was frustrated for ways to voice its concerns, make
its demands, and respond to O'Neill's overtures; it was out of step with the slowly
changing ambitions of the traditional nationalist movement, and although new
nationalist parties were formed, these largely were unsuccessful.

Far more significant was the growth in the mid-1960s of extra-parliamentary pressure groups, such as the Campaign for Social Justice, the Northern
Ireland Civil Rights Association, and People's Democracy. Such groups followed the example of the international civil rights movement by employing
techniques of peaceful protest—particularly the mass march—to campaign
against discrimination, gerrymandering, the slow pace of reform, and the
partisan character of security services. Often articulate and sophisticated,
such groups were careful to avoid making claims that could be misinterpreted
as political and astutely couched their campaigns in terms of the internationally fashionable language of civil liberties.

Nevertheless, O'Neill's policy of liberalization and the Catholic middle
class's largely sympathetic and constructive response produced a Protestant
backlash. Although a wide variety of Protestants became concerned about
O'Neill's reformism, its most trenchant opponent was Ian Paisley, who,
throughout the 1960s, mobilized demagoguery and sometimes quite violent
street politics behind his fanatical and provocative brand of Protestantism.[33]
Paisley appealed mainly to working-class Protestants, who felt most threatened by the reformism. Thus, Paisley's involvement led to a split between
unionism's middle-class and working-class supporters. When, as O'Neill put
it, the "lid blew off the pot,"[34] it was largely the result of confrontation between extra-parliamentary Catholic and Protestant groups.

The lid began to blow off in late 1968. A Catholic civil rights march in
Londonderry ended in violent clashes with police, provoked rioting throughout the city, and signaled a new phase of "the troubles." Catholic marches
and Protestant countermarches succeeded one another in Derry over the following two months, and as nationalist forces began to coalesce behind the
civil rights movement, Protestant fears began to rise. In January 1969 further clashes occurred, and by April public buildings were being bombed. More
sectarian rioting occurred in July and August, as well as the growth of paramilitary and self-defense groups, which persuaded Westminster to deploy
British troops. Catholics initially welcomed these nationalist organizations,
particularly a resurgent IRA.[35] By late 1970 these groups had succeeded in
reducing the violence; by 1971 they had convinced the Catholic community
that the British troops were partisan (they were under the executive control
of the Protestant-dominated government); and by the end of that year the
friction between Catholics and Protestants was as fierce as it had ever been.
The "Bloody Sunday" massacre, in which British troops killed thirteen un-

armed people in early 1972 (the year in which more people were killed in political violence in Ireland than in any other year),[36] drew world attention to the problem. This forced Britain to announce Direct Rule over the province at the beginning of April, putting an end to fifty-odd years of "benign neglect."[37]

The imposition of Direct Rule was intended as a short-term measure, but in some ways it became entrenched. Direct Rule provided the IRA with a new, "legitimate" target—British imperialism—and because the IRA employed guerrilla tactics British troops could not defeat the IRA through straightforward military means. As a result, the conflict between the IRA and the British government settled into a stalemate in the 1970s and early 1980s, underpinned by an economic downturn throughout the United Kingdom. Even official attempts to manage economic competition and prevent its politicization were unsuccessful. For example, the Fair Employment Act of 1976 attempted to eliminate sectarian inequality in employment, but in an environment where there simply were not enough jobs to go around, every job that went to a Catholic was one that didn't go to a Protestant. As the lives of working-class Protestants and Catholics became more difficult (certainly compared to their respective middle classes), moderate political leaders were sidelined, exclusivist extremists on both sides attracted a good deal of support, and the prospects for progress became extremely bleak.

Concerned moderates on both sides of the sectarian divide tended to look to unconventional means for a solution. Since politics was so antagonistic and unpromising, and unelected British officials handled the day-to-day administration of the province, "some of the brightest talents [chose] to put their energies into the voluntary sector rather than into formal politics."[38] Voluntary groups also emerged as a result of the increasing popularity of notions of popular participation, a growing awareness of poverty, and the evident incapacity or unwillingness of government services to meet social needs—all of these changes resulted in part from the fact that the most important issue in the 1970s and 1980s became once again Northern Ireland's constitutional status, so that social and economic issues got less attention. For Catholics, this sort of community involvement represented simply the development and elaboration of an established style of civil rights activism, but for Protestants it represented a new form of social organization. Apart from the dearth of appealing alternatives for political and social activists, other factors promoted growth in the voluntary sector, as well. For instance, in 1969 the British government established the Ministry for Community Relations to improve community relations in Northern Ireland, and the Department of Education provided financial support for voluntary organizations involved in community relations work.[39]

There were few political developments in Northern Ireland until the early 1980s. In 1976, IRA prisoners in the Maze Prison in Belfast were deprived of prisoner-of-war privileges and treated as ordinary criminals. By 1979, their resistance to this measure took the form of high-profile, internationally covered hunger strikes. Embarrassed by the attention the issue was attracting, the British government began to look more energetically for a solution to the Northern Ireland problem, and in 1980 met with the Irish government to explore cooperative means for achieving that goal.[40] Although the prominent nationalist Social Democratic and Labour Party rejected one proposal for a British withdrawal from Ireland (a "rolling devolution," in which elected representatives gradually would return to power, provided that widespread support for their return existed), the ground was laid for the Anglo-Irish Agreement of 1985.

Remarkably, the agreement satisfied both British and Irish concerns about Northern Ireland: Westminster recognized Dublin's interest in Northern Ireland, but a unionist majority was guaranteed the right to veto unification with the South; and Ireland supported Britain's policy of encouraging moderation and constitutionalism in Northern Ireland, furthering devolution of power on the basis of power-sharing, and combating terrorism.[41] Effectively, Ireland accepted that Britain maintain Direct Rule and a military presence while searching for a negotiated settlement. Unionist opposition to the agreement was almost total but ineffectual, and sectarian violence lessened after the agreement.

By 1991, the Anglo-Irish Agreement had been established long enough (and enough "talks about talks" had taken place in the background) so that discussions about superceding it could begin between the Irish and British governments and the main Northern Irish constitutional parties. No settlement was reached, but there was a consensus about which principles should underlie any new political institutions in Northern Ireland.[42] At this point the British government revealed that it had been communicating secretly with the revolutionary nationalist movement for some three years, and although this disclosure angered Protestants, it indicated to Catholics that the British government was sincere about finding a solution for Northern Ireland.

Amid an upswing in violence in late 1993, the British government released the Downing Street Declaration in an attempt to nullify the IRA's justification for violence in Northern Ireland—that is, British imperialism. In it the British government denied any "selfish strategic or economic interest in Northern Ireland," and asserted that its objectives for the province were solely "peace, stability and reconciliation."[43] Although it did not regard the Declaration as adequate, the IRA declared a cease-fire in late August 1994 in order to explore the possibility of peace through negotiation.[44] Unionist paramilitaries reciprocated in October, with the provision that they would not tolerate any change in the constitutional status of Northern Ireland.

The British and Irish governments published their joint discussion document, *Framework for the Future*, in January 1995, but unionists felt that the document was too generous to the nationalist movement and clashes occurred again in mid-1995. Although a massive IRA bomb in February 1996 delayed talks scheduled for the end of that month (and the peace process was jeopardized, in general), the cease-fire was reinstated in 1997 and negotiations continued. In May 1998 a countrywide referendum showed widespread support for a new Northern Irish Assembly to include representatives from both unionist and nationalist parties.

Israel/Palestine

There was a Jewish presence—albeit small—in Palestine well before the waves of Jewish immigration of the late nineteenth century. In 1881, Palestine had close to half a million inhabitants, and only 25,000 of these (about 5 percent) were Jews.[45] Most of these Jews were in Palestine to worship and study. Their small and unassertive community enabled them to coexist with the Arab majority in a sort of loveless harmony, although sporadic conflict did occur as early as the 1880s. By World War I, however, the first of several waves of Jewish immigration into Palestine more than doubled the Jewish population. Under the influence of Zionism and the mistaken impression that Palestine was "a land without a people awaiting a people without a land,"[46] some came with the intention of making Palestine a Jewish homeland.[47] This ambition largely contributed to a situation in which conflict became a part of everyday life in the following decades.

When World War I erupted, the Ottoman Empire—of which Palestine was then a part—sided with Germany. In order to influence the non-Turkish inhabitants of the Empire, Britain "made many promises, some of them mutually exclusive" to Jews (i.e., the Balfour Declaration) and Arabs (i.e., the Hussein-McMahon Correspondence) in the Middle East.[48] Thus, at the end of the war both groups believed that they had claims to Palestine. After a period of military rule and much discussion, the matter was settled in 1922: under a League of Nations mandate, Britain controlled Palestine and was to "facilitate Jewish immigration under suitable conditions" and encourage "close settlement by the Jews on the land," while ensuring that "the rights and position of other sectors of the population [were] not prejudiced"[49] and preparing the region for political independence.

This proved a difficult task. The Palestinian Arabs, who agreed on little else, were unanimously opposed to Jewish settlement. They constantly thwarted British attempts to establish self-governing institutions, fearing that their participation would indicate acceptance of and legitimize the growing Jewish presence in Palestine. Relations between Arabs and Jews—who became increasingly numerous, organized, and confident—were poor. Outbreaks of violence became more frequent and lethal as the Jews formed self-defense units in response to the anti-Jewish riots that erupted when they began to purchase land in 1920 and 1921. Much more serious violence flared up again in 1929 and again in the mid-1930s when Jews began to stream out of Nazi Germany into Palestine.

The development of a peace-advocating NGO sector was still decades away, but during the 1920s and 1930s academics and intellectuals formed several small organizations that argued for a binational state and restrictions on immigration into Palestine.[50] Although one of these organizations lasted (or languished) into the 1950s, these groups had little impact on mainstream Zionist thinking and Palestinians were equally unsympathetic to their proposals for compromise. The main effect that these organizations had was to lead the Jewish public to equate peace activism with naïve, extreme utopianism—an association P/CROs in Israel/Palestine still struggle to overcome.[51]

The British response to the deteriorating situation was equally ineffectual: "Policy was shaped by a series of 'white papers' issued usually in response to outbreaks of violence over land or immigration issues . . . [T]he British seemed to be muddling through, while trying to keep the peace."[52] This process, which sometimes favored Jews and at other times Arabs, had severely damaged Britain's relationship with both communities by the late 1930s. Three years prior to World War II, there were massive Arab strikes and anti-British violence, as well as some Jewish terrorism. By the outbreak of the war, Palestine was in chaos. Jews and Arabs had developed a zero-sum perspective on their claims to Palestine, and neither community endorsed the continuation of Britain's mandate. Although the final white paper published before the war granted most of the Arabs' demands, the Jews, despite their great bitterness, had no choice but to support the Allies against the Nazis when the war broke out.[53] On the other hand, the Arabs sided with the Axis powers.

The political climate during the war years was comparatively calm. A major British military presence meant that active resistance from Jews or Arabs to the mandatory authorities was minimal, although Jews did flout the restrictions on immigration that the 1939 white paper had imposed. They also campaigned to raise international awareness of Jewish aspirations and clarified the concept of a Jewish national home. When Allied victory was assured late in the war and with British policy still based on the 1939 white paper, Jewish guerrilla resistance to the mandatory authorities resumed, with the aim of forcing Britain to partition Palestine between Jews and Arabs. With emerging evidence of the horror of the Holocaust many Jews felt they had an irresistible right to compensation, but Allied policymakers curiously were unmoved. Arab political activism also increased as the war ended, and Arab Palestinians, along with the Arab countries that surrounded them, demanded independent statehood for a unitary, Arab-dominated Palestine.

The British, in conjunction with the United States, initially tried to find a solution to the problem; when that failed in 1947 they turned the entire matter over to the United Nations for resolution. The UN Special Committee on Palestine decided that the partition of Palestine between Jews and Arabs was the best solution, and in November 1947 the General Assembly supported the proposal. Arab protests and Jewish celebrations followed, and clashes between the two communities soon escalated into a full-scale civil war. The conflict became increasingly widespread and vicious as the date approached for the implementation of the partition and as Arabs from neighboring countries became involved. When the British mandate terminated and the state of Israel declared its independence in May 1948, the armies of Egypt, Transjordan, Syria, Lebanon, and Iraq—a total of 25,000 troops—invaded. Thus began the war-studded history of Israel.[54]

Initially the newly constituted Israeli Defense Force (IDF) struggled against the Arab troops, but it soon took the upper hand against a poorly coordinated Arab campaign. In fact, the IDF was so successful that it pushed the Arab armies beyond the partition boundaries and came to occupy an additional two thousand square miles (20 percent) of Palestine. When armistices were signed in 1949, the Israelis retained nearly all of the land they had captured during the fighting. More significant, the war created about 750,000 Arab refugees (about 70 percent of Israel/Palestine's Arab population), including almost the whole Palestinian intellectual and political elite; understandably, Arabs have since referred to this migration as al-Nakhba—"the disaster." Most of these refugees fled to what were to become the West Bank and the Gaza Strip (then parts of Jordan and Egypt, respectively) or to other Arab states, while the rest became internal refugees.

Half a century after the event, there is still little consensus about just who caused the refugee problem. At the time, the Jewish authorities disclaimed all responsibility, and maintained that the Arab states had encouraged the Palestinian Arabs to depart temporarily and to return when the Jews had been defeated; at the least, Syria did make such a call.[55] On the other hand, the Palestinians maintained that Jewish forces had deliberately driven them from Palestine (the particularly gruesome civilian massacre at the village of Deir Yasin was part of this strategy), and there is evidence for this claim, too.[56] In any case, the refugee problem became a major issue in Arab-Israeli relations, with the Israeli state firmly rejecting all proposals for general repatriation and even compensation.

Most of the decade after the civil war was a period of great austerity for the new state. It spent vastly on defense, as guerrilla raids into Israel were common, and vigilance and protection were required.[57] The cost of integrating hundreds of thousands of Middle Eastern Jewish immigrants, the Arab states' total economic boycott of Israel, and the closure of the Suez Canal to Israeli shipping further weakened the economy. Protective of its new and still somewhat precarious sovereignty, the new state—especially under David Ben-Gurion—energetically constrained extra-parliamentary activity. Therefore, the 1950s were a lean time for nonconformist activists of any kind, but especially for those who sought an accommodation with the Palestinians. Furthermore, with the Israeli state increasingly entrenched, Israeli activists recognized that their pre-1948 goal of a binational state founded on Israeli-Palestinian parity had become all but impossible, and so began to advocate the very opposite—the division of Palestine between Jews and Arabs.[58] This radical proposal did little to redeem the radical image of peace activism in Israel/Palestine.

Not surprisingly, Jewish-Arab relations worsened with the establishment of the Israeli state, and in October 1956 the IDF, in collusion with Britain and France, attacked Egypt. The IDF regarded the attack as a preemptive strike since Egypt was armed by the Soviet Union and was fomenting a pan-Arab coalition against the young nation-state.[59] While Britain and France failed to regain the regional ascendancy that they had hoped, Israel secured the demilitarization of the Sinai Peninsula and the deployment of UN forces in trouble spots, and regained access to the Gulf of Aqaba. During the postwar period, Israel made important advances in its foreign relations, enjoyed growing prosperity, and began to mature politically and culturally. Nevertheless, the civil society remained weak and NGOs were scarce and unimportant. The consumerism and improving standards of living that accompanied prosperity combined with the fatigue of warfare and years of mobilization focused most Israelis' attention on the private rather than the public sphere.[60] Moreover, the state continued quite actively to discourage unofficial sociopolitical initiatives.

The end of the Suez War initiated a period of tense but nonviolent coexistence between the Israeli and Arab states; this lasted until the Six-Day War a decade later. But the attitude of the Arab states remained antagonistic and fearful, and there even developed something of an inter-Arab rivalry in championing the anti-Israel cause. In 1964 the Palestine Liberation Organization (PLO) was formed with the aims of destroying Israel, returning the refugees to Palestine, and establishing a Palestinian state—although for some years it "was primarily an instrument of the Arab governments, especially Egypt."[61] For their part, Palestinians began to organize themselves politically for the first time since the 1948–49 war. In 1959, Yasser Arafat formed al-Fatah, which initially competed with the PLO. Al-Fatah was most active militarily, carrying out raids into Israel from bases in Jordan and Syria, which was becoming increasingly anti-Israel; the Israeli IDF units retaliated, sometimes excessively.

In the months and weeks preceding the 1967 War, Israel's relationship with Syria and Egypt increasingly became strained. A number of factors contributed to Egypt's remilitarization of the Sinai Peninsula in May 1967. Egypt had ambitions to become the leader of the Arab nation-states and a false estimation of its military capacity. The USSR had supplied Egypt with misinformation about Israeli troop movements in the hope of strengthening the 1966 Egypt-Syria defense pact; both Arab countries had become Soviet clients. International diplomatic attempts to avert the impending crisis failed, and Israel's government, weakly led at the time, displayed little assurance.

When war broke out in early June, however, Israel acted decisively. It smashed the armed forces of Egypt, Jordan, and Syria, and occupied the fertile and economically developed West Bank, the oil-bearing Sinai Peninsula, the Gaza Strip, and the Golan Heights, increasing its territory by threefold. The official resolution of the conflict was UN Resolution 242, which, although ambiguous, proposed the idea of peace in exchange for territory. Its acceptance by the Arab states (with the exception of Syria) constituted an implicit acknowledgement of Israel's right to exist, but the fleeting opportunity to achieve a more stable, lasting peace was not taken, and matters settled into a belligerent stalemate once again. In fact, Israel and Egypt were soon involved in the two-year War of Attrition in the Sinai; the absence of a negotiated settlement, along with Arab discontent and humiliation, made another round of conflict almost inevitable.

In the years after the Six-Day War, there were significant developments in Arab-Israeli relations. Along with the territory Israel had conquered came well over a million Palestinian refugees in Gaza and the West Bank. Moreover, the specifically Palestinian nationalism that had simmered while these refugees lived under Arab governments now began to grow and spread. Since 1974 the PLO—with Arafat now as president—served as an umbrella organization for guerrilla groups, among which al-Fatah was still the most important and effective. In 1974 the Arab League also acknowledged the PLO as the legitimate representative of the Palestinian people, and the PLO was granted observer status at the UN. Two years later the PLO became a full member of the Arab League, although relations between the PLO and the Arab states were often fraught.[62] Thus, in the words of one commentator, the conflict became "Palestinianized"[63] for all of the parties involved in it.

The performances of Syria and Egypt in the 1973 Yom Kippur War bolstered their confidence, although their success was partly due to materials from the USSR. Egypt became so self-assured that it was willing to try conventional diplomacy to resolve the dispute with Israel.[64] In 1977 Anwar Sadat, Egypt's president, visited Israel and set the scene for his meeting with Menachim Begin, Israel's prime minister, at Camp David outside Washington, D.C., the following year. The negotiations resulted in a peace treaty between the two countries, which was supposed to lead to Palestinian autonomy and in due course to Israel's withdrawal from the Sinai and parts of Gaza. Mutual suspicion, recalcitrance, and Palestinian resistance to the terms of the treaty hindered the implementation of the autonomy provisions, and the process was finally stymied when Israel invaded Lebanon in 1982. Israel destroyed PLO bases in Southern Lebanon (called "Fatahland"), but the PLO rapidly reestablished itself after the war.[65] More importantly, the invasion was condemned internationally, and the PLO gained more credibility among Palestinians, as well as international recognition and some international support.

There were also important domestic developments within Israel during the late 1960s and 1970s. The ease with which Israel had won the 1967 War and the territorial buffer zones established on Israel's borders meant increased security and confidence, and the collectivist and semi-authoritarian political culture that had checked the growth of civil society relaxed. In addition, as the state consolidated its power, it came to tolerate more extra-parliamentary activism. The civil rights movement in the United States and the student movements worldwide also legitimized such activism, and the Israelis that came of political age in the early 1970s began to organize themselves into NGOs to address such issues as civil rights, education, environmental protection, and medical care. A small number of organizations also emerged to press for dialogue with the Palestinians and negotiation about the Occupied Territories. The Yom Kippur War and its aftereffects also strengthened participation in NGOs. Although Israel ultimately had prevailed, it failed to anticipate Egypt's attack and was caught dramatically off guard. A judicial inquiry found that the upper echelons of the military command were at fault. This finding, along with a wave of protest after the war, left many Israelis concerned about "the inability of the society, its leadership and institutions to deal adequately with some of its basic, central, internal and external problems."[66]

When Menachem Begin became prime minister of a right-wing government in 1977 and indicated unequivocal support for settlement in the Occupied Territories, many left-wing Israelis feared that the peace talks with Egypt would be jeopardized and mobilized to form Peace Now, the largest P/CRO in Israel's history. When the treaty was indeed signed in 1979, Peace Now broadened its scope and began to protest the ongoing settlement of the Occupied Territories and the IDF's treatment of Palestinians. Its zenith was its high-profile role in the massive protest over the 1982 invasion of Lebanon, which was regarded as an aggressive and unnecessary "war of choice."[67] However, cognizant of the stigma Israeli peace groups had acquired, Peace Now was careful not to threaten the broad fabric of Israeli society. While the voluntary sector in general began to expand in the 1980s as the state cut back its level of social service provision and NGOs stepped in to fill the gaps,[68] the period after the end of the war in Lebanon was one of "concerted inactivity"[69] for peace organizations: the government encountered many political grievances and had to mollify moderate activists; Begin's resignation in 1983 reduced the passions involved in politics; and the rate of settlement in the Occupied Territories slowed.

During the 1980s there were also some promising developments in the Middle East. Although influential Israelis opposed them, peace negotiations began between Jordan and Israel, and the Arab League reinstated Egypt as a member (it had been expelled for the 1977 peace agreement with Israel). But these developments rarely reflected Palestinian concerns or involved Palestinians, and at the 1987 Arab summit in Amman Palestinian interests were low on the agenda. A sense of marginalization, the increasing militarization of Palestinian youth in the 1980s, no viable remedy for longstanding grievances about arbitrary legislation, the inequitable apportionment of water between Jews and Arabs, and unemployment in the Occupied Territories meant that "only a spark was needed to set off an explosion."[70] In December, an IDF truck accidentally killed four Palestinians, and their funerals in a refugee camp in Gaza became the occasion for a massive Palestinian demonstration against the occupation. Unlike earlier protests, this one spread and grew, and thus began the Intifada (resistance).

The Intifada's ramifications were extensive. The Israeli state responded with tough measures, but the Intifada simply became more organized and sophisticated; while some Israelis, especially settlers in the Occupied Territories, concluded that yet greater force was required, more concluded that some sort of land-for-peace deal was the only solution. The moribund peace movement resurrected itself and expanded (a daily newspaper identified at least 46 such groups in 1988),[71] and skillful use of the mass media ensured that its voice was heard, if still warily. For much of the 1970s and 1980s the Israeli peace movement had been ridiculed for not having an "Arab equivalent,"[72] and for the first time, large numbers of grassroots Israeli-Palestinian dialogue groups emerged.

Media coverage of the Intifada made it difficult to sustain the self-deception that the occupation was benign, and when Iraqi missiles later fell on Israel during the Gulf War many Israelis were persuaded that "security through territorial depth was a dangerous illusion in the context of contemporary warfare," and began to question the value of retaining the Occupied Territories.[73] Although different Arab nations stood to profit more or less from the Intifada, "at the all-Arab level [the Intifada] in general and the PLO in particular received considerable rhetorical, political and diplomatic support."[74] The unrest in the West Bank led Jordan to announce in 1988 that it was severing judicial and administrative ties with the area; both Israel and the United States had assumed that Jordan would partner with the Palestinians in a West Bank–Jordan federation if Israel ever withdrew from the West Bank. This move meant that eventually Israel would have to negotiate directly with the PLO. The Intifada also pushed the PLO into positive action: a Palestinian state was declared, while accommodationist overtures were made to Israel.

Although the Gulf War briefly superseded the Palestinian problem, Israeli leaders began to realize that PLO participation in talks was essential. However, because the PLO supported Saddam Hussein, it lost the crucial sponsorship of the Persian Gulf states and its options were reduced. Little was achieved at the formal peace talks in Madrid in 1991, where the PLO could participate only as part of the Jordanian delegation. However, Norwegian diplomats facilitated secret negotiations in Oslo just over a year later, during which the PLO explicitly acknowledged Israel's right to exist and renounced terrorism, and Israel recognized the PLO as the official Palestinian representative in peace negotiations. In September 1993, the Washington, D.C., Declaration of Principles set the mutually agreed upon framework for further discussions about the status of Palestine over the following five years.

This declaration was vague enough that both Israel and the PLO could commit to it; but this meant that determining the details of the agreement was painfully slow business. Both right-wing religious Jewish settlers in the Occupied Territories and militant Islamic groups opposed the peace process. Peace activists relaxed their efforts—many of them were exhausted after their unrewarded struggle and were hopeful that the government would safely lead the peace process. Reservations among NGOs about the peace process were downplayed so as not to lend weight to Israeli right-wing criticism. The sometimes fatal clashes between the IDF and Palestinian demonstrators were a constant backdrop to the negotiations during the next few years. When a right-wing Jew killed 29 Muslim worshipers in 1994, the guerrilla organization, Hamas, responded with two suicide bombings. Nonetheless, by mid-1994 the negotiations in Cairo led to an IDF withdrawal from Gaza and Jericho and to Palestinian self-rule in those areas. Later negotiations at Taba determined that self-rule for 90 percent of Palestinians would be expanded in early 1996, although the fates of Hebron and East Jerusalem still had to be decided and settler resistance was frenzied. Meanwhile, concessions and substantial cooperation had prepared the way for a peace treaty between Jordan and Israel in mid-1994, although Syria and Israel were unable to reach a similar agreement.

In November 1995 a right-wing Israeli assassinated Yitzhak Rabin, Israel's pro-peace prime minister. Israelis were horrified, but the assassination "also helped to silence the most violent anti-peace rhetoric and shifted public opinion toward a greater acceptance of the peace process."[75] Arafat and Shimon Peres, Rabin's successor, both appeared committed to peace negotiations. Arafat's mandate to continue the talks was broadly confirmed when he garnered 90 percent of the vote in the January 1996 election of a self-governing Palestinian assembly.[76] It was widely expected that Israelis would give Peres similar ratification in Israel's general election that May. But radical Islamic groups launched more suicide bombings in early 1996, and this swayed many Israeli voters towards Peres's opponent, Binyamin Netanyahu of the right-wing Likud Party, whose campaign stressed security and the concerns of Israeli settlers in the Occupied Territories. Netanyahu also proved himself more adept than Peres at the political horse-trading with small parties that is often crucial to success in Israeli elections, and although his margin of victory was minute, he became Prime minister in May 1996.

Although Netanyahu agreed to honor the peace agreements that already had been concluded, he slowed down the withdrawal of IDF troops from Palestine, despite the fact that their retreat had been agreed upon at Taba. In addition, Palestinian riots, in response to what seemed to be Israeli designs on a Muslim holy place in Jerusalem, left fifty people dead by late 1996. International criticism and pressure from the United States led Netanyahu and Arafat to resume talks, and after several months of tortured negotiations, they reached agreements about the future of Hebron, the status of the West Bank, the release of political prisoners, and other matters. However, Israeli P/CROs were conspicuous during this process mainly because of their absence; after demobilizing in the early 1990s, they failed to rise to the challenge that the victory of Netanyahu's Likud Party had presented.

Conclusion

There are some broad, very basic comparisons that can be made between the conflicts presented in this chapter. First, in some sense land was at issue in each country. This was truest for Northern Ireland and Israel/Palestine, where the conflicts were most obviously over which community had the right to occupy a specific territory; but even for South Africa the crucial question was whether and how the space was to be shared between conflicting communities. Relatedly, to a certain degree all three conflicts had their origins in one population's forced settlement of and ensuing rule over another population's territory; moreover, in part a religious mythology of national destiny and election was used to justify this imperialism in all three regions.[77] Thus, another feature common to all three conflicts was ethno-national division, with religious identities further complicating the situations in Northern Ireland and Israel/Palestine. These ascriptive divisions, in turn, largely coincided with and reinforced class borders: blacks, Palestinians, and Catholics in South Africa, Israel/Palestine, and Northern Ireland, respectively, all tended to be proletarian, have less access to the state, and receive fewer opportunities than did whites, Jewish Israelis, and Protestants.

There were also some distinct differences between the conflicts. For instance, what constituted a P/CRO varied among the countries according to the roots of the conflict and what was considered a workable, just solution. This difference will be fully examined in later chapters of the book. The conflicts also were—to greater or lesser degrees—specific regional conflicts, in which the international community had an interest. For instance, it is difficult to understand the history of Israel/Palestine without understanding the history of its relationship with its middle-eastern neighbors or its geopolitical importance to the superpowers. Although South Africa's sub-Saharan African region was less of a factor in the conflict there, international pressure played a very important role in putting an end to apartheid. Comparatively speaking, the conflict in Northern Ireland was both local and insulated.

Notes

1. See Dan O'Meara, *Volkskapitalisme: Class, Capital and Ideology in the Development of Afrikaner Nationalism* (Johannesburg: Ravan Press, 1983).

2. See Deborah Posel, *The Making of Apartheid 1948–1961: Conflict and Compromise* (Oxford: Clarendon Press, 1991).

3. Nigel Worden, *The Making of Modern South Africa: Conquest, Segregation and Apartheid* (Oxford: Blackwell, 1994), pp. 99–103; Tom Lodge, *Black Politics in South Africa since 1945* (London: Ravan Press, 1983).

4. Harold Wolpe, *Race, Class and the Apartheid State* (London: James Currey, 1988), pp. 88–89.

5. Worden, *The Making of Modern South Africa*, p. 109.

6. Frank Molteno, "The Historical Significance of the Bantustan Strategy," *Social Dynamics* 3 (1977): 23.

7. Hermann Giliomee, "The Changing Political Function of the Homelands," in *Up against the Fences: Poverty, Passes and Privilege in South Africa*, ed. Hermann Giliomee and Lawrence Schlemmer (Cape Town: David Philip, 1985).

8. Lodge, *Black Politics*, p. 330.

9. Martin Murray, *South Africa: Time of Agony, Time of Destiny: The Upsurge of Popular Protest* (London: Verso, 1987), p. 112.

10. See Eddie Webster, "The Rise of Social-Movement Unionism: The Two Faces of the Black Trade Union Movement in South Africa," in *State, Resistance and Change in South Africa*, ed. Philip Frankel, Noam Pines, and Mark Swilling (London: Croom Helm, 1988), p. 192.

11. See Tom Lodge, "State of Exile: The African National Congress of South Africa, 1976–1986," in *State, Resistance and Change*, ed. Philip Frankel, Noam Pines, and Mark Swilling (London: Croom Helm, 1988); Mark Swilling, "The United Democratic Front and Township Revolt," in *Popular Struggles in South Africa*, ed. William Cobbett and Richard Cohen (London: James Currey, 1988).

12. Sampie Terreblanche and Nicoli Nattrass, "A Periodization of the Political Economy," in *The Political Economy of South Africa*, ed. N. Nattrass and E. Ardington (Cape Town: Oxford University Press, 1990), pp. 18–19.

13. Mann, "The Giant Stirs: South African Business in the Age of Reform," in *State, Resistance and Change*, ed. Philip Frankel, Noam Pines, and Mark Swilling (London: Croom Helm, 1988), p. 80.

14. Terreblanche and Nattrass, "A Periodization of the Political Economy," p. 18.

15. Worden, *The Making of Modern South Africa*, p. 138.

16. John Darby, "Conflict in Northern Ireland: A Background Essay," in *Facets of the Conflict in Northern Ireland*, ed. Seamus Dunn (Basingstoke: Macmillan, 1995), p. 16.

17. Patrick Buckland, *A History of Northern Ireland* (New York: Holmes and Meier Publishers, 1981), p. 23.

18. Paul Arthur, *Government and Politics of Northern Ireland* (London: Longman, 1984), p. 17.

19. Sabine Wichert, *Northern Ireland Since 1945* (London: Longman, 1991), p. 17.

20. D. Kennedy, "Catholics in Northern Ireland 1926–1939," in *Years of the Great Test 1926–1939*, ed. F. MacManus (Cork: Cork University Press, 1967), p. 148.

21. Buckland, *A History of Northern Ireland*, p. 55.

22. Denis P. Barritt and Charles F. Carter, *The Northern Ireland Problem: A Study in Group Relations* (London: Oxford University Press, 1962), p. 24.

23. Feargal Cochrane and Seamus Dunn, Final Country Report, Northern Ireland, 1998, p. 39.

24. Wichert, *Northern Ireland Since 1945*, p. 47.

25. R. J. Lawrence, *The Government of Northern Ireland* (Oxford: Clarendon Press, 1965), p. 152.

26. The Irish Free State became the Republic of Ireland in 1949.

27. Wichert, *Northern Ireland Since 1945*, p. 75.

28. Barritt and Carter, *The Northern Ireland Problem*, p. 153.

29. Dervla Murphy, *A Place Apart* (London: J. Murray, 1978). Cited in Wichert, *Northern Ireland Since 1945*, p. 99.

30. Richard Rose, *Governing without Consensus: An Irish Perspective* (London: Faber and Faber, 1971), pp. 297–306.

31. Ibid., p. 228.

32. Ibid., pp. 300–302.

33. Thomas Hennessey, *A History of Northern Ireland, 1920–1996* (Basingstoke: Macmillan, 1997), pp. 138–139.

34. Wichert, *Northern Ireland Since 1945*, p. 91.

35. In December 1969 the Provisional IRA was formed when a more radical faction of the IRA decided that deliberate military action was necessary to defend Catholics in Northern Ireland and that the IRA was unwilling to undertake it. J. Bowyer Bell, *The Secret Army: The IRA 1916–1979* (Dublin: Academy, 1979), pp. 366–370.

36. Darby, "Conflict in Northern Ireland," p. 19.

37. Richard Rose, *Northern Ireland: A Time of Choice* (London: Macmillan, 1976). Cited in Wichert, *Northern Ireland Since 1945*, p. 55.

38. Pollak, ed., *A Citizen's Inquiry: The Opsahl Report on Northern Ireland* (Dublin: The Lilliput Press, 1993). Cited in Cochrane and Dunn, Final Country Report, p. 45.

39. Cochrane and Dunn, Final Country Report, p. 48.

40. Paul Arthur and Jeffrey Keith, *Northern Ireland since 1968* (Oxford: Blackwell, 1988), p. 15.

41. Wichert, *Northern Ireland Since 1945*, pp. 194–195.

42. Hennessey, *A History of Northern Ireland*, p. 282.

43. Ibid., p. 287.

44. See Paul Bew and Gordon Gillespie, *The Northern Ireland Peace Process, 1993–1996* (London: Serif, 1996), p. 63.

45. Yossi Beilin, *Israel: A Concise Political History* (London: Weidenfeld and Nicolson, 1992), p. 15.

46. British Zionist, Israel Zangwill, quoted in Don Peretz, *The Arab-Israeli Dispute* (New York: Facts on File, 1996), p. 10.

47. Yossi Melman writes of Theodor Herzl, the father of modern Zionism, that he "did not really consider the question of how the local Arabs would feel about the immigrating and colonizing Jews. . . . He avoid[ed] the problem by hoping for mutual tolerance between Arabs and Jews. With this kind of thinking, Herzl laid the spiritual cornerstone for the approach of Zionists toward their Arab neighbours in the Middle East," in Yossi Melman, *The New Israelis: An Intimate View of a Changing People* (New York: Carol Publishing Group, 1992), p. 31.

48. Adam M. Garfinkle, "Genesis," in *The Arab-Israeli Conflict: Perspectives*, ed. Alvin Z. Rubinstein (New York: Harper Collins, 1991), p. 15.

49. Ian J. Bickerton and Carla L. Klausner, *A Concise History of the Arab-Israeli Conflict* (Englewood Cliffs, N.J.: Prentice-Hall, 1995), p. 43.

50. Michael Jansen, *Dissonance in Zion* (London: Zed Books, 1987), pp. 6–7.

51. Tamar Hermann, Final Country Report, Israel, 1998, p. 42.

52. Bickerton and Klausner, *A Concise History*, p. 48.

53. Once war broke out, Ben-Gurion famously declared: "We shall fight the war as if there were no white paper; we shall fight the white paper as if there were no war," quoted in Peretz, *Arab-Israeli Dispute*, p. 27.

54. One historian (although one might dispute his enumeration) has described the history of Israel as "seven wars and one peace treaty." See Itamar Rabinovich, "Seven Wars and One Peace Treaty," in *The Arab-Israeli Conflict: Perspectives*, ed. Alvin Z. Rubinstein (New York: Harper Collins, 1991), pp. 34–58.

55. See Chaim Herzog, *The Arab-Israeli Wars: War and Peace in the Middle East from the War of Independence through Lebanon* (New York: Random House, 1982), p. 38. Herzog, a former Israeli Prime Minister, also noted that "the Jews endeavored . . . to dissuade the Arab population from [fleeing]," but that the "Arabs were torn by doubts and beset by an atmosphere of panic," and left nonetheless. Herzog, *The Arab-Israeli Wars*, p. 37. There is very strong although not entirely conclusive evidence that some Jews tried to persuade Arabs not to leave.

56. See Benny Morris, *The Birth of the Palestinian Refugee Problem, 1947–1949* (Cambridge: Cambridge University Press, 1987) and Ritchie Ovendale, *The Origins of the Arab-Israeli Wars* (London: Longman, 1992).

57. Melman, *The New Israelis*, pp. 131–148. Some maintain that most of these "guerrilla raids" were in fact merely Palestinian Arabs "attempting to return to their property in Israel." Peretz, *Arab-Israeli Dispute*, p. 57. Michael Jansen describes the militarization of Israeli society in *Dissonance in Zion*, chapters 2 and 3.

58. David Hall-Cathala, *The Peace Movement in Israel, 1967–1987* (Basingstoke: Macmillan, 1990), p. 29.

59. Rabinovich, "Seven Wars," pp. 38–39.

60. Hermann, Final Country Report, p. 32.

61. Bickerton and Klausner, *A Concise History*, p. 144.

62. See Helena Cobban, *The Palestinian Liberation Organization: People, Power, and Politics* (New York: Cambridge University Press, 1984).

63. Herbert C. Kelman, "The Palestinianization of the Conflict," in *The Arab-Israeli Conflict: Two Decades of Change*, ed. Yehuda Lukacs and Abdalla M. Battah (Boulder: Westview Press, 1988), p. 334.

64. See Ann Mosely Lesch and Mark Tessler, *Israel, Egypt and the Palestinians: From Camp David to Intifada* (Bloomington: Indiana University Press, 1989).

65. See Itamar Rabinovich, *The War for Lebanon, 1970–1983* (Ithaca: Cornell University Press, 1984).

66. S. N. Eisenstadt, *The Transformation of Israeli Society: An Essay in Interpretation* (Boulder: Westview Press, 1985), p. 389.

67. Colin Shindler, *Ploughshares into Swords? Israelis and Jews in the Shadow of the Intifada* (London: I.B. Tauris, 1991), pp. 206–207.

68. Samuel Lehman-Wilzig, *Stiff-Necked People, Bottle-Necked System: The Evolution and Roots of Israeli Public Protest, 1949–1986* (Bloomington: Indiana University Press, 1990).

69. Shindler, *Ploughshares into Swords?*, p. 207.

70. Peretz, *Arab-Israeli Dispute*, p. 89.

71. Reuven Kaminer, "The Protest Movement in Israel," in *Intifada: The Palestinian Uprising against Israeli Occupation*, ed. Zachary Lockman and Joel Beinin (Boston: South End Press, 1990), p. 231.

72. Shindler, *Ploughshares into Swords?*, p. 209.

73. James Ciment, *Palestine/Israel: The Long Conflict* (New York: Facts on File, 1997), p. 58.

74. F. Gregory Cause, "The Arab World and the *Intifada*," in *The Intifada: Its Impact on Israel, the Arab World and the Superpowers*, ed. Robert O. Freedman (Miami: Florida International University Press, 1991), p. 196.

75. Ciment, *Palestine/Israel*, p. 212.

76. *The Economist*, January 27 1996.

77. See Donald Akenson, *God's Peoples: Covenant and Land in South Africa, Israel, and Ulster* (Ithaca: Cornell University Press, 1992).

Part III

Peace and Conflict-Resolution Organizations in the Four Locales Studied

4

SOUTH AFRICA: THE ROLE OF PEACE AND CONFLICT-RESOLUTION ORGANIZATIONS IN THE STRUGGLE AGAINST APARTHEID

RUPERT TAYLOR

Apartheid South Africa was one of the most unjust and oppressive societies the world has known, with the widespread suppression of human freedoms enforced through systematic race classification and draconian security legislation. Apartheid's most notorious features included the denial of voting and land rights to the majority of South Africans, an exploitative system of migrant labor and pass laws, segregated education and public amenities, and complex residential arrangements designed to ensure the "separate development" of black and white South Africans. As the *Truth and Reconciliation Commission Report* stated: "For at least 3.5 million black South Africans it [apartheid] meant collective expulsions, forced migration, bulldozing, gutting or seizure of homes, the mandatory carrying of passes, forced removals into rural ghettos and increased poverty and desperation."[1]

The 1980s, in particular, were dark times. Under National Party (NP) rule, South Africa was highly militarized: it was fighting wars in Angola and Namibia, aggressively destabilizing the Frontline States, and within its own borders systematic and violent official repression of the resistance movement rose to unprecedented levels.[2] By the end of 1985, the South African Defence Force (SADF) had deployed over 32,000 troops in ninety-six of the country's townships. In July 1985, a partial state of emergency was declared. It was lifted in March 1986, but a nationwide state of emergency followed in June 1986 that remained in force for four years. Between 1985 and 1988, over five thousand people were killed in political violence in South Africa, and approximately fifty thousand people were detained. By the end of 1988, thirty-two nonviolent anti-apartheid organizations had been banned.[3] In these years it was little exaggeration to say that South Africa was "a terrorist state."[4]

Not surprisingly, in 1968 the United Nations had declared the apartheid system "a crime against humanity." Later, the World Council of Churches was moved to describe apartheid as a sin against God and humanity, and in 1985 the Kairos Document labeled the apartheid state "satanic."[5] The apartheid state's attempts "to achieve the maximum possible separation between the races" and its prevention "of contact on a basis of equality" quite clearly violated the notion of a common humanity and subjected Africans to a daily routine of humiliation and deprivation.[6]

Such repression, injustice, and discrimination provided powerful motives for protest and challenge, but those seeking peaceful progressive change faced immense obstacles. The prospects for successful nonviolent direct action virtually had been eliminated in the 1950s when it "was shown to be an impotent and ineffective counter to state action."[7] It was for this very reason that the African National Congress (ANC)—after being banned in 1960—formed its military wing, Umkhonto we Sizwe (MK), and turned to armed struggle. Increasingly, the South African situation was interpreted as an irresolvable zero-sum communal conflict between blacks and whites, between African and Afrikaner nationalism, between the ANC and NP, in which the use of force was inevitable.

Nonetheless, nonviolent direct action tactics were continually used. During the 1970s there were three clear waves of protest—the student protests of 1972, the Durban labor strikes of 1973, and the Soweto uprising of 1976—all of which the state contained with ever increasing repression.[8] In the 1980s, mass-based social movements deploying a broad repertoire of noncooperative and defiance strategies arose, at the center of which were the United Democratic Front (UDF) and the Congress of South African Trade Unions (Cosatu). Students, workers, and community activists engaged in school, consumer, and election boycotts; demonstrations; labor strikes; and stayaways.

The UDF, formed as an umbrella organization in August 1983 to protest the National Party's reform agenda (which included a tricameral parliament that continued to exclude the majority of the population), united about eight hundred organizations and approximately 3 million people. On February 24, 1988, however, it was prohibited—along with sixteen other anti-apartheid organizations—from performing any activities or acts whatsoever.[9] Cosatu was formed in November 1985 as a federation of independent trade unions and soon came to represent 1 million workers. Trade unions had developed through a decade-and-a-half struggle to build strong and democratic shop-floor organizations. Building on this, Cosatu forged close alliances with community politics and sought to contest apartheid through large-scale strike action and stayaways, as well as supporting the call for international economic sanctions. Under the states of emergency, however, the police detained many labor leaders, and in February 1988 Cosatu was prohibited from engaging in political activities.[10] Those engaged in any form of anti-apartheid work operated in an ever-contracting public realm, often under intensive surveillance from the security police, and increasingly faced the threat of imprisonment and death. Peace seemed extremely elusive.

Peace and Conflict-Resolution Organizations

In apartheid South Africa, anti-apartheid activists had a very narrow space in which to pursue peaceful progressive change. Just about the only options available to them were nongovernmental organization (NGO) advocacy and activism for peace, reconciliation, and negotiation between conflicting parties on the basis of mutual recognition, and the use of dispute-resolution strategies in conflicts at both the national and subnational levels. A number of legally constituted NGOs positioned themselves somewhere between the ideological "extremes" of African and Afrikaner nationalism, argued that black and white South Africans did not face a "win-lose" situation, and sought to bring people together in order to change values, attitudes, and patterns of interaction. Broadly following the agency model of relationship building, such interventions aimed specifically at promoting grassroots contact between black and white South Africans and facilitating dialogue between political actors. Nevertheless, peace and conflict resolution work in apartheid South Africa was inherently subversive; it could hardly be otherwise: although the NGOs outwardly professed political neutrality, impartiality, and objectivity, these very notions are definitionally grounded in a democratic framework, within taken-for-granted progressive assumptions.

According to this book's definition of a peace and conflict resolution organization (P/CRO), the most vibrant, active, and well-known P/CROs in apartheid South Africa were those listed in table 4.1.[11] These P/CROs engaged in a wide variety of activities, and, as will be argued below, together constituted a network within which group memberships circulated and overlapped. In the 1980s, the organizational characteristics of NGOs engaged in peace and conflict resolution work were well suited to the strategies and tactics of protest and change they adopted. Most important, these P/CROs were integrated into social networks, which insulated their personnel from the severe restrictions the apartheid state imposed on their rights to organize, speak, and demonstrate.

South African P/CROs exhibited a number of clear similarities in their modes of operation, above all a great degree of centralization and formalization. Although a superficial examination of P/CRO structures might suggest relatively high levels of organizational democracy, in practice most decision-making authority rested with the organizations' leaders. In all of the organizations—regardless of whether their anti-apartheid activities involved protesting and campaigning or the provision of services in research, community development, or mediation—operational decisions were made by execu-

TABLE 4.1.   The Leading Peace and Conflict-Resolution Organizations in Apartheid South Africa

Organization	Acronym	Dates of existence
South African Institute of Race Relations	SAIRR	1929–
Black Sash		1955–
Justice and Peace Commission, SACBC	J&P	1967–
Centre for Intergroup Studies	CIS	1968–
End Conscription Campaign	ECC	1983–1994
Independent Mediation Service of South Africa	IMSSA	1984–2000
Institute for a Democratic Alternative for South Africa	Idasa	1986–
Koinonia Southern Africa	KSA	1986–1992
Project for the Study of Violence	PSV	1988–
Quaker Peace Centre	QPC	1988–

tive committees, which the organization leaders usually controlled, and strategic decision making generally was the prerogative of a board of trustees comprising people of high social standing and reputation (such as the former leader of the parliamentary opposition, Frederik van Zyl Slabbert, and Soweto civic leader, Dr. Nthato Motlana). Leadership was a crucial factor, particularly because in the early years of these organizations very few staff were employed. It is true to say that, with the exception of the End Conscription Campaign (ECC), all of the organizations listed in table 4.1 were dominated by their leaderships.

P/CRO leaders tended to share a common set of socioeconomic characteristics. They were all South African, predominantly university-educated, white, and male; several of them, such as H. W. van der Merwe of the Centre for Intergroup Studies (CIS) and Rommel Roberts of the Quaker Peace Centre (QPC), were Quakers. Many of the leaders held, or had held, faculty posts at leading South African universities, and—especially among Afrikaans-speakers—had backgrounds in theology. The leaderships of CIS, the Institute for a Democratic Alternative for South Africa (Idasa), Koinonia Southern Africa (KSA), and QPC included both English and Afrikaans speakers. A significant number of English-speaking leaders, notably Charles Nupen of the Independent Mediation Service of South Africa (IMSSA) and Laurie Nathan of ECC, had long been involved in broader anti-apartheid activity, especially through the National Union of South African Students (Nusas) and other NGOs.

Below the leadership level, P/CROs comprised largely a white, liberal, English-speaking constituency, often with professional training in service-providing P/CROs. Although a significant number of black South Africans were active in all of these organizations, the P/CROs' social base was relatively homogenous—the white liberal middle class. During the 1980s, active supporters of these ten organizations probably never numbered more than ten thousand people, and the total number of full-time paid staff never exceeded two hundred. Over time, though, service-providing P/CROs did expand their staff complements and increase the representation of black employees.[12]

South Africa's administrative and legal environment, especially its tax laws, discouraged philanthropy and corporate-giving to NGOs, so securing overseas funding was absolutely crucial for the P/CROs' survival and expansion.[13] Astute leadership secured regularly increasing levels of funding, from thousands of rands in the 1980s to millions in the 1990s. Particularly important was funding from Scandinavian countries, the European Union, and American foundations.

Under apartheid, one of the key funders of peace and conflict resolution work was US-AID, which provided funds to IMSSA, CIS, Idasa, and the South African Institute of Race Relations (SAIRR). The Ford Foundation was also a major funder of the sector, providing initial funding for IMSSA (for whom this funding was essential) and giving financial support to Idasa and Black Sash. Another key funder was the UK-based Joseph Rowntree Charitable Trust, a Quaker organization that funds work for nonviolence and mediation. It has had a long-standing commitment to South Africa, providing important funding for CIS, IMSSA, QPC, Idasa, and Koinonia, all of which the Trust regarded as working for "peaceful social change." Throughout the apartheid years the proportion of funding from overseas and domestic sources was constant, approximately 83 percent and 17 percent, respectively.

It is quite evident that South Africa's P/CROs were highly interlocked and are best understood as constituting an interorganizational network, or as occupying the center of a multiorganizational field concerned with peace and conflict-resolution work. Their activities can be divided into five distinct but overlapping clusters: antimilitarization, conflict resolution and mediation, promoting "contact," initiating dialogue, and pursuing "objective research."[14]

It is necessary to analyze South African peace and conflict-resolution work in terms of these clusters—rather than detailing each individual organization's contribution—because, in the apartheid years, most P/CROs did not understand themselves as single-purpose peace and conflict-resolution organizations. The P/CROs typically engaged in more than one type of work; leaders and activists described their organizations as pursuing multiple ends and could not easily identify their most important tactic. In the following section, the five clusters of P/CRO activities are discussed sequentially.

Peace and Conflict-Resolution Work

Antimilitarization

The closest thing to a South African "peace movement" (in the usual sense of the term) is the cluster of organizations that opposed the militarization of South African society, maintaining not just—to put it loosely—that the country should move toward an end to war, but also that it should seek to establish a "just peace." The Black Sash, the Justice and Peace Commission of the Southern African Catholic Bishops Conference (SACBC), and ECC all formed part of this cluster in the 1980s, protesting the South African Defence Force's involvement in Angola and Namibia and its role in defending apartheid within South Africa. Compulsory conscription was a particular target. Between 1976 and 1990, conscription was extended to all white male South African citizens; during this period it was illegal to encourage people not to serve in the apartheid army, and conscientious objection was not recognized in law. It was possible, though, to call for an end to conscription, and the ECC made this call trenchantly, recognizing—as Albert Einstein argued—that personal refusal to take part in war is the best way to abolish it.[15]

The ECC was formed in 1983 as a cooperative grouping of some 18 organizations, emerging from concerned groups, such as the South African Council of Churches, Southern African Catholic Bishops Conference, Nusas, and the Black Sash. The ECC adopted a fairly encompassing political stance, which embraced both universal and situational pacifists. Perhaps its most significant contributions were its 1985 "Troops Out of the Townships" campaign, involving three-week fasts and a rally of four thousand people at Cape Town city hall, and a 1986 "Working for a Just Peace" campaign, which advanced alternatives to military service centered around developing community projects in townships.[16] ECC, along with the Black Sash, J&P, and Koinonia, also upheld an individual's right to refuse to do military service for reasons of conscience.

All of this resistance to militarization worked to weaken the apartheid state: it affected the apartheid state's assessment of its military capacity, resulting in the state's crackdown on the ECC in August 1988, when it became the first white organization to be banned in more than twenty-five years (since the Congress of Democrats in 1962).[17] Beyond this, J&P's ongoing work in Namibia led to the 1985 publication of a *Report on War in Namibia* and the ensuing trial of Archbishop Denis Hurley, South African Catholic Bishops Conference president, for accusing South African counterinsurgency forces of perpetrating atrocities.[18] In the event, the state withdrew its charges one half hour into the trial.

Conflict Resolution and Mediation

Other clusters of organizations concerned themselves with conflict resolution and mediation, notably the CIS and IMSSA, and more recently the Quaker Peace Center and the Project for the Study of Violence (PSV). Evincing a strong commitment to impartiality, these organizations offered a variety of professional services: third-party assistance, mediation and facilitation of community and political conflicts, and skills training for groups in conflict.

Under its Quaker director, H. W. van der Merwe, the Centre for Inter-group Studies was the first organization to "specifically offer courses on, or training in, communication skills for mediators or third-party intervenors in the field of community and political conflict."[19] In the field of industrial relations, IMSSA served as an independent industrial dispute-resolution organization, promoting mediation and arbitration as alternatives to conventional approaches (in labor dispute mediation IMSSA had a more than 50 percent success rate).[20] Informally linked to the CIS, the Quaker Peace Centre, which was founded in response to conflict in Cape Town townships, also engaged in community conflict resolution; as did the PSV, which was established at the University of the Witwatersrand in Johannesburg (Wits). For these organizations, conflict resolution and mediation were not about decisively resolving conflicts (which were analyzed as multicausal, multidimensional, complex, and not necessarily undesirable), but about providing skills for constructive conflict management. Successful interventions resulted in increasing faith in the processes of mediation and negotiation.

Promoting "Contact"

Among the cluster of P/CROs that promoted "contact," the aim was to change personal attitudes about race, especially among the white community. Following the precepts of the "contact hypothesis," these organizations focused on arranging "encounters."[21] Koinonia, SAIRR, Black Sash, and Idasa were at the forefront of such work. At the launch of Koinonia ("belonging together") in 1986, Nico Smith, the founding national director, stated that the organization's aim was "to promote contact between people of different race groups in a polarized South African society."[22] Koinonia assessed the South African situation as "a conflict of the unknown," where whites did not know blacks, and vice versa, and from 1988 onwards it organized "encounters" with around three hundred people at a time in various townships. Koinonia also arranged informal meal groups in people's homes, group trips to restaurants and cinemas, and joint community projects.

Similarly, the SAIRR initially was established to "promote interracial goodwill," and before most of its regional branches were phased out, actively sought to bring young people together.[23] In addition, the Black Sash consistently worked to promote interracial contact and is largely regarded as having played a bridge-building role.[24] Idasa also arranged township visits and various workshops to promote "contact." All of this "contact" work brought about changes in people's perceptions and represented a direct challenge to apartheid ideology, which insidiously maintained that "contact" led to "friction" and therefore justified segregation.[25]

Initiating Dialogue

Another cluster of organizations—the SAIRR, CIS, and Idasa, at different points in time—worked to encourage dialogue at the elite level between Afrikanerdom and the extra-parliamentary opposition in the belief that it would prepare the ground for a negotiated solution to the conflict. Partly out of necessity, these organizations promoted interaction through informal channels. In the early years of apartheid, the SAIRR facilitated contact between the National Party and the anti-apartheid movement.[26] In December 1984, H. W. van der Merwe of the CIS attempted to initiate a dialogue between the senior members of the NP and the ANC by arranging a five-hour clandestine meeting in Lusaka (Zambia) between senior ANC officials—namely, Thabo Mbeki and Simon Makana—and Dr. Piet Muller, an assistant editor of a leading Afrikaans pro-government newspaper. In doing so, he established direct communication between the ANC and the Afrikaner establishment for the first time in twenty-four years.[27]

Idasa, which overtly positioned itself as a nonaligned NGO and was founded by former parliamentarians Alex Boraine and Frederik van Zyl Slabbert, also played a crucial role by initiating and organizing a meeting in Dakar (Senegal) on July 9–12, 1987, between more than fifty prominent, reform-minded Afrikaners and seventeen key ANC members.[28] Idasa also held later conferences in Leverkusen, Harare, and Lusaka, and informally encouraged and facilitated other third-party mediation initiatives.[29] Such endeavors promoted "public acceptance of the possibility of a negotiated settlement and growing recognition of the ANC as a legitimate contending party within South Africa,"[30] and forced those in power to see "that the ANC was not part of the problem, but part of the solution."[31]

Pursuing "Objective Research"

Finally, some P/CROs sought to "objectively" reveal and challenge apartheid "facts" through strategic analysis and research. The ECC, SAIRR, and the Black Sash exposed the "objective facts" of apartheid—concentrating on the migrant labor system, forced removals, and the role of the SADF—in order to educate and sensitize people to their human and economic costs. The SAIRR devoted most of its resources to the accumulation and dissemination of data on apartheid South Africa; its internationally known *Survey of Race Relations*, first published in 1936, documents "all matters affecting race relations" in hundreds of pages annually.[32] According to the author Ellen Hellmann, "the systematic seeking out of facts relating to the conditions which determine the quality of life of the disadvantaged groups in South Africa would increase public awareness and promote inter-racial understanding, an understanding without which there could be no peaceful future for South Africa."[33]

The Black Sash also did much to publicize apartheid's injustices, especially forced removals (such as the plight of the people of Crossroads outside of Cape Town). Sheena Duncan, a Black Sash national president, recalled: "*The Rand Daily Mail, The Star* . . . there were ways in which those newspapers took the stuff we gave them, and they ran big exposures. I think that if we hadn't been there, the newspapers wouldn't have had half of the things they did expose. Nobody else knew about, ever thought about, the pass laws. So the Black Sash was the source of information about what was going on."[34] The ECC focused on the cost of the wars in Angola and Namibia, and the repressive function of the SADF in the townships. Altogether, "objective research" attempted to explode the myths of apartheid by showing statistically that apartheid did not work and that its social, political, and economic costs were immense. The many publications that the P/CROs produced induced both South African and international communities to support the anti-apartheid movement.[35]

It is important to realize that significant personnel overlap existed across these organizations—for ordinary members, leaders, and board members—that other networks formed through family ties and institutional attachments reinforced. In fact, the Black Sash deliberately networked with other organizations. Sheena Duncan recalled: "I used to tell Black Sash people that they must have at least one other area in which they were active. This was long ago, way back. I used to say we all need to be involved somewhere else."[36] The ECC, with its coalition structure, was itself a network, and the PSV "had broad networks . . . [and] crossed boundaries at different levels."[37]

It is a mistake, then, to perceive either P/CROs or P/CRO clusters as discrete, hermetically sealed entities. In practice they were dynamic groups that were always interacting. Many P/CROs spanned more than one cluster of peace and conflict-resolution work. Their links with one another were central to their formation, their cooperation on projects and programs, and the sharing of resources.

It is also important to note that P/CROs actually engaged in many unorthodox forms of peace and conflict-resolution work. For example, the ECC engaged in creative activities, such as fun-runs, kite-flying, street theater, rock concerts, and art exhibitions; the Black Sash undertook court-monitoring, sit-ins, and silent vigils; and J&P workers helped prepare special prayers for important occasions and placed symbols of oppression—like barbed wire, tear gas canisters, and rubber bullets—on the altar to remind congregation members that they were worshiping in a time of oppression. Furthermore, the real significance of P/CROs in South Africa lay in how they complemented the broader anti-apartheid struggle, how they meshed with other social actors struggling for progressive social change.

The Multi-Organizational Field

Not only did P/CROs constitute a densely interlocked network themselves, but they were also part of a broader anti-apartheid organizational network. P/CROs engaged in joint activities and campaigns with other anti-apartheid NGOs and were also connected to the more prominent mass-based social movements. Examining these connections reveals that P/CROs shared with the NGOs and social movements a broader peace-building paradigm, and suggests that P/CROs may have made a larger contribution to change in South Africa than most analysts have realized.[38]

The mass-based social movements stood at the core of the struggle and were the most important agents of social change. P/CROs were linked to the mass-based movements through their association with the broad network of anti-apartheid NGOs, which provided services for the poor and oppressed, furthered mobilization, and created space—above all, legal—for the United Democratic Front and the labor movement (primarily the Congress of South African Trade Unions). Anti-apartheid NGOs were those that took a more radically anti-apartheid stand than the P/CROs being considered here, whose activists faced greater risk of arrest and detention, and in which some participants maintained that "the correct role for people with education, training, skills, wealth, and facilities is to put themselves and their tools at the service and under the direction of the oppressed people. There is no alternative."[39] The most prominent anti-apartheid nongovernmental organizations are listed in table 4.2.[40]

Almost all of the anti-apartheid NGO leaders and activists experienced some degree of confrontation with the state during the 1980s. Constantly under investigation by the security police and secret spy networks, some leaders and activists were subjected to bans, arrests, detentions without trial,

TABLE 4.2. The Leading Anti-Apartheid Nongovernmental Organizations in Apartheid South Africa

Organization	Acronym	Date formed
National Union of South African Students	Nusas	1924
SA Council on Higher Education	Sached	1959
South African Council of Churches	SACC	1968
Centre for Applied Legal Studies	CALS	1978
Lawyers for Human Rights	LHR	1979
Legal Resources Centre	LRC	1979
National Medical and Dental Association	Namda	1981
Organization for Alternative Social Services for SA	Oasssa	1981
Transvaal Rural Action Committee	TRAC	1983
Five Freedoms Forum	FFF	1986
National Education Crisis Committee	NECC	1986
Human Rights Commission	HRC	1988

death threats, and even assassination attempts. Beyers Naudé, general secretary of the South African Council of Churches (SACC) from 1984 to 1987, stated that, "I simply had to accept the fact that whatever I did, you know, could lead to the fact that I could be liquidated."[41] In fact, the SACC headquarters, Khotso (*Peace*) House in Johannesburg—which was also the UDF's national headquarters—was bombed on August 31, 1988. Twenty-three people were wounded in this attack, which—it has now been revealed—was carried out on the direct orders of President P. W. Botha.[42] Most sinisterly, an apartheid death squad assassinated David Webster, a founding member of the Five Freedoms Forum, on May 1, 1989.[43]

During the 1980s, the anti-apartheid NGOs listed in table 4.2 were among the most generally representative bodies in the country. The SACC, the National Medical and Dental Association (Namda), and the National Education Crisis Committee (NECC) had a majority of black members, but whatever their racial composition, the organizations were all explicitly nonracial and sought to enhance the capacity of the struggle against apartheid; most were connected to or affiliated with the UDF.[44]

Working together, anti-apartheid NGOs provided services to the disenfranchised, offering a kind of shadow welfare system in support of the mass-based movements and the poor. As Bishop Paul Verryn reflected: "My sense was that these organizations were like a resource base for mass-based movements, these organizations were the people who were really the Department of Welfare."[45] At the forefront was the SACC, which, through its eighty staff at Khotso House, provided a shield for a wide variety of social welfare programs.[46] These included paying for the legal defense of anti-apartheid activists, providing financial assistance to the dependents of political prisoners, assisting strike-affected families, promoting community projects, and making church buildings available for meetings.[47] Other anti-apartheid NGOs provided ameliorative and alternative services, primarily in the areas of education, health, and legal rights.

In the area of education, Nusas, the South African Council on Higher Education (Sached), and NECC vigorously campaigned against the injustices of apartheid education. Both Nusas and Sached provided bursaries for black tertiary-level students, as well as facilities and resources for the education of political prisoners. Former Nusas president, Charles Nupen, remarked that "We supplied books and money to political prisoners on Robben Island so that they could study. And that I know is regarded by the movement as a crucially important contribution."[48] Nusas and the NECC were also affiliated with the UDF.[49]

In the field of health, Namda addressed inequities in health provision, and the Organization for Alternative Social Services for South Africa (Oasssa) provided a forum for psychiatrists, psychologists, and social service workers to expose torture and human rights abuse. During the state of emergency,

Namda set up an Emergency Services Group "to treat people in the townships then occupied by the SADF, to treat survivors of torture, to treat those just released from detention and to provide medical services within riot areas."[50] Both Namda and Oasssa worked closely with the UDF to plan joint operations and exchange information.

In the area of legal rights, the Transvaal Rural Action Committee's (TRAC) fieldworkers actively championed the land rights of and acted as resource brokers for rural communities facing forced removal (notably the Mogopa people). The Human Rights Commission (HRC) sought to monitor and publicize human rights violations by the state. More generally, the Legal Resources Centre (LRC), the Centre for Applied Legal Studies (CALS), and Lawyers for Human Rights (LHR) challenged and exploited the contradictions of apartheid legislation through the courts. The goal was to win back legal space, expand the existing set of rights, and narrow the gap between apartheid law and justice.[51] As Nicholas Haysom, legal advisor to President Nelson Mandela, argued, "We were using legality as an umbrella within which mass-based organization could take place; challenging prohibitions on gatherings, providing space for publications, providing legal space for people not to be charged for what they were doing and put in jail, all of that [was] a material condition for mass organization."[52] Most significantly, perhaps, LRC and CALS provided the defense counsel in the 1988 Delmas treason trial in which a number of high-profile UDF leaders were charged with treason and furthering the aims of the ANC.[53]

Anti-apartheid NGOs probably made their largest impact through their support for the trade union movement. According to academic and activist, Neville Alexander, the importance of anti-apartheid NGOs lay "in the fact that they did work closely with the union movement. I would say that the union movement itself could not have been as successful as it was without that sort of support, because they were supported in many different ways by all these organizations, people drafting papers, people training people."[54] Nusas, in particular, played a very important role in supporting the independent trade union movement through the work of its wages commission and workers advice offices.[55] The SACC offered leadership training for workers and took the initiative in promoting mediation in labor disputes.[56] Anti-apartheid NGOs contributed so much to the union movement that Jay Naidoo, former general secretary of Cosatu, described them as "a very important support in mobilization."[57]

In addition, anti-apartheid NGOs smuggled considerable amounts of foreign money into the country for the mass-based social movements. The state constantly attempted to stop the foreign funding of anti-apartheid work— with the Affected Organizations Act of 1974, the Fund Raising Act of 1978, and the Disclosure of Foreign Funding Act of 1989—but to little avail. During the 1980s the SACC and to a lesser extent the SACBC, as church bodies, could legally bring foreign grants and donations into the country and were conduits for many millions of rands, especially from Scandinavia.[58] For example, overseas funds were channeled through SACC and the Black Sash for the Port Elizabeth Black Civic Organization. SACC and SACBC even relayed overseas funding support to the End Conscription Campaign.

P/CROs not only cooperated with these anti-apartheid NGOs, some were directly involved in the same kind of service provision, and most participated in their campaigns against detentions without trial, homeland consolidations, and forced removals. Reciprocally, anti-apartheid NGOs participated in P/CRO activities and campaigns. Nusas, SACC, and the Five Freedoms Forum (FFF) regularly involved themselves in ECC initiatives, and the Black Sash could count on support from most of the NGOs. Also, several of the anti-apartheid NGOs—notably LRC, TRAC, and FFF—were established at the initiative of leading P/CRO activists.

Some of the P/CROs were supportive of (but not formally affiliated with) the UDF. The ECC was close to the UDF, and the Black Sash and J&P were present at its launch. Some P/CROs were linked to the UDF through the provision of support services; most prominent among these was the Black Sash, which established volunteer-staffed advice offices to offer paralegal advice about pass laws and forced removals and to assist thousands of black South Africans enmeshed in the bureaucratic red tape of apartheid laws.[59] According to civic leader Moses Mayekiso, "the Black Sash was an NGO trying to oil the wheels of misery, therefore we would use them, channel people to those structures."[60] Black Sash and ECC members often attended the funerals of UDF activists in the townships, providing both moral support and a degree of protection from security force violence; as Sheena Duncan stated, "People used to ask the Black Sash to come to funerals in Alexandra [township] because they knew that if there were white women there in their black sashes, the police sitting around the cemetery would be highly unlikely to shoot."[61]

P/CROs also assisted the trade union movement, which turned to the Black Sash "because it provided an effective legal service"[62] and to IMSSA because it "had a skill when it comes to issues like elections, issues like mediation."[63] IMSSA, which in fact developed alongside the independent trade union movement, was important because it challenged the notion that labor and capital could relate only as antagonists by showing "that dialogue is a normal activity, not an abnormal activity."[64]

Several P/CROs combined forces with the legal service anti-apartheid NGOs to win important court victories for the anti-apartheid struggle. The LRC, in conjunction with the Black Sash and TRAC, litigated the Rikhoto case, a landmark intervention that established a precedent of urban residence rights for black South Africans with a ten-year unbroken employment record in a city. Together, CALS and the ECC also challenged the Emergency Regulations.[65]

Clearly, P/CROs were a part of the broader anti-apartheid NGO network and became increasingly integral to it as the 1980s progressed. Although the P/CROs' social base remained for the most part white and middle class, they tended to shift their sympathies increasingly toward the UDF. In general, this multi-organizational field of interconnecting personalities, activities, and campaigns served as a rich pool of resources for the victims and opponents of apartheid, strengthened local communities' capacity to organize and resist apartheid policies, and created additional legal and political space for the operation of mass-based movements and for "very poor people to actually have a voice."[66] As Pat Horn, a labor union activist, stated, "These organizations provided confidence to people and enabled them to conceive of achieving political change."[67]

It is also important to recognize the ramifications that P/CRO activism had on the broader anti-apartheid network. For example, news of Idasa's Dakar meeting rippled through the anti-apartheid NGO community, prompting other organizations to do the same—such as the Five Freedoms Forum, which "trekked" north to Lusaka in late June 1989 with over one hundred white leaders to meet a fifty-member ANC delegation that included Thabo Mbeki, Pallo Jordan, and Joe Slovo.[68] IMSSA's introduction of democratic processes into labor relations laid the groundwork for a culture of negotiation; not only were wage negotiations more amicable as a result but trade union figures—especially Cyril Ramaphosa—who were later crucial to the constitutional negotiations that preceded elections, learned their skills in IMSSA's mediation workshops.[69] More generally, as Afrikaner academic Willie Breytenbach maintained, "the relative success of the [Codesa] negotiations could be attributed to the fact that the main actors met before, via the avenues created by these organizations."[70]

What this analysis suggests is that P/CRO and anti-apartheid NGO work are best understood on a continuum. This is all the more reasonable because for many of the people who were engaged in anti-apartheid peace and conflict-resolution work the notion of peace was linked to total social transformation and reconstruction, as evidenced in slogans like "peace with justice" and "just peace." Certainly, those who worked for reconciliation and negotiation did have severe critics on the left, who maintained that "the time for these was long past," that "peace" was a bankrupt notion because in the vocabulary of the apartheid state it was synonymous with acquiescence to the status quo, or "that the very nature of apartheid means that there is no middle ground."[71]

Nonetheless, the distinction between peace and conflict-resolution work and the broader anti-apartheid struggle should not be drawn too sharply; the existence of this liberal-left multi-organizational field with a common commitment to the abolition of apartheid cannot be denied. Indeed, the apartheid state itself provides confirmation for this claim: the state harassed almost all of the P/CROs to some degree, with phone taps, mail interceptions, meeting disruptions, and infiltrations of their structures, especially as the 1980s progressed. The apartheid state also sponsored counterorganizations—such as the Catholic Defence League, National Student Federation, and Veterans for Victory—to compete with and discredit the P/CROs.

Also highly significant is the contact that P/CROs had with the banned and exiled ANC and South African Communist Party (SACP). Several P/CRO leaders and activists—such as Nico Smith and Ivor Jenkins of Koinonia—were sympathetic to the ANC and SACP and took the initiative to visit their leaderships overseas on a number of occasions. Some even joined the ANC and SACP, thereby establishing direct links—albeit obviously clandestine ones—with these parties. The ANC and SACP very much included P/CROs in their strategic thinking.[72] In the 1980s there were ANC members working in the ECC, Black Sash, and Idasa; from its beginning, ECC included ANC members, and Idasa not only had links with the ANC, but it had been founded with the ANC's blessing, and two of its regional directors were MK members. The ANC also appears to have been diligent in respecting the P/CROs' autonomy. As Mac Maharaj, a prominent ANC and SACP member, recalled: "I was very clear when I was secretary of the ANC underground, I was clear that we were not going to be there in any of these organizations to subvert them, to take them over . . . [We were there] to get an accurate political intelligence reading of what was happening in the country."[73] Thus, although at least eight people within ECC were recruited to the ANC, they did not operate as a caucus within ECC; leading activist Gavin Evans revealed that the eight members "weren't connected to each other within the ANC, they weren't necessarily part of the same cell."[74]

Thus, as figure 4.1 depicts, anti-apartheid work in South Africa was a heavily interlocked field consisting of three types of interconnected and interdependent organizations, as the circles in figure 4.1 represent. This diagram illustrates that P/CROs did not operate in isolation and suggests instead that their impact resulted from interactions with the other components of a complex multi-organizational field characterized by manifold reciprocal interorganizational links and influences. This powerful synergistic dynamic between P/CROs, the anti-apartheid NGO network, the mass-based movements, and ANC/SACP has largely remained unknown and unacknowledged.

Transforming South Africa

Thus, during the 1980s, P/CROs were part of a multi-organizational field, characterized by intensive interactions between organizations and individuals, which reinforced their relationships in a variety of ways. A leading activist, Don Foster, recognized this situation: "I suppose politically what is just so terribly

FIGURE 4.1.   The Multi-Organizational Field (1980s). Each line represents an interlock between organizations in terms of leaders, campaigns, and activities. Although it is not shown, many of the organizations in the second circle—the anti-apartheid NGOs—are also interlocked with each other.

important is how important all of these [organizations] are to each other. There's the constant interlocking of entirely different people, connecting count-less individuals in entirely different ways. . . . Actually, the more you look at it—in what sense was I not connected to any of these organizations?"[75]

Given this multi-organizational field, it is not enough to simply isolate in-dividual P/CROs in order to gauge their impact. As ANC Cabinet Minister Kader Asmal said with regard to which P/CRO had the greatest impact, "You can't have a beauty contest, you can't have a beauty contest, it would be wrong. . . . It was a cumulative effect, really. It was networking, it was a cu-mulative effect and in the end I would say that these NGOs were part of the great mobilization against apartheid."[76] Likewise, when questioned about Idasa's impact, Frederik van Zyl Slabbert made the following analogy: "Chaos theory says that the flutter of a butterfly's wings eventually ends up in a hur-ricane. Does it cause a hurricane? No, but it was part of it."[77]

Therefore, P/CROs' contributions and impact cannot be abstracted from the interorganizational context or adequately grasped by simply studying each P/CRO as a separate entity. Rather, the interdependence and complexity of the multi-organizational field means that P/CROs can only be properly understood by analyzing their individual, relational, and transformational aspects. So far this chapter has highlighted the individual and relational aspects of P/CRO work; attention must be turned now to the transformational dimension. How did the work of P/CROs form part of a broader interactive process that evolved and transformed people?

As the components of the multi-organizational field interacted, a collectively engendered consequence became discernible. These organizations overlapped and combined, influenced and penetrated each other, evolved together, and eventually came to project a new "emergent reality"—namely, a virtual nonracial democratic South Africa. The multi-organizational field was concerned not only with improving relationships and providing services but with projecting and creating a nonracial democratic future. As one activist pointed out: "People in the eighties said, 'You do not start anew in a liberated era, you carry the developments in which you have been involved with through into the next era. So it's going to be very important for us to start creating the new society that we want now.'"[78] Richard Turner's prophetic book, *The Eye of the Needle*, also described this position clearly: "On the organizational level we must ensure that all organizations we work in . . . prefigure the future."[79] Accordingly, people within these organizations attempted to live as if they were already living in a nonracial democratic South Africa, and in doing so, they helped to facilitate that future. It seems as if people implicitly built upon Albert Einstein's insight that "no problem can be solved from the same consciousness that created it."[80]

There were various ways in which P/CROs and anti-apartheid NGOs imagined and projected a postapartheid future within their own domains. Among the P/CROs, for example, IMSSA aimed "to present credible alternatives to systems that the apartheid state offered,"[81] the ECC sought an alternative national service system, and J&P argued that the church should be an alternative society. The anti-apartheid NGOs advanced an even wider range of alternative visions. The SACC was particularly forward-looking—especially through the "prescient vision" of Beyers Naudé[82]—and promoted itself as "a prototype of the future South Africa."[83] Even before the 1980s, SACC leaders worked toward the racial integration of black and colored churches, called for black advancement through the church itself, and launched the Study Project on Christianity in Apartheid Society (Spro-cas), a five-year project involving 130 members of six study commissions to explore future alternatives.[84] Later, during the 1980s, various religious youth groups within the ambit of the SACC and SACBC called for a "people's church."

Nusas, Sached, and NECC presented alternative nonracial education policies—at the primary, secondary, and tertiary levels—targeting access, curriculum, and governance. In particular, Sached developed creative educational options for adult education and established Khanya College (with campuses in Johannesburg and Cape Town), which provided full scholarships to black students.[85] More visibly, the NECC, as a sector-driven coordinating structure, spearheaded a call for "people's education for people's power," and was "able to establish a forum for innovation," especially through Education Policy Units, which were established at Wits in 1987 and the University of Natal in 1988.[86]

Namda and Oasssa advanced alternatives to apartheid health and welfare, promoting wide-ranging proposals for postapartheid social policy, especially for a national health service and progressive mental health institutions.[87] The legal service organizations (LRC, CALS, and LHR) provided alternatives to the apartheid legal system by orienting themselves toward the realization of substantive human rights for all under a just constitutional and legal order.[88] More broadly, the Five Freedoms Forum's bridge-building projects—such as the 1988 "One City, Open City" campaign—were intended, in the words of David Webster, "to focus attention on the fact that an alternative vision for South Africa does exist and is very much alive."[89] The FFF's main supporting organizations included the Black Sash and ECC.

Moreover, P/CROs and anti-apartheid NGOs clearly made nonracial democracy a reality in their micro-practice, as Bishop Paul Verryn noted: "In fact, a lot of these organizations were places of empowerment and places for clarifying the thinking processes for many people, both black and white. They were a forum in which black people could express themselves without fear."[90] Within these organizations many people found a new sense of solidarity and fraternity. Of course, in the 1980s there were material and strategic incentives to adopt and maintain nonracial practices for organizations that otherwise might not have recruited many black members. Not only were nonracial organizations more attractive to rich and powerful international funders seeking to hasten social change, but they enjoyed more freedom to operate because the apartheid state was reluctant to act forcefully against organizations that involved whites.[91]

The ANC and SACP stimulated such developments through their underground links with these organizations. There is no doubt that the anti-apartheid network, including P/CROs, accorded well with the ANC/SACP's commitment to nonracialism,[92] and organizations like Idasa and FFF were definitely encouraged in their attempts to draw whites away from the racist regime. In addition, P/CRO and anti-apartheid NGO attempts to build alternative structures were paralleled by the UDF's attempts to elaborate a grassroots notion of "people's power" and to establish nonracial governance structures, such as street committees and people's courts.[93] Moreover, these moves articulated with the trade union movements' concern with—as reflected in the title of Steven Friedman's book—*Building Tomorrow Today*.[94]

Centrally, what arose from the multi-organizational field were the ideology and practice of nonracialism. As an emergent cosmological dimension, nonracialism provided a new way of understanding South Africa that increasingly drew together a whole range of social forces working for change.[95] It created a new vision of how social relationships could and should be constructed around a common South African citizenship irrespective of race and ethnicity, it pointed the way toward a future that would be, in the words of Nobel Prize-winning author Nadine Gordimer, "vastly different from that built to the specifications of white power and privilege."[96] As Laurie Nathan put it, nonracialism "was a matter of ideology and idealism, it was a matter of analysis, in other words we've misunderstood, we've misdiagnosed the nature of the problem if you see this as white versus black."[97]

Nonracialism, premised upon a discourse of equality and the principled rejection of race, provided an alternative understanding of South African society that increasingly enabled activists to comprehend their social worlds outside the warped logic of apartheid; as Nicholas Haysom declared, "In fact being a member of the broad non-racial struggle, you loose your colour."[98] As people's activism transformed them and their worlds, the struggle against apartheid was pushed "off its black and white track."[99] Significantly, the National Party's chief constitutional negotiator, Roelf Meyer, admitted that "One's image of the conflict certainly changed over a period of time. . . . It's true that in the eighties, in general, there developed in my own mind a more non-racial image, especially if one looks at these organizations."[100]

In conclusion, when the whole network of relationships in which P/CROs were involved is taken into account, it is clear that the impact of these organizations was profound. It is not simply that there were connections between P/CROs, anti-apartheid NGOs, and the ANC/SACP, but that these connections were multiple, with individual, relational, and transformational effects. Peace and conflict-resolution organizations dealt with and interacted with tens of thousands of people, they addressed both grassroots concerns and confronted the rulers of the apartheid state. Their cumulative effect was crucial to the undermining of the apartheid social order and the advent of a nonracial democratic South Africa—they "ripened" the climate for the ANC and other anti-apartheid organizations to be unbanned in February 1990, and they "softened" the process of constitutional negotiation, which led to the democratic election of April 1994.[101] Most activists were not aware of how this complex multi-organizational field coalesced; it was not discussed or articulated in a formalized or systematic way, but it emerged nonetheless. In a sense, people's practice forged ahead of theory. As philosopher Johan Degenaar stated, "The point is that people needn't be conscious of the fact that they interrelate. . . . Things are related to one another in a way that we cannot always see."[102]

Notes

This chapter draws upon research reports compiled by ISPO-South Africa team members: Mark Shaw, Adam Habib, Jacklyn Cock, Aubrey Lekwane, Simon Stacey, Jo-Ansie van Wyk, Anthony Egan, Pat Waugh, and Carol Coary Taylor. Special thanks to Adam Habib and Anthony Egan for their comments on draft versions of the chapter. The author is also grateful for the comments of Adrian Guelke, Tom Karis, Mervyn Shear, Henrik Sommer, and Elke Zuern.

1. *Truth and Reconciliation Commission of South Africa Report* (Cape Town: Juta, 1998), vol. 1, p. 34.

2. Kenneth Grundy, *The Militarization of South African Politics* (Bloomington: Indiana University Press, 1986).

3. Max Coleman, ed., *A Crime Against Humanity: Analysing the Repression of the Apartheid State* (Johannesburg: Human Rights Committee, 1998). Also see, South African Institute of Race Relations, *Survey of Race Relations* (Johannesburg: SAIRR, annual).

4. Jacklyn Cock, "The Role of Violence in Current State Security Strategy," in *Views on the South African State*, ed. Mark Swilling (Pretoria: Human Sciences Research Council, 1990), pp. 85–108.

5. *Challenge to the Church: The Kairos Document* (Johannesburg: Institute for Contextual Theology, 1985).

6. Leo Kuper, *Genocide* (Harmondsworth: Penguin, 1981), p. 197.

7. *Truth and Reconciliation Commission of South Africa Report*, vol. 1, p. 36.

8. Henrik Sommer, "Nonviolent Direct Action, The Cycle of Protest and the Demise of Apartheid in South Africa, 1970–1994" (Ph.D. thesis, University of Colorado, Boulder, 1998).

9. Anthony W. Marx, *Lessons of Struggle: South African Internal Opposition, 1960–1990* (New York: Oxford University Press, 1992). The UDF disbanded on August 20, 1991.

10. Jeremy Baskin, *Striking Back: A History of Cosatu* (Johannesburg: Ravan, 1991).

11. These were the organizations selected for detailed study in the South African case. The details that follow are drawn from the individual research reports. The following P/CRO name changes should be noted: from 1981 to 1987 the Justice and Peace Commission, which is part of the South African Catholic Bishops Conference (SACBC), was called Justice and Reconciliation, but in 1987 it reverted back to Justice and Peace; the Project for the Study of Violence changed its name to the Center for the Study of Violence and Reconciliation in 1993; the Center for Intergroup Studies, earlier known as the Abe Bailey Institute, became the Center for Conflict Resolution in 1994; and Idasa became the Institute for Democracy in South Africa in 1994.

12. In the 1990s, both Idasa and IMSSA appointed black national directors, Wilmot James and Thandi Orlyn, respectively.

13. More detailed information on funding can be found in the ISPO-South Africa report on "Funding." Also see, Robin Lee and Fran Buntman, *The Future*

of the *Nonprofit Voluntary Sector in South Africa*, Research Report No. 5 (Johannesburg: Centre for Policy Studies, 1989).

14. For more information on "clusters," see Sam Marullo and John Lofland, eds., *Peace Action in the Eighties: Social Science Perspectives* (New Brunswick: Rutgers University Press, 1990).

15. Otto Nathan and Heinz Norden, eds., *Einstein on Peace* (New York: Schocken Books, 1981).

16. Laurie Nathan, "Force of Arms: Force of Conscience" (M.Phil. thesis, Bradford University, UK, 1990).

17. The ECC was fully and legally reconstituted in February 1990 (when it was unbanned). The ECC decided to disband in 1994, the year in which compulsory national service ended.

18. South African Catholic Bishops Conference, *Report on War in Namibia* (Pretoria: SACBC, 1985).

19. Renate Winkler, Hendrik W. van der Merwe, and Odette Geldenhuys, *An Overview of Peace Initiatives, Movements and Organisations in South Africa*, Conflict and Peace Studies Series No. 4 (Cape Town: Centre for Intergroup Studies, 1987), preface.

20. "On the Frontline: Ten Years of the Independent Mediation Service of South Africa, 1984–1994," *IMSSA Review* 16 (1994).

21. For a discussion of the "contact hypothesis," see Miles Hewstone and Rupert Brown, eds., *Contact and Conflict in Intergroup Encounters* (Oxford: Blackwell, 1986).

22. Nico Smith, quoted in "Launch of New Church Group," *The Citizen*, February 15, 1986.

23. Devan Pillay (anti-apartheid activist), interview with Rupert Taylor, March 23, 1998.

24. A popular journalistic book on the Black Sash by Kathryn Spink is in fact entitled *Black Sash: The Beginning of a Bridge for South Africa* (London: Methuen, 1991).

25. On the central tenets of apartheid ideology, see Hermann Giliomee and Lawrence Schlemmer, *From Apartheid to Nation-Building* (Cape Town: Oxford University Press, 1989).

26. Mac Maharaj (ANC Cabinet Minister), interview with Rupert Taylor and Adam Habib, April 21, 1998.

27. Simon Makana, "Meeting with Professor van der Merwe and Dr. Piet Muller, Lusaka, 4–12–1984," ANC archives, University of Fort Hare. Also see H. W. van der Merwe, *Peacemaking in South Africa: A Life in Conflict Resolution* (Cape Town: Tafelberg, 2000).

28. Alex Boraine and Frederik van Zyl Slabbert secured funding for Idasa's Dakar trip following a fortuitous lunch meeting with billionaire George Soros in New York; Alex Boraine (Idasa co-founder) interview with Rupert Taylor and Adam Habib, May 12, 1998. Also see Frederik van Zyl Slabbert, *Tough Choices: Reflections of an Afrikaner African* (Cape Town: Tafelberg, 2000).

29. Richard Rosenthal, *Mission Improbable: A Piece of the South African Story* (Cape Town: David Philip, 1998).

30. H. W. van der Merwe, *Pursuing Peace and Justice in South Africa* (London: Routledge, 1989), p. 102.

31. Willem de Klerk (Afrikaner academic), interview with Jo-Ansie van Wyk, March 9, 1998.

32. Formerly the *Race Relations Survey*, and recently retitled *South African Survey*.

33. Ellen Hellmann, "Fifty Years of the South African Institute of Race Relations," in *Conflict and Progress: Fifty Years of Race Relations in South Africa*, ed. Ellen Hellmann and Henry Lever (Johannesburg: Macmillan, 1979), p. 9.

34. Sheena Duncan (Black Sash leader), interview with Rupert Taylor and Jacklyn Cock, February 8, 1998.

35. Judge Albie Sachs (Constitutional Court), interview with Rupert Taylor and Aubrey Lekwane, March 24, 1998.

36. Sheena Duncan interview, February 8, 1998.

37. Graeme Simpson (Centre for the Study of Violence and Reconciliation leader), interview with Rupert Taylor and Jacklyn Cock, April 3, 1998.

38. Most analysts have focused primarily on the behavior and decisions of elites and the formal negotiation process; see, for example, Allister Sparks, *Tomorrow Is Another Country: The Inside Story of South Africa's Negotiated Revolution* (Johannesburg: Struik, 1994); Patti Waldmeir, *Anatomy of a Miracle: The End of Apartheid and the Birth of the New South Africa* (London: Viking, 1997).

39. Cedric Mayson, *A Certain Sound* (London: Epworth Press, 1984), p. 69.

40. All of these organizations were studied in the first phase of the ISPO-South Africa research process, and much of what follows in this section is drawn from the individual research reports. The following organizational developments should be noted: Nusas merged with the South African National Council Students Council in 1991 to form the South African Students Congress; Namda and Oasssa came together with other health care organizations to form the South African Health and Social Services Organization in 1992; the Five Freedoms Forum disbanded in 1993; the Human Rights Commission was renamed the Human Rights Committee in 1994; the National Education Crisis Committee, banned in 1988, was reestablished as the National Education Co-ordinating Committee in late 1989, and was dissolved in 1995; and TRAC is an affiliate of the National Land Committee.

41. Beyers Naudé (leading Afrikaner dissident), interview with Henrik Sommer, April 12, 1999.

42. *Truth and Reconciliation Commission of South Africa Report*, vol. 2, pp. 291–293.

43. Patrick Laurence, *Death Squads: Apartheid's Secret Weapon* (Johannesburg: Penguin, 1990).

44. Jeremy Cronin (South African Communist Party general secretary), interview with Rupert Taylor and Jacklyn Cock, January 1, 1999.

45. Bishop Paul Verryn (Methodist Church), interview with Rupert Taylor and Aubrey Lekwane, March 13, 1998.

46. Tristan Anne Borer, *Challenging the State: Churches as Political Actors in South Africa, 1980–1994* (Notre Dame, Ind.: University of Notre Dame Press, 1998), pp. 130–131.

47. The SACC's funding for some of this work was very surreptitiously tied to the fund-raising work of the International Defence and Aid Fund based in London.

48. Charles Nupen (IMSSA leader), interview with Rupert Taylor and Aubrey Lekwane, April 24, 1998.

49. Nusas was declared an "affected organization" in 1974 (under the Affected Organisations Act of 1974), which meant that it could not legally secure foreign funds. In February 1988, the NECC was banned, by which time all national office bearers had been detained.

50. David Greene (Namda leader), interview with Catharine Payze, 1996.

51. Consider, Stephen Ellmann, *In a Time of Trouble: Law and Liberty in South Africa's State of Emergency* (Oxford: Clarendon Press, 1992).

52. Nicholas Haysom (legal advisor to President Nelson Mandela), interview with Rupert Taylor and Aubrey Lekwane, February 18, 1998.

53. Even though the defense did not win this case, they did much to raise the national and international profile of the UDF and the convictions were reversed thirteen months later; George Bizos (LRC leader), interview with Rupert Taylor and Aubrey Lekwane, February 16, 1998.

54. Neville Alexander (academic/activist), interview with Rupert Taylor and Adam Habib, March 25, 1998.

55. David Lewis, "Black Workers and Trade Unions," in Thomas G. Karis and Gail M. Gerhart, *From Protest to Challenge: A Documentary History of African Politics in South Africa, 1882–1990, Volume 5: Nadir and Resurgence, 1964–1979* (Pretoria: Unisa Press, 1997), pp. 198–199.

56. James Cochrane, "The Churches and the Trade Unions," in *Resistance and Hope: South African Essays in Honour of Beyers Naudé*, ed. Charles Villa-Vicencio and John W. de Gruchy (Cape Town: David Philip, 1985), pp. 174–188.

57. Jay Naidoo (ANC Cabinet Minister), interview with Rupert Taylor and Aubrey Lekwane, February 27, 1998.

58. The SACC did not, however, escape state attention with regard to funding; consider, *South African Outlook*, August 1984, issue on the Eloff Commission of Inquiry.

59. Jennifer Scott, "The Black Sash: A Study in Liberalism in South Africa, 1955–1995," (Ph.D. thesis, Oxford University, 1991).

60. Moses Mayekiso (civic leader), interview with Mcebisi Ndletyana, April 20, 1998.

61. Sheena Duncan (Black Sash leader), interview with Henrik Sommer, March 4, 1999.

62. Pat Horn (trade union activist), interview with Adam Habib, April 15, 1998.

63. Moses Mayekiso interview, April 20, 1998.

64. Jeremy Routledge (QPC leader), interview with Rupert Taylor, April 20, 1998.

65. Richard L. Abel, *Politics by Other Means: Law in the Struggle against Apartheid, 1980–1994* (New York: Routledge, 1995).

66. Mamphela Ramphele (vice-chancellor of the University of Cape Town), interview with Rupert Taylor, April 4, 1998.

67. Pat Horn interview, April 15, 1998.

68. Five Freedoms Forum, *Four Days in Lusaka* (Johannesburg: Five Freedoms Forum, 1989). Four months later Namda met with the ANC in Harare, Zimbabwe.

69. Paul Pretorius, "Negotiating a New Constitution," unpublished paper, 1994.

70. Willie Breytenbach (Afrikaner academic), interview with Jo-Ansie van Wyk, March 23, 1998.

71. M. L. [Michael Lapsley], "Letter from Lesotho," *Sechaba*, July 1980, pp. 24–27.

72. Pallo Jordan (ANC Cabinet Minister), interview with Rupert Taylor and Adam Habib, March 28, 1998.

73. Mac Maharaj interview, April 21, 1998.

74. Gavin Evans (ECC activist), interview with Stephen Louw, May 5, 1998. Also see Gavin Evans, interview with Howard Barrell, January 28, 1991, Karis-Gerhart Collection, William Cullen Library, University of the Witwatersrand, Johannesburg.

75. Don Foster (academic/activist), interview with Rupert Taylor and Anthony Egan, March 28, 1998.

76. Kader Asmal (ANC Cabinet Minister), interview with Rupert Taylor and Adam Habib, May 11, 1998.

77. Frederik van Zyl Slabbert (Idasa co-founder), interview with Rupert Taylor and Adam Habib, March 24, 1998. On the butterfly effect in chaos theory, see James Gleick, *Chaos* (New York: Viking, 1987).

78. Sheila Meintjes (academic/activist), interview with Rupert Taylor, March 13, 1998.

79. Richard Turner, *The Eye of the Needle: Toward Participatory Democracy in South Africa* (Maryknoll, N.Y.: Orbis Books, 1978), p. 93. Richard Turner, who was active in Nusas and trade union organizations, was assassinated by agents of the apartheid state on January 8, 1978.

80. Albert Einstein, quoted in E. Sam Overman, "The New Sciences of Administration: Chaos and Quantum Theory," *Public Administration Review* 56 (1996): 490.

81. Charles Nupen interview, April 24, 1998.

82. Mark Orkin (Community Agency for Social Enquiry leader), interview with Rupert Taylor and Mark Shaw, May 26, 1998.

83. Peter Storey, "SACC: Walking in the Spirit," *South African Outlook*, February 1982, p. 23.

84. Peter Randall, "Spro-cas Revisited: The Christian Contribution to Political Debate," in *Resistance and Hope: South African Essays in Honour of Beyers Naudé*, ed. Charles Villa-Vicencio and John W. de Gruchy (Cape Town: David Philip, 1985), pp. 165–173.

85. Gareth Coleman, "A History of Sached, 1959–1987," (M.A. thesis, University of Natal, Durban, 1989).

86. "Strategic Evaluation of the National Education Co-ordinating Committee, 1992," confidential NECC report, p. 8 (copy held by Resource Centre, Education Policy Unit, University of the Witwatersrand, Johannesburg).

87. See, for example, H. M. Coovadia, "New Directions in Health Care: From Apartheid to Democracy" (paper presented at the Institute of Social Studies, Transnational Institute, Amsterdam); proceedings of Oasssa national conferences: "Apartheid and Mental Health," 1986; "Mental Health in Transition," 1987; "Mental Health: Struggle and Transformation," 1988; "Social Services in a Changing South Africa," 1989.

88. John Dugard (CALS leader), interview with Rupert Taylor, March 11, 1998.

89. David Webster, "Republic Day—A Time to Renounce Apartheid," *The Star* [Johannesburg], May 30, 1988.

90. Bishop Paul Verryn interview, March 3, 1998.

91. Also see Robert Price, "Race and Reconciliation in the New South Africa," *Politics & Society* 25 (1997): 149–178.

92. Julie Frederikse, *The Unbreakable Thread: Non-Racialism in South Africa* (London: Zed Press, 1990).

93. See, for example, Steven Mufson, *Fighting Years: Black Resistance and the Struggle for a New South Africa* (Boston: Beacon Press, 1990).

94. Steven Friedman, *Building Tomorrow Today: African Workers in Trade Unions, 1970–1984* (Johannesburg: Ravan, 1987).

95. On the cosmological dimensions of social movements, see Ron Eyerman and Andrew Jamison, *Social Movements: A Cognitive Approach* (University Park: Pennsylvania State University Press, 1991).

96. Nadine Gordimer, "Living in the Interregnum," *New York Review of Books*, January 20, 1983, p. 21.

97. Laurie Nathan (ECC leader), interview with Rupert Taylor and Mark Shaw, March 26, 1998.

98. Nicholas Haysom interview, February 18, 1998. Also see Aletta Norval, *Deconstructing Apartheid Discourse* (London: Verso, 1996).

99. Ebrahim Rasool (ANC Member of Parliament), interview with Nida Farooqui, September 30, 1998.

100. Roelf Meyer (former NP Cabinet Minister), interview with Rupert Taylor and Adam Habib, June 9, 1998.

101. Willem de Klerk interview, March 9, 1998; Judge Albie Sachs interview, March 24, 1998.

102. Johan Degenaar (philosopher), interview with Rupert Taylor and Jo-Ansie van Wyk, March 25, 1998.

5

THE SOUR TASTE OF SUCCESS: THE ISRAELI PEACE MOVEMENT, 1967–1998

TAMAR HERMANN

In July 1994, Israel's prime minister, Yitzhak Rabin, went to the United States to sign the Washington Declaration, a preliminary peace agreement with Jordan. He invited twelve carefully selected Israeli citizens of various ethnic origins, ages, social strata, and occupations to attend this important and symbolic event. Not inadvertently, most of these individuals had been personally involved in or affected by Israel's violent conflict with the Arabs—they included members of bereaved families, victims who had been wounded in terrorist attacks, soldiers who had participated in particularly deadly battles or had been held as prisoners of war by Syria or Egypt, and some who had even endured a number of these harrowing experiences. The group also included an academic specializing in Israeli-Jordanian affairs and several people who had conducted positive diplomatic relations or some form of cooperation with the Arab world. In a speech to the U.S. Congress the day after the declaration was signed, Rabin referred to his guests as living reminders of the agonies of the bloody past, who nonetheless were imbued with a fervent hope for a better future, and whose symbolic presence was meant to encourage both sides to overcome the immense obstacles to peace.[1]

Apparently neither Rabin, his audience, nor indeed most Israelis noticed that not even one member of the Israeli peace movement was included in this group. The fact that no representatives of the Israeli peace movement were invited to this ceremony—or to any other formal occasions marking progress in the Israeli-Arab peace process—demonstrates the prevalent and ongoing disregard of this movement's contributions to cultivating and facilitating the peace process. It also illustrates the intensely frustrating situation in which the movement found itself after the launching of the Oslo process: official Israeli decision makers had adopted the very same agenda for which the movement had struggled for years—Israeli-Palestinian rapprochement based on mutual recognition and negation of the prevalent and previously unchallenged zero-sum definition of their relations—yet they did not give the movement any role in this process.

The movement, for its part, considered the Oslo Accords a great success; indeed most members, except for some small radical factions, publicly applauded and supported the Labor government's move in this direction from the beginning. However, almost immediately after the signing of the Oslo Declaration of Principles, it became apparent that while the government had adopted significant parts of its agenda, the movement itself was excluded from the peace negotiations. Furthermore, the Israeli decision makers refused to credit the movement for its past efforts and sometimes even publicly derided it, all in an apparently calculated effort to disassociate the peace process from the peace movement.

Prior to the Oslo Accords, the Israeli peace movement had been the first and most persistent advocate of Israeli-Arab coexistence, with considerable public visibility and political presence. This chapter explains how and why the peace movement was marginalized and denied credit for facilitating the formal peacemaking process, and discusses how this situation affected the movement. It argues that a combination of perceptual, socio-demographic, and organizational/functional factors separated the Israeli movement from both the political establishment and the general public. These factors—which only magnified the huge obstacles that nonconformist social movements normally confront when striving to introduce their aims into the national agenda—prevented the movement from rightfully enjoying the sweet taste of success when Israeli-Palestinian peace finally became a feasible political option.

The chapter develops this hypothesis in several stages. First, it outlines the historical development of the Israeli peace movement from 1967 to 1998 and its prolonged dispute with the political mainstream. Second, it presents the movement's political agenda and its problems in "selling" it to the Israeli public and decision makers. Third, it describes the movement's obstacles in establishing itself as a significant political actor and shows how those difficulties were linked to the movement's unique socio-demographic, organizational, and functional features. Finally, it assesses the movement's efficacy, maintaining that the prevalent negative judgment of the Israeli peace movement's achievements can be modified if more sensitive criteria are used. That is, the two classical indicators of a social movement's success—bringing about a policy transformation and the movement's own institutional consolidation—turned out to be quite problematic when applied to the Israeli peace movement. Owing to the extremely complicated relations between the movement and the political mainstream, no causal relations between the movement's activity and the policy change invested in the Oslo process could be sufficiently established. Moreover, contrary to theoretical predictions, the stabilization of Israeli peace movement activity—that is, the institutionalization of various peace organizations—did not strengthen the movement but in fact contributed significantly to its decline.

Methodology

Two important methodological points need to be made. First, the term "Israeli peace movement" is, in fact, an analytical construct rather than a concrete entity. What we refer to as a "movement" was actually a highly decentralized aggregate of organizations—with different sizes, worldviews, and fairly diverse goals—that usually developed ideological and strategic programs independently of one another. Many of these entities did not even cooperate with each other on a tactical level, although interorganizational cooperation had increased considerably over the past few years, giving more meaning to the term "peace movement." The use of this umbrella term also is justified insofar as the groups to which it refers saw themselves as forming something of a political camp, particularly in juxtaposition to the "national camp"—that is, the parties and groups of the Right.[2] Furthermore, although the Israeli peace groups were quite distinct, most politicians and citizens perceived them as an amalgamated political entity. In fact, most outsiders failed—or did not bother—to notice the various ideological nuances that often seemed so critical to the peace activists themselves.

The second point concerns the data-collection process. The data on which this chapter is based were collected within the framework of an international study of peace organizations. The Israeli research team was composed of four members, all professional social scientists or students in this field.[3] Three of the four had been involved in peace activism in the past and thus had connections with various peace activists and groups. This proved to be of utmost importance for gaining access to highly relevant but often quite inaccessible data. Furthermore, the stage of "confidence building," which is so crucial in semi-ethnographic studies, was fairly brief and "painless" because of these personal connections. However, since personal involvement and acquaintance with the subject of inquiry could have caused problems of objectivity—particularly given the socio-demographic and political similarities between the researchers and peace activists—a great effort was made to substantiate the analysis with abundant indisputable facts and to support all arguments with reliable and sufficient documentation.[4]

It also should be noted that in contrast to the Northern Irish and South African studies, where research teams from both sides of the conflict worked in tandem, the Israeli-Palestinian study was conducted by two autonomous research teams—Israeli and Palestinian. The state of political affairs at the national level during the study period (1996–1998) made it extremely difficult to conduct a joint study, in part because of the frequent closures and security precautions that researchers encountered when entering certain areas. However, both the Israeli and the Palestinian teams also realized almost from the beginning that a joint team never would have been able to penetrate the surface and get at the "real" stories of the Israeli and Palestinian peace organizations, including the ideological and practical difficulties they had experienced, particularly those stemming from relations with the other side. In addition, developing a joint Israeli-Palestinian interpretation of the data seemed very difficult or even impossible owing to the very dissimilar historical and national narratives each side employed, as well as the clearly unbalanced power relations between the occupiers (Israelis) and the occupied (Palestinians).[5]

The data collection was conducted in four sequential stages. First, we explored and mapped all of the groups and movements dealing with peace-related issues that were active from 1967 to the present. Approximately ninety peace groups and organizations were identified. Second, we selected a sample of twenty active peace groups, with different ideologies and organizational structures, for exploratory analysis.[6] This analysis enabled us to capture the main ideological and organizational features of Israeli peace activism during the period under study, and to make a general estimate of the different organizations' relative importance. The third and most important stage of data collection involved an in-depth analysis of nine of the peace organizations that already had been analyzed in the second stage.[7] In the fourth and final stage, all of the materials collected in the first three stages were reviewed, integrated, and summarized for this report. We use the information to present what we hope is an accurate and comprehensive account of the Israeli peace movement's ideological outlooks, human composition, organizational features, modi operandi, internal and external relations, and, perhaps most importantly, an assessment of its overall efficacy over the past thirty years.

Historical Development: An Overview

Throughout the twentieth century, Jewish-Arab relations have been mostly hostile and often violent, the major point of contention being the historical and moral claim to Palestine/Israel.[8] Although this conflict cost many lives on both sides, no significant peace movements emerged in the region until the 1970s. On the Arab-Palestinian side, several groups advocating peaceful coexistence with Israel developed in the 1980s; however, almost none of them defined themselves as "peace groups."[9] The first, and thus far only, self-declared Arab peace movement was established in Egypt in 1998. Likewise, up to the mid-1970s, there was a lack of extensive, grassroots peace activism in Israel. As will be discussed below, the various peace groups that did emerge faced severe difficulties in establishing and maintaining their presence.[10]

Nevertheless, the roots of Israeli peace activism date back to the mid-1920s. The first organized peace group to emerge within the Jewish community in Mandatory Palestine was the Peace Covenant (Brit Shalom), which was founded in Jerusalem in 1925. This small association sought to persuade the Zionist leadership and the British Mandatory authorities to adopt a binational state model—whereby the Jewish and Arab communities residing in the same area would have had equal political representation, regardless of their demographic size—so as to prevent the growing Jewish-Arab tensions from developing into a deadly struggle. In the late 1920s, following a series of violent Arab attacks on Jewish neighborhoods and while the Jewish community was still mourning its dead, the Peace Covenant issued a statement that the Jews were partly responsible for the deterioration of Jewish-Arab relations, and advocated that the Zionist movement relinquish its central aspiration to build a Jewish majority in Palestine.

The Peace Covenant, which saw itself as a think tank rather than a political movement, numbered only a few dozen registered members, who were mostly newcomers from Central and Western Europe (mainly Germany). The group was very homogeneous and highly elitist; its leading members were either prominent academics at the newly established Hebrew University or high-level administrators in the Mandatory Palestine civil service or the Zionist establishment. The socio-demographic composition and dissident political views of the Peace Covenant clearly inhibited the group's ability to "sell" its message to the Yishuv (the pre-state Jewish community in Palestine), whose leaders denounced the group for elitism and naive bourgeois pacifism. The severest critics accused the Peace Covenant of anti-Zionism, defeatism, and pandering to enemy interests. Although the Peace Covenant existed formally for eight years (1925–1933), it was only active for six frustrating years, during which time all of its recommendations were rejected and the Arab-Jewish conflict became increasingly violent. Moreover, the group's negative public image was projected onto peace activism, in general, which many Israelis still associate with political naivete, academic sequestration, and parochial class motivations.

Not surprisingly, this negative public attitude also was projected onto the highly visible but notably unpopular Union (Ihud) peace group, which Martin Buber, a prominent philosopher, and Dr. Judah Magnes, the president of the Hebrew University—both of whom had been politically though not formally connected to Brit Shalom—established early in 1942. The Union also advocated bi-nationalism and its activists were motivated by a strong moral pacifism. Unlike some other peace groups of the time, the Union was unconcerned about provoking the Jewish mainstream. Some of its members— Magnes, in particular—already had been branded political outsiders, so it was futile to try to disguise their recommendations as consensual in order to gain public approval. Moreover, they believed that the situation in Palestine was at such a decisive stage that the choice of policy to be pursued was more critical than ever.

Nevertheless, the Union failed to alter, or even slightly influence, the course of events: binationalism was rejected, in 1947 the Zionist establishment accepted the UN Partition Plan, and in 1948 an independent Jewish state of Israel was declared, constituting a fatal blow to the binational vision. During the 1950s, the group tried to promote antimilitarism as a traditional Jewish core value. When it failed to convey this message to the public, it concentrated, almost desperately, on warning the country's policymakers against turning Israel into a modern Sparta. These efforts also were ineffective, and the group slowly dissolved, leaving the activists pessimistic and the public wary of peace activism.

The Israeli Peace Committee (Va'ad Ha'shalom Ha'Yisraeli) was another—although very different—group that was engaged in peace and antinuclear activism during the 1950s. The Committee was successful for a short time in Israeli politics, but ultimately failed to make an impact. It was formed as the Israeli branch of the World Peace Council, which was noted for its worldwide, antinuclear Stockholm Petition campaign. The Committee was able to collect 400,000 signatures for the petition—almost one-third of Israel's adult population at the time (although its opponents maintained that many of the signatures were forged). However, the Committee violated a number of local political taboos and therefore lost its momentum in less than three years: it attempted to organize wide-ranging, grassroots political activity outside of the dominant political-party framework; identified itself with a universal, non-Jewish, non-Zionist organization; and maintained close relations with the USSR. Moreover, it received backing from two left-wing parties: Mapam, the Zionist competitor to the ruling Mapai Party; and Maki, the Israeli Communist Party, which was non-Zionist and lacked national legitimacy. The Committee's rapid decline added to the legacy of failure among Israeli peace groups, and, during the late 1950s and early 1960s, no significant peace activism occurred.

The Israeli peace camp regained some momentum following the 1967 War, which brought new issues to the forefront of the national agenda thereby increasing the legitimacy of extra-parliamentary tactics. The turning point came in 1968 when the Movement for Peace and Security (Ha'tnua Le'shalom U'bitachon) was established in response to the Movement for a Greater Israel, an extra-parliamentary, right-wing movement that advocated the immediate and total annexation of the Occupied Territories.[11] The Movement for Peace and Security had only several hundred members, but was fairly conspicuous between 1968 and 1970. It was the first Israeli organization to publicly warn of the occupation's political, military, and social dangers, and strongly urged that the idea of occupation be abandoned before it became rooted in Israel's political, economic, and psychological mindset. The Movement advocated direct dialogue with any Arab leader or group willing to discuss peace and tried to convince the Israeli public and decision makers that significant territorial concessions were a necessary and reasonable price to pay for peace with the Arabs. It also warned that if Israel administered the Occupied Territories too harshly, a violent Palestinian rebellion would result eventually.

The Movement for Peace and Security gained the support of a number of prominent academics, intellectuals, artists, and other public figures, and tried to integrate itself into the Israeli mainstream so as to avoid its predecessors' fate. Nonetheless, the combination of the immense military victory of 1967—which many euphoric Israelis interpreted as divine intervention—and the Movement's inability to identify any Arab partners for peace talks led to mounting criticism.[12] Its opponents maintained that the Movement's ideas were unrealistic and could critically jeopardize Israel's security. Not surprisingly, the strongest attacks came from the Right. However, Mapai—still the dominant political party representing the mainstream public—also directed caustic criticism and fierce attacks on the Movement's patriotism and political rationality. Thus, the Movement was badly stigmatized and isolated, and its political influence remained negligible. In the early 1970s it faded, and following the traumatic 1973 War, it disappeared. In retrospect, however, the Movement established a new discourse on the options for peace and war and their costs, thereby paving the way for more successful peace activism toward the end of the decade.

Following the 1973 October War, in which the Arabs perpetrated a well-coordinated surprise attack on Israel, the national consensus on security issues was shattered as many Israelis became increasingly convinced that long-term national security depended on a political rather than military solution to the conflict. Reserve soldiers who returned from the war even organized a massive protest campaign demanding that those responsible for the military fiasco resign. Thus, the political atmosphere was becoming more conducive to grassroots political activism, as evidenced by the emergence in the mid-1970s of Strength and Peace (Oz Ve'shalom), a small, religious peace group. The group's founders, many of whom were connected with the universities, aimed to provide a religious counterbalance to Bloc of the Faithful (Gush Emunim), a rapidly expanding, right-wing nationalistic movement that had gained wide support within the religious-Zionist sector. Strength and Peace tried to convince its main target audience, the religious Zionists, that, contrary to Bloc of the Faithful's ideology, using force to establish claims over the Occupied Territories ran counter to Jewish religious tradition. It also tried to convince the secular public that not all religious Zionists supported the Bloc's messianic, expansionist ideology. Nevertheless, the group's activities did not elicit much positive response: the group failed to win the support of rabbis with significant religious authority or that of the religious public, toward whom its message was basically directed. Moreover, the group's religious affiliation isolated it from the secular peace movements that were gaining momentum. Although the group was still active at the time of this study, it remained very small and had not attained much ideological or political influence.

Another peace group that emerged amid this favorable political atmosphere was the Israeli Council for Israeli-Palestinian Peace (Ha'moetza Ha'yisraelit Le'shalom Israel-Falestine), which was established in 1976. This small organization was the first to dare to suggest that Israel negotiate directly with the PLO and recognize it as the legitimate representative of the Palestinian people. The Council's founders, most of whom had widely acknowledged political or military expertise, developed close relations with prominent Palestinian leaders. The meetings often took place in European countries, such as France and Italy, and were declared private since the Israeli activists had no official authorization to negotiate with their Palestinian counterparts, who were usually PLO officials. Nonetheless, the most prominent Israeli decision makers—including then Prime Minister Yitzhak Rabin—usually were apprised of these meetings, thereby implicitly acknowledging that communication with the PLO was valuable.[13] Still, the Council remained a tiny and exclusive body, a virtual think tank with only minimal political power and almost no public appeal.

The heyday of Israeli peace activism began in early 1978 with the emergence of Peace Now (Shalom Achshav), a movement that grew out of a fear among some Israelis that the right-wing, Likud-led government had no genuine interest in concluding the peace talks it had begun with Egypt. The group demanded that the government continue the talks until a peace agreement was reached, and mobilized unprecedented public support in a very short period of time. It should be noted, however, that in addition to its pro-peace components, this support also reflected the anti-Likud sentiments of many in the moderate Left, who could not come to terms with the Labor Party's unprecedented defeat in the 1977 elections.

After the signing of the peace treaty with Egypt in 1979, Peace Now—by then a large grassroots movement—needed a new and viable cause. The group's overarching goal became the promotion of a sane, humanistic version of Zionism in response to the growing popularity of the nationalist Zionism espoused by the right-wing Bloc of the Faithful. The movement also protested the Israeli army's harsh treatment of the Palestinians in the Occupied Territories, which, it claimed, proved that the occupation was far from benign, and that, contrary to government propaganda, occupation, by its very definition, could not be truly "enlightened."

At the same time, to sustain its popularity, Peace Now also was aware that it had to demonstrate allegiance to collective core values and maintain a lawful character. Thus it refrained—and, at the time of the study, continued to refrain—from opposing the clearly delineated political consensus, as the more radical peace groups often did by advocating conscientious objection, for example. This nonconfrontational stand became particularly apparent when Israel invaded Lebanon in 1982. Although by that time Peace Now aspired to leadership of the peace camp, it did not denounce this "war of choice" for ten days—well after several other, much smaller and weaker peace groups had done so. Hence, the more radical peace activists publicly challenged Peace Now's right to lead the peace camp. Its most conspicuous challenger was the There Is a Limit (Yesh Gvul) group, whose program advocated—for the first time in Israel's history—the option of (selective) conscientious objection and whose members refused to serve in Lebanon and the Occupied Territories and consequently often were jailed. This position directly contravened the Israeli mainstream belief that military service had to be separated from individual political views.

During the 1980s a new, particularistic style of peace activism emerged that still existed at the time this study was conducted. A notable example of this sort of activism was Parents against Silence (Horim Neged Shtika). Its members were all parents of soldiers serving in Lebanon and had no other goal than the withdrawal of Israeli forces from Lebanese territory. When this was achieved in 1984 (although the last Israeli soldier only left Lebanon in June 2000), the group indeed dissolved. Parents against Silence served, however, as a model for subsequent peace groups with limited goals and specific membership composition, most notably the Four Mothers Movement, discussed below, which in fact adopted the same goal.

A number of women's peace groups also were formed during these years, as well as Mizrachi (of Middle Eastern descent) groups, such as East for Peace (Ha'mizrach Le'shalom), whose members felt alienated from the existing peace organizations.[14] These groups called for far-reaching social, economic, and political reforms, and met publicly with PLO officials. The establishment denounced them as "dangerous to the nation's interest," and in 1986 the Knesset enacted a law that prohibited meetings between Israeli citizens and PLO officials. Although some peace activists were sentenced to short prison terms, the law failed to halt the vigorous wave of peace activism that emerged in late 1987 following the eruption of the Intifada, the Palestinian uprising.[15]

Many of the new groups that emerged in the late 1980s worked in tandem with the earlier ones. Although most of them were small, their self-confidence, close connections with the mass media, and eloquence in articulating their ideologies brought them considerable public attention, though not necessarily approval. Somewhat paradoxically, the most visible of these groups, Women in Black (Nashim Be'shachor), was the least institutionalized. From 1988 to 1993 this authentic, women-only, grassroots movement held Friday vigils at noon in central public squares and intersections throughout the country, demanding an end to the occupation.[16] The participants suffered severe public criticism, and even violent assaults by passing drivers and pedestrians, who called them "Arab lovers" and traitors. Still, their ritualistic protest delivered a clear message and gained wide public attention.

Other groups embraced this unequivocal and uncompromising anti-occupation stance, as well. Some of them identified openly with the Palestinian national liberation struggle, and a few of the more radical ones even rebuked the Zionist endeavor for instigating the ongoing strife. Both moderate and radical groups propagated the anti-occupation message in public appearances with Palestinians and in discussion forums, both within and outside of the country. Hundreds of Israeli-Palestinian grassroots dialogue groups of various sizes and orientations also emerged throughout the country. Thus, in the late 1980s peace activism became an integral—though certainly not the most popular—part of Israeli political life, and it resonated strongly in public discourse on security matters.

Bowing to intense American pressure, Israel participated in the Madrid Conference in 1991. The peace movement, for its part, did not regard this as very significant since the Likud-led government showed no intention of changing its security policies. However, the peace movement largely supported the newly elected Labor government's launching of the Oslo process in 1993, even though this process greatly contributed to the movement's decline and may even lead to its demise. The Oslo Accords caused an acute ideological split within the peace movement. Although most peace groups warmly welcomed the shift in national policy, the movement's more radical elements rejected the "Two States for the Two Peoples" formula, arguing that it was only a scheme to stop the Intifada, and that the Palestinians would end up with limited self-government and not the independent state to which they were entitled. Even while the negotiations were in progress, the radical groups maintained that peace activism and anti-government protests should continue. On the other hand, the moderate and much larger peace groups withheld criticism of the government's peace policy so as to thwart the right-wing opposition. As we shall see below, this policy cost the movement both momentum and political visibility. Although peace activists occasionally rallied against the Netanyahu government's anti-peace tactics, these sporadic events did not revitalize the peace camp, which had receded since the early 1990s.

Despite the peace movement's loss of vitality, several important and promising developments occurred during the late 1990s. Although they cannot be referred to as peace groups, per se, a number of institutionalized bodies emerged that promoted Israeli-Palestinian rapprochement. The best example is the Peres Center for Peace, established in September 1997 and headed by Shimon Peres, who is perhaps most closely associated with the Oslo process and the vision of a New Middle East. At the time of the study, the Center organized various dialogue forums, raised enormous sums of money for joint Israeli-Palestinian ventures, and encouraged foreign interest—mainly European—in the Middle East peace process. Its success, however, may well undermine other Israeli peace groups' ability to gain visibility and financial support.

Ad hoc coalitions of peace and human rights groups, who utilized their combined numbers to achieve common goals, also developed in recent years. Some coalitions were established for a single undertaking (e.g., a mass demonstration), while others were more multipurpose and enduring. The latter coalitions generally were formed to protest or take legal action against a specific practice, such as the "silent transfer" of Palestinian residents from Jerusalem (in order to maintain the city's Jewish majority), or the administrative detention of Palestinians accused or suspected of hostile acts. While participating in these coalitions, each of the organizations maintained its distinct goals and specific character. When the study was conducted, one of the most active of these coalitions was the Israeli Committee against the Demolition of Homes, which included Bat Shalom, Women for Peace, Rabbis for Human Rights, Peace Now, and the (Palestinian) Land Defense Committee. This grouping was formed to protest Israel's policy of destroying houses that Palestinians had built on their own property in the Occupied Territories without permits. Although the coalition had not succeeded yet in preventing these acts, it had drawn media attention to the hardships and injustices this policy inflicted on the Palestinians.

Finally, there was a reemergence in recent years of various small groups—in particular, the Four Mothers Movement—demanding that Israel unilaterally withdraw from southern Lebanon. These groups were not perceptually, strategically, or tactically innovative; instead they demonstrated the routinization of peace activism in Israel. However, they succeeded in drawing the attention of both the media and the political establishment, which may indicate that the peace movement had become a legitimate voice in the discourse on national security matters.

Figure 5.1 shows the establishment of new Israeli peace groups from the 1940s to the 1990s and thus outlines the progress of Israeli peace activism.[17] The dearth of such groups up to the late 1970s reflects the difficulties that peace activism faced during this era, whereas the large numbers of peace groups established in the late 1980s and early 1990s suggest that this period was the heyday of Israeli peace activism. Figure 5.1 also indicates the negative impact of the Oslo process on Israeli peace activism.

Findings

As maintained at the beginning of this chapter, the Israeli peace movement's tireless efforts to convince the public of its political relevance and concern for the national interest, and thus to expand, gain recognition, and become an

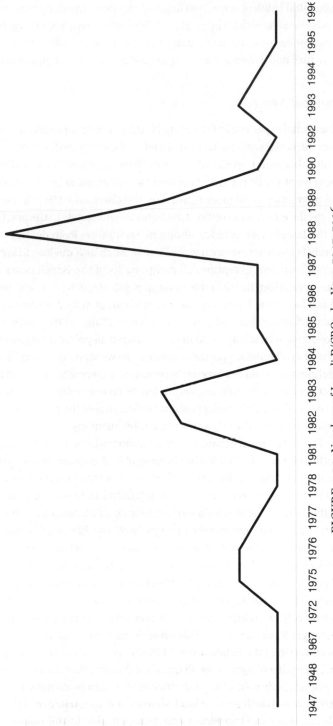

FIGURE 5.1. Numbers of Israeli P/CROs, by Year, 1947–1996

influential political actor, had failed at the time this study was conducted. It is suggested here that the origins of this failing stem from three different factors, concerning the movement's (1) political agenda, (2) organizational structure and dynamics, and (3) socio-demographic composition.

Political Agenda

The dismal experience of the early Israeli peace groups served as a red flag to their successors, who tried to avoid what they regarded as their predecessors' major deficiency—political naivete. Thus, over the years, the Israeli peace movement's political agenda became less dominated by moralistic, ideological orientations and more focused on the "here and now." In fact, since the 1970s the movement confined itself almost completely to the practical aspects of the Israeli-Arab conflict, altogether refraining from dealing with armed conflicts elsewhere or with global issues, such as a nuclear freeze.

Still, without exception, all components of the Israeli peace movement were located on the left of the national political spectrum ("left" being defined in the local Israeli political context in terms of attitudes toward the Israeli-Palestinian conflict and how to resolve it). Thus, in this respect, the peace movement as a whole stood in opposition to all political parties of the Right, as well as all religious parties. However, as we shall see, a significant perceptual gap also could be observed between the movement's political agenda and that of center and even somewhat left-of-center political actors, as they, together with the right-wing political bodies, shared the postulates of the mainstream security ethos that the peace movement rejected.

The Israeli mainstream's security ethos, which all of the major political parties espoused and which has been analyzed extensively, particularly in the context of "the new historians debate,"[18] is based on the following tenets: (1) Power politics are central to international and intercommunal relations. In this context, the Israeli-Palestinian relationship is seen as a zero-sum struggle between two peoples over the same piece of land; hence, recognizing Palestinian national rights and interests necessarily means that Jewish rights will be undermined. (2) Israel's struggle with its neighboring states is part of a pattern of persecutions and catastrophes that has occurred throughout Jewish history. Thus, Israel is envisaged as playing a passive role in the conflict and as acting defensively, with little ability to prevent the recurring violent clashes that endanger its existence. (3) This underlying existential anxiety has led to the glorification of the Israeli army. Military service is considered a primary and indispensable obligation of all qualified citizens, thereby excluding from the legitimate body politic the Arab citizens of Israel who do not serve in the army. (4) Control of the historical land of Israel and maintenance of the state's Jewish character are connected and indispensable to the nation's existence.

Thus, significant territorial compromises would affect Israel's national character and jeopardize its very raison d'être.

In contrast, the peace movement rejected the logic of power politics and its practical ramifications, such as the zero-sum definition of the regional conflict. Instead it advocated win-win definitions of the situation, and usually considered military resolutions as more costly and less effective than political ones. The peace movement also regarded democratic values as equal to or more important than Jewish ones in determining the national character of the state of Israel. Unlike the Israeli mainstream, all of the peace groups long recognized the Palestinians' right to self-determination and the PLO as their legitimate representative. They also believed that neither side could achieve a decisive military victory; therefore significant territorial concessions, painful as they may be, could contribute to Israel's long-term security.

At the same time, there was considerable ideological diversity within the peace movement, which damaged both its political status and its public image. The most significant ideological cleavage occurred between the Zionist majority and the non- or anti-Zionist minority. The Zionist peace groups endorsed the Jewish nature of the state of Israel, defined Israel as the Jewish homeland, and often maintained strong relations with Jewish communities in the Diaspora. Although Zionist peace organizations were devoted to promoting Israeli-Arab peace, most limited their activities to opposing the occupation of the territories or advocating a political solution to the conflict. They rarely emphasized Jewish-Palestinian social or cultural integration, either because of disinterest or a desire to mobilize widespread public support. The few groups that advocated integration were the tiny and short-lived East for Peace Mizrachi peace group, which strongly supported cultural integration, and the joint Israeli-Palestinian women's groups, which often promoted social interactions between the two sides. In addition, the Zionist peace groups frequently used their members' military service and rank to legitimize their participation in the security debate. For example, Peace Now was virtually founded on the basis of the "Officers' Letter," in which the signers used their high military rank to justify their demand that Prime Minister Begin reach a peace agreement with Egypt. It should be noted, however, that while their conformity with the Zionist creed enabled these peace groups to establish a more fruitful dialogue with the mainstream, it also hindered their relations with Palestinian groups, as well as international peace organizations that identified Zionism with the occupation and colonialism.

The non-Zionist peace groups, on the other hand, made no effort to appease the mainstream. Instead of forging contacts with Jewish communities in the Diaspora, these groups established links with foreign, non-Jewish organizations that purported to be politically progressive, such as European bodies of the new-Left and Green types, as well as Christian churches. Along with certain Palestinian critics of the Israeli peace movement, the non-Zionist groups argued that their Zionist counterparts unintentionally served as a smokescreen behind which the abuses of the Israeli occupation could continue. Some non-Zionist groups, such as the Alternative Information Center,[19] even maintained that the Arab-Israeli conflict was the direct result of the Zionist movement's colonialist nature and expansionist policies that flourished in Israel/Palestine and later in the state of Israel. Thus, they viewed the Israeli army as an instrument to suppress the Palestinians and urged their members to avoid military service at all costs until the occupation was terminated. Not surprisingly, these "heretic" views isolated the non-Zionist groups from the Israeli public, and the negative image associated with them was reflected on the entire peace movement, contributing greatly to its political marginalization.

In addition to their disparate views about the causes of the Arab-Israeli conflict, Zionist and non-Zionist peace organizations proposed different solutions. At the time of the study, the Zionist peace groups advocated the Two States for the Two Peoples solution—that is, the establishment of a Palestinian state that would coexist with the state of Israel. Although the non-Zionist groups were the first to openly support this alternative, most of them preferred a binational state as a solution at the time the study was conducted. A separate Palestinian state, they argued, would be too economically, militarily, and politically weak to be genuinely independent, and would merely serve Zionism's colonialist aspirations; only a joint framework, rather than political and economic separation, could provide the Palestinians with a commensurate degree of prosperity and thus prevent further bloodshed.

The ideological differences between the Zionist and non-Zionist peace groups also extended to issues of social justice and economic equality. The Zionist peace groups usually addressed these problems only when trying to mobilize working-class supporters, and even then in a very limited capacity. In this context, rather than fully elucidate the connection between domestic social conditions and the country's external relations, they focused on one small aspect of the problem: the large amounts of money the Israeli government was spending in the Occupied Territories on construction, roadwork, and Jewish settlements instead of using it to improve the living conditions of their target audience, Israelis of the lower socioeconomic strata. Thus, the moderate but larger peace groups sustained the movement's public image as a body with middle-class interests, and the movement often was accused of being overly concerned with Palestinian interests at the expense of Israel's underprivileged sectors.[20]

On the other hand, socioeconomic issues formed a more central part of the non-Zionist peace groups' discourse. These groups, which often espoused traditional or new Marxist ideologies, sought to expose the connection between the protracted conflict in the Middle East and the socioeconomic problems within Israeli society, as well as the growing economic disparity between Israelis, on the one hand, and Palestinians and most Arabs in the region, on the other. They believed that the growing oppression of Palestinians in the Occupied Territories and of weaker groups within Israel—such as the working class, new immigrants, women, Israeli-Arab citizens, and Jews of Mizrachi origin—stemmed from the same conflict. Furthermore, they contended that as a colonialist ethno-national entity, Ashkenazi-Zionist Israel could not come to terms with either its non-Ashkenazi Jewish and Arab minorities or with the existence of an adjacent Palestinian state. Thus, they did not regard the establishment of a Palestinian state, in and of itself, as a remedy for the conflict; instead the radical non-Zionist peace activists advocated a structural change in the dominant Israeli political and social orientation. Ironically, most members of the weaker Jewish groups in Israeli society strongly rejected this argument because it associated them with the Israeli Arabs and Palestinians.

Despite their diversity, all of the political agendas the peace movement put forth were criticized over the years, mostly by centrist and right-wing organizations or individuals, although the left-wing establishment also expressed reservations about certain tenets. The most mild criticism was that the peace activists were politically naive: they were ignorant of the dominant role that power played in interstate and inter-community relations, and did not fully understand that Israel's existence depended on its ability to maintain military superiority. [21] Critics also questioned the movement's basic loyalty to Zionism and the Israeli national interest. The peace activists were virtually accused of lacking patriotism, preferring the Arab/Palestinian cause over the Israeli/Jewish one, and giving precedence to "bleeding-heart," universalistic values.[22]

Such reservations about the peace movement's political agenda were recently publicized in a well-articulated article by Yuval Steinitz,[23] in which he denigrated three of the peace camp's basic assumptions as false and misleading: (1) that regional economic prosperity would necessarily bring peace; (2) that peace automatically would engender prosperity; and (3) that democratization and normalization could produce peace and, conversely, that peace would promote democratization and normalization.[24] He maintained that the first assumption reflected a sort of bourgeois pacifism since it overemphasized economic factors while underemphasizing the Arabs' national aspirations and their deeply structured, religiously based antagonism toward Israel. It also led to a misunderstanding of Mizrachi Israelis who, by and large, rejected rapprochement between Israel and the Arabs on religious and nationalistic grounds. The second assumption, Steinitz argued, reflected "leftist-messianic megalomania," which ignored the fact that neither peace nor war with Israel would have any substantial impact on the economy of the Middle East. The third assumption, he believed, was rooted in a mistaken cosmopolitan humanism that refused to realize that primordial national, almost tribal, affiliations motivate most people, and peace-making, in and of itself, is of little value. In his view, under the influence of the peace camp, these three basic, erroneous assumptions already had led Israel to such fateful decisions as the launching of the Oslo process, which may result in a national catastrophe.

Organizational Structure and Dynamics

Organizational factors also affected the Israeli peace movement's political status and its relations with the mainstream. First, the negative effects of the movement's extra-parliamentary tactics cannot be underestimated, even though extra-parliamentary activism had become an integral and legitimate part of Israeli political life since the early 1970s. The first two decades of statehood (1948 to the late 1960s) were characterized by centralist and collectivist tendencies, and extra-parliamentary endeavors were discouraged since they were considered contrary to the state's interests. Especially in the 1950s, when the Israeli government was preoccupied with establishing, exercising, and demonstrating its authority, many at both the elite and the grassroots levels felt that such nonestablishment efforts undermined the government's supremacy. This statist orientation—promoted with considerable zeal by David Ben-Gurion, Israel's highly charismatic first prime minister during the formative years of the late 1940s and the 1950s—attributed utmost importance to the agencies of the political establishment and downgraded the political aspirations of small and voluntary groups, labeling them as petty, parochial, and counterproductive to the collective national interest. The country's leaders and the general public shared this collectivist orientation, which was reinforced by the ever-present reality—or perception—of an external existential threat and by the frequent military confrontations with neighboring Arab countries.[25]

This attitude began to change in the late 1960s. By then the Israeli political system's stability and the decision makers' authority had become well established, and nonestablishment-style activism was less threatening to the political elite. Moreover, the security threat declined significantly following the 1967 War, greatly relieving existential anxieties and increasing the tolerance for nonconformist attitudes and actions. News reports about the American civil rights movement and student revolts in Europe also made the Israeli public and elite more receptive to ordinary citizens' participation in "high politics." Furthermore, a new generation of young Israeli political activists came of age in the late 1960s and early 1970s. Having been politically socialized in the Israeli milieu and never having experienced first-hand such collective traumas as the Holocaust, the insecurity of the pre-state days, or the bloody struggle for independence, these new political participants had a stronger sense of security and self-reliance than their parents' generation, and therefore opted for noncompliance and alternative means of political expression.

The combination of these developments and the shock of the October War in 1973 led to dramatic changes in the repertoire of Israeli political tactics. The soldiers' massive postwar protests prompted open debate over the decision makers' competence and greatly contributed to the legitimization of active extra-parliamentary activity. In the late 1970s and 1980s, manifestations of civil discontent increased in Israel, challenging the state's monopoly on political power and various spheres of social and economic activity. Together with the peace groups, these newly empowered grassroots actors contested the national ideology, including fervently held ideas about state security.

The development of extra-parliamentary activity, however, raised new conceptual and practical problems. Since the groups that promoted such activity were not elected and hence could not be held accountable, the political establishment and the broad public often questioned their right to try to change the national consensus and influence decision-making processes, particularly when sensitive national-security matters were involved. Furthermore, the sharp increase in the number of nonestablishment bodies undermined the authorities' control over the political arena, which they tried to regain using means that were legal but did not always conform to the democratic value of free association. Indeed, today, according to Israeli law, extra-parliamentary bodies have to be registered with and acknowledged by the authorities in order to gain benefits, such as tax exemptions and formal recognition as legitimate sociopolitical actors.[26] Not surprisingly, those groups that propounded radical programs were not granted such status and therefore faced severe financial and other hardships. Thus, although extra-parliamentary groups had gained much more acceptance over the years, Israeli peace groups, particularly those that blatantly opposed the Zionist creed, were still limited in their ability to gain formal and informal recognition as legitimate participants in the public discourse on important political issues.

The relatively small size of the peace groups also hindered the movement's ability to gain influence. With the exception of a few large organizations, most Israeli peace groups were small or medium size. Even at the height of their popularity, the largest Israeli peace organizations had no more than a few hundred inner-core activists and some ten thousand latent supporters. The combined membership of most groups did not exceed one hundred activists and supporters, and many had fewer members. The size of Israeli peace organizations seemed to be directly related to their function. Since visibility and hence large size are crucial for organizations engaged in protest, the groups focusing on this kind of activity devoted much of their resources to mobilization efforts. Dialogue and advocacy-oriented organizations generally were smallest in size since they were engaged in face-to-face interactions either with Palestinian counterparts or with policymakers. Size was often of minor importance to service-oriented organizations, as well, since many preferred to maintain the minimal membership necessary to efficiently deliver their particular service. At the same time, the fact that the total number of peace activists was small clearly undermined the movement's ability to gain political weight and reduced politicians' motivation to attend to its demands.

The strategies that the various peace groups employed over the years affected their success, as well. In the 1970s and 1980s, most peace groups focused on consciousness-raising and protest activities in order to mobilize grassroots support for the newly emerged movement. In addition, its founders were influenced to a large extent by the anti-Vietnam War campaign in the United States and comparable European activities. This strategy also was relatively easy and inexpensive to implement, a serious consideration for entirely voluntary bodies. Moreover, while consciousness-raising and protest activities involved substantial organizational efforts and resources, they did not demand extremely high personal sacrifice or necessitate ongoing massive mobilization efforts. However, the effect of demonstrations and other means of protest eroded over the years and many participants simply were burned out. Furthermore, right-wing nationalists criticized these peace groups for continuing to concentrate on less demanding activities, particularly since their own members "put their money where their mouths were" and, for example, went to live in settlements in the Occupied Territories. This undoubtedly contributed to a growing frustration among some peace activists who had to admit that there were limits to the personal sacrifices they were willing to make.[27]

Compared to organizing mass demonstrations, the strategy of establishing a dialogue with pro-peace Palestinians also required limited organizational effort, resources, and professional skills, but was difficult for the peace movement to employ for many years because of the Israeli taboo against "speaking with the enemy." More problematic, however, was the difficulty peace activists encountered in identifying Palestinians and other Arabs who were willing or unafraid to communicate with them. This situation began to change in the mid-1970s, when the Israeli Council for Israeli-Palestinian Peace became the first group to conduct an ongoing and practical dialogue with Arab/Palestinian representatives. In the 1980s, however, when the popularity and impact of mass protest activities declined, open dialogue with the Palestinians became the preferred alternative, and almost all of the Israeli peace groups became involved in organizing such meetings both inside and outside of the country.[28]

Furthermore, and somewhat paradoxically, during the Palestinian Intifada (late 1980s to early 1990s) many small Israeli-Palestinian dialogue groups were established. These groups usually targeted specific audiences, particularly youths, professionals, and women. However, at a certain point— particularly after the signing of the Oslo Accords—dialogue with the Palestinians on the grassroots level not only ceased to be an attractive novelty but also seemed redundant while the leaders of the two sides were engaged in direct peace talks; thus participation decreased. Moreover, as the peace process stalled from 1996 onward, the Palestinians' desire to communicate with Israelis declined noticeably and more concrete modes of cooperation, such as joint economic ventures, professional courses, and so on, were employed.

Relatively few Israeli peace groups opted to offer professional services as their primary strategy. At the time of the study, less than a quarter of the peace organizations provided medical, legal, psychological, educational, economic, and interorganizational coordination services. Until the 1980s, the only group to offer some type of service was the tiny, pacifist Israeli War Resisters, which was founded in the early 1950s. Although it never defined itself as a service organization, this group provided men who had refused military service with legal advice and information about pacifist refusal. The first group to declare itself a service organization was the Alternative Information Center, which offered media services to the foreign and local press, as well as publishing and distribution services to Israeli pro-peace organizations and groups. Since the late 1980s, providing services had become more widespread in the Israeli peace movement because of the objectively greater need for certain services (e.g., medical care in the Occupied Territories) and the growing realization among activists that service-giving helped to maintain an organization and raise funds for other activities. However, as mentioned earlier, certain organizations also made this strategic shift because of declining participation in mass protest activities, as well as the growing fear that the movement would dwindle if its grassroots support disappeared and there was no organizational alternative. However, if for some reason the provided service was no longer needed—as was the case with Physicians for Human Rights, which could no longer perform its task after the IDF's withdrawal from large parts of the West Bank and Gaza—then the organization was most likely to fade away or find another pursuit; both of these options left a hole in the fabric of the peace movement.

Advocating a pro-peace message to the political establishment was another strategy that certain Israeli peace organizations employed. This approach required open communication with the authorities, and success often was highly dependent on whether a peace group espoused a moderate or radical ideology. The radical groups, which often espoused non- or anti-Zionist ideologies, were almost completely dissociated from the political establishment; moreover, they generally did not regard advocacy as feasible because they believed that the authorities never would adopt the type of peace policy they favored. On the other hand, most moderate peace groups believed that the decision makers could be influenced—particularly under massive pro-peace pressure—and therefore interacted regularly with individuals, groups, and organizations close to or within the political establishment, such as political parties, government agencies, and office holders. To maintain good relations with the political elite, these moderate groups generally disassociated themselves from the more radical peace organizations and the negative public image they engendered. Their success often depended on their ability to identify and co-opt allies within the political establishment. For example, during the Rabin-Peres government (1992–1996) some Knesset members (MKs) from the ruling Labor Party and all the MKs from the Meretz Party often functioned as unofficial peace movement lobbyists and had particularly close relations with Peace Now and the women-only organization, Bat Shalom. Later, when the Likud Party returned to power and the government coalition was composed only of right-wing and religious parties, the peace movement rarely used advocacy as a strategy. When the Labor Party won the 1999 elections, the new prime minister, Ehud Barak, adopted a rather unsympathetic approach toward the peace movement in an attempt to reinforce his government security-oriented image, which apparently had won him the voters' loyalty.

Finally, the Israeli peace movement underwent an accelerated process of institutional consolidation in recent years that affected its political status. In his suggestive book on Israeli peace activism and the Palestinian Intifada, Reuven Kaminer observed that this organizational restructuring had had positive effects on the movement: "[There is a] remarkable amount of continuity and innovation . . . in the Israeli peace movement. . . . In this sense, the movement has accumulated a wealth of organizational tools and experience, which enable it to respond to new crises. . . . The plethora of protest groups, among them the appearance and success of organization by profession, enabled the protest movement to tap the energy and the talents of wide sectors in the population."[29] However, these rapid institutional changes also proved quite problematic for the movement, primarily—although not solely—in terms of its intraorganizational relations. Our study indicated that those peace organizations that underwent an intensive institutionalization process lost much of their grassroots support. In addition, the new, highly institutionalized peace groups formed in the 1990s found it difficult to create a wide base of public support (e.g., Bat Shalom).

There also was a recent trend toward professionalization within the peace movement, indicated by a sharp increase in the number of hired professional staff. As the volunteer membership within the movement dropped, the proportional influence of these "professionals" increased, thereby reversing the balance of power within many peace organizations. In fact, two distinct sectors—each considering the organization to be its "own"—could be observed within certain peace groups (e.g., Physicians for Human Rights and Bat Shalom), creating inefficiency and mounting internal tensions. Professionalization also had a significant affect on the peace groups' budgets, as the proportion devoted to salaries increased and the amount allocated to activities, advertisement, and so on, diminished.

Institutionalization also impeded collaboration between different peace groups. The smaller, less institutionalized organizations accused the larger groups of using their highly developed organizational apparatus and skills to appropriate all of the available resources, thereby virtually eliminating ideological pluralism and creating an internally conformist, mainstream movement. Therefore, although the process of institutional consolidation helped maintain the movement after the massive demobilization of its grassroots support, it also led to internal dissension among those activists who resented the movement's new, highly institutionalized character.

Socio-Demographic Features

The Israeli peace movement's political status also was strongly influenced by its socio-demographic features, which resembled those of most new social movements.[30] The movement's unique characteristics created a clear delineation between it and most of the Israeli public, making it an exclusive group despite its efforts to be inclusive. The movement's most visible characteristic was its extreme social homogeneity, which made it a sort of subculture. The peace movement was almost entirely composed of middle-class, highly educated, urban Ashkenazi Jews—Ashkenazi being both the national majority and the dominant ethnic group in Israel; relatively few members were Mizrachi/Sephardic Jews, and even fewer were Israeli-Arabs.

Mizrachi Jews did establish several peace groups in the past—most notably East for Peace—aiming to present an authentic Mizrachi peace program and to serve as a bridge to the Arab world. Although the number and visibility of Mizrachi groups had increased in general in recent years, those few that engaged in peace activism went largely unnoticed, with no discernible political impact. This was primarily due to a lack of support among non-Ashkenazi Israelis, most of whom identified with the political Right. Moreover, many of the core Mizrachi activists abandoned their groups in frustration over what they considered to be a structural, ethnically based inability to create a fruitful, eye-to-eye dialogue with their Ashkenazi counterparts, thereby widening the schism between the peace movement and large sectors of Israeli society.

Another factor that influenced the movement's image was the disproportionate number of members who were born in the United States and other English-speaking countries. To these activists, many of whom were politically socialized on European and American campuses during the 1960s, values such as liberalism, human rights, and participatory democracy were "natural." To the majority of Israelis, however, these ideas were much less self-evident and acceptable. This discrepancy created a high cognitive barrier between the activists and the Israeli mainstream.

Thus, because of its distinct and allegedly elitist orientation and composition, many less privileged Israelis questioned both the peace camp and its motives. Some even contended that the movement was actually motivated by its members' particularistic class interests since they would have been the first to benefit from a peace settlement. This prevalent impression apparently impeded almost all of the peace movement's efforts to mobilize support among the lower classes and non-Ashkenazi Israelis. For example, Peace Now tried for years to overcome this obstacle with little success. Its leaders met with heads of citizens' groups in poor neighborhoods to try to facilitate joint actions,[31] and their message was epitomized in the slogan, "Money for the neighborhoods and not for the settlements." Recently, Peace Now invited new immigrants from the former USSR—who were known to be quite hawkish and therefore had no representatives in the peace movement—to participate in daytrips to West Bank settlements to expose them to the problematic realities of the territories. Although Peace Now activists argued that their message was well absorbed, others contended that the new immigrants—most of whom not only felt alienated from the social center to which most of the peace activists belonged but also suffered from severe economic difficulties—were unmoved by the organizers' anti-settlement message and instead had become interested in buying houses in the West Bank settlements.[32]

Bat Shalom, the largest women's peace organization, also tried unsuccessfully to mobilize non-Ashkenazi and working-class Israelis. In 1995, its Social Justice and Peace Program launched an outreach project aimed at poorly educated, low-income Jewish Mizrachi women living in development towns and inner-city neighborhoods to introduce them to the group's ideas about peace, feminism, and social justice. Over the next few years, Bat Shalom community workers organized several women's clubs—mainly in Jerusalem, with a few in Tel Aviv—that held weekly meetings to discuss issues such as family violence, women's health, parenthood, and other subjects of special interest to women. Those women who attended regularly were expected to become local opinion-leaders, who would mobilize other women from their neighborhoods to participate in Bat Shalom's activities. Although it may have been too early to assess the long-term effectiveness of this effort, the Bat Shalom leaders and activists with whom we spoke were fairly pessimistic since the program's participants voted for either religious or right-wing parties in the 1996 and 1999 elections.

Another socio-demographic feature of the peace movement that shaped its public image and affected the extent of its support was the high level of education among its members, most of whom held academic degrees, usually in the humanities or social sciences.[33] This was reflected in the movement's highly sophisticated slogans, ads, and publications, as well as its emphasis on written documents. Input from university faculty members enabled the peace movement to develop a critical, nonconformist view of the conflict and its possible resolutions; however, it also stigmatized the peace movement as politically naive and detached from the harsh realities of life. Furthermore, it impeded the movement's ability to present a simple program that the general public could comprehend.

Many Israelis also believed that the peace movement was led by kibbutz members, and claimed that the kibbutz movement logistically and financially supported peace activism. This perception invested the peace movement with an even more negative image since kibbutzim were perceived as Ashkenazi, affluent, and politically dominant. The truth, however, was that most Israeli peace activists were now city dwellers (primarily in Tel Aviv, Jerusalem, or Haifa),[34] while activism among kibbutz members had waned in recent years, due partly to economic difficulties and ideological crises within the kibbutz movement.

Age also was a distinguishing feature of the peace movement, although it affected the movement's image less than ethnic origin and education. Until the mid-1970s, peace activism was not a popular activity among young people and most members were over age forty. With the appearance of Peace Now and its young participants, peace activism came to be associated with the youth counterculture, whose "make-love-not-war" message projected an image of political naivete. However, as the number of new recruits diminished over the next two decades and the average age of the existing members increased, the movement's youthful image gradually eroded and it came to be viewed as middle-aged and anachronistic.[35] Since the mid-1990s, the movement had attempted to reverse this image by creating a youth movement, which numbered about 5,000 members at the time of the study. Their presence, however, apparently had had little effect on the movement's agenda, activities, and image.

Gender was another socio-demographic feature that affected the peace movement's political status and efficacy. As in peace organizations worldwide, women played a very large role in the Israeli groups.[36] In fact, during the 1980s the women's groups became the spearhead of the entire peace movement, particularly toward the end of the decade,[37] from Mothers against Silence in the early 1980s to Women in Black in the late 1980s, Reshet and Bat Shalom in the early and mid-1990s, and more recently the Four Mothers, Women and Mothers for Peace, and Women for the Sanctity of Life groups that were quite visible at the time of the study, particularly given the peace movement's low levels of activity, in general.

Since the socio-demographic profiles of the women's peace groups so closely resembled those of the mixed-gender groups, two primary rationales were used to justify their presence: (1) according to the feminist perspective, women are less prone to sanction war, and tend toward nonviolent modes of conflict resolution;[38] hence, they had to be able to organize their own activities so that their special voice could be heard; and (2) some of the women activists had suffered humiliating experiences in the mixed-gender peace organizations. Their male colleagues too often dismissed or simply ignored their views, despite these organizations' professed egalitarianism.[39]

Although the women activists believed that their involvement in the peace movement was important in terms of gaining a political voice, unfortunately their overwhelming presence impeded the movement's credibility as a participant in the public discourse on security matters.[40] Because many Israelis believed that these women advocated Palestinian/Arab interests and used somewhat emotional and often moralistic anti-war/pro-peace arguments to do so, their participation evoked atavistic, hostile feelings at the grassroots level. The women often were stigmatized as treasonous Arab lovers, and were even called "whores."[41] Furthermore, male participants in the security discourse often based their recommendations on their military experience, putting Israeli women at a clear disadvantage.

Religiosity was another factor that affected both the peace movement's status and its political agenda. Unlike many European, American, or Asian peace movements for which religion often serves as a frame of reference and whose core activists sometimes are religious people, the Israeli peace movement was almost entirely secular in its ideology and social composition. This was largely because Judaism does not have a historical legacy of theological pacifism. Moreover, most of the peace movement's members were openly secular and even antireligious. Nevertheless, religion played a significant role in the Israeli security debate. In fact, its visibility in these matters increased sharply over the years, particularly after the 1967 War when Israel's right to retain the territories it had captured was questioned. Since the war, the mainstream Orthodox community's views became similar to those of the right-wing groups.[42] Therefore, it was not surprising that very few religious peace organizations existed (Strength and Peace/Paths to Peace—Oz Ve'shalom/Netivot Shalom) and that religious arguments formed a minimal part of the peace movement's agenda.

The Sour Taste of Success

The Israeli peace movement's distinct perceptual and organizational/functional features at times served conflicting purposes: they enabled the movement to establish itself outside of the political mainstream and to present alternate views on the Israeli-Arab conflict; however, they also distanced the movement from the Israeli public and the political establishment. This contradictory situation raises the theoretical and practical question of whether or not the Israeli peace movement can be considered successful.

As we saw earlier, gauging the movement's achievements according to the classical indicators of a social movement's success—namely, accomplishing policy transformation and institutional consolidation[43]—is problematic since no causal relationship between the movement's activities and the policy change evidenced by the Oslo process could be sufficiently established.

Judging the movement's success by the criterion of institutional consolidation also is unsatisfactory since, contrary to theoretical predictions, the stabilization of Israeli peace activism—that is, the institutionalization of various peace organizations—contributed significantly to the movement's decline.

A more recently defined criterion of a social movement's success—namely, the gradual introduction of a desired attitude change into the collective public agenda[44]—is more applicable to the Israeli peace movement. According to this criterion, the peace movement, despite its marginal political status and limited popularity, can be credited for its contributions to the cognitive change that facilitated Israeli-Palestinian rapprochement and resulted in the Oslo process. Nevertheless, during the years of this study, Israeli peace activism displayed an extremely complex set of features, making judgments about its success difficult. The movement was rife with internal contradictions: it was small, but publicly assertive; it existed at the political periphery, but its members belonged to the upper socioeconomic strata of Israeli society; it offered political and intellectual alternatives to the mainstream security ethos, but nonetheless retained some of the basic postulates of that ethos; and finally, while most decision makers repeatedly rejected its program, in a rapid turnabout, the government embraced certain main components of the movement's agenda and with relatively minor changes turned it into the country's official foreign policy—only to abandon it four years later, then reembrace it with Barak's election in 2000, all the while turning a cold shoulder to the peace activists themselves, thereby leaving the movement weak and frustrated.

In addition to its inherent complexity, assessing the peace movement's achievements depends on the observer's political interests. Paradoxically, the Labor Party was the main political actor to deny the peace movement's contributions to the peace process, in general, and to the Oslo process, in particular. This was necessary so as to rationalize its own policy transformation without admitting any past mistakes in unequivocally rejecting the peace movement's ideas. By adopting this perspective, the party could claim full credit for the process and hence increase its chances for reelection. To refute the movement's argument that the new, official pro-peace policy could or should have been adopted years earlier, the Labor Party maintained that the shift had resulted from far-reaching changes in the global and regional environments, and in particular the Palestinians' unprecedented willingness to abandon their aim of destroying Israel.[45]

It was particularly important for the Labor Party to disassociate itself from the stigma of unpatriotic capitulation that had tainted the peace movement's readiness for far-reaching territorial and other concessions to the Palestinians. Any such association between the Labor Party and the peace movement could easily have delegitimized the entire peace process in the public's eyes. In addition, close and overt relations with the peace movement at that time could have bolstered allegations among the Labor Party's political rivals that certain nongovernmental, nonmainstream interest groups had manipulated the party into launching the Oslo process. Moreover, from the Labor Party's perspective, recognizing the movement's role in the peace process might have worsened power relations within the center-left political camp since crediting the movement would have strengthened the Meretz Party, which was closest to the peace movement and the Labor Party in this camp. This might explain why Rabin was said to have been very annoyed by a sticker that the Left distributed in the fall of 1995—"Peace is Meretz's work," using a clever play on the words *work* and *labor*, which are the same word in Hebrew. Always personally disaffected from the peace movement, Rabin also was annoyed by the large number of Meretz placards prominently displayed at the peace rallies at which he spoke, including the November 4, 1995, rally where he was assassinated.

Whereas the Labor Party disregarded the peace movement's contributions, the Right attempted to delegitimize the Oslo process by claiming that the peace movement had succeeded in manipulating the Labor government into initiating it. Since most of the Labor leaders who had launched the peace process were recognized for their patriotism and security backgrounds (in fact, Rabin was elected in 1992 because of his "Mr. Security" image), the Right had to blame someone else for this allegedly unpatriotic policy shift. Under the circumstances, blaming the Left, in general, and the peace movement, in particular, made perfect tactical sense. For many years right-wing politicians, publicists, and other representatives had portrayed the peace activists as being unpatriotic, obsessed with abstract moralistic ideals, and lacking a sense of Jewish solidarity. Thus, the Right claimed that the peace movement had "contaminated" the Labor Party—formerly the spearhead of the Zionist enterprise—as evidenced by the Labor leaders' willingness to surrender religiously and militarily significant national assets in return for a dubious peace agreement that often was referred to in this context as "a piece of paper."[46]

The peace movement developed a narrative of its own, in which it tried to portray itself as a small political body, with no official standing, that had been the first and only to foresee the inevitable course of events and to propose the correct solution for the region's plight. The peace movement, however, could not claim to have directly influenced the decision-making process that facilitated the Oslo process since it was widely known that the movement's practical access to the nation's upper echelons always had been minimal, even while the Labor Party was in power from 1992 to1996. Therefore the movement praised itself for laying the groundwork that led to the official policy transformation that the Labor government finally implemented.[47]

Thus, the peace movement's narrative openly called for some broad public recognition that it had opened communication with the Palestinian side. It disclosed the fact that after the formal peace talks were launched, Rabin and Peres had hesitated more than once before taking decisive steps toward reconciliation and that they often had wavered in making necessary compromises.[48] The peace movement purported that its indispensable grassroots pressures had encouraged—and sometimes even forced—the Labor government to make the necessary though painful concessions it otherwise might have failed to do.

Rabin's assassination on November 4, 1995, together with the Labor Party's defeat in the 1996 elections a few months later, shattered the still-fragile peace process, and with it the self-confidence of its adherents. Yet the repercussions of these two events were particularly devastating to the peace movement because they seemed to indicate that the movement had failed to convey its peace message to large parts of the Israeli public even after the upper political echelons had adopted it. While the assassination could be interpreted as the act of a solitary individual, the election of Binyamin Netanyahu, the Likud Party candidate who promised "peace with security," over Shimon Peres, the architect of the "New Middle East" vision,[49] indicated that the Israeli public considered security to be much more important than peace, at least as the Labor Party had conceived it under the Oslo process. Furthermore, when Netanyahu's government employed tactics that seemed to the peace movement to be anti-peace, the Israeli public as a whole remained silent. This suggested that the peace movement's grassroots support had eroded during the four years in which the movement had kept a low profile so as to facilitate the Labor government's peace efforts. This long hiatus strengthened the Right's claim that the peace movement was driven by baseless panic, and eroded the peace activists' self-confidence, as well. When violence erupted between Israelis and Palestinians in September 2000, however, it was so severe that the hard-core activists of the peace movement, whose fundamental belief was the need for peace and its feasibility, found it extremely difficult to mobilize even limited public support for their demand that the peace talks be continued.

These combined realities led to growing skepticism among observers about the movement's ability to make either an ideological or a practical impact on the Israeli political arena. A recent statement in a newspaper article about Peace Now can be applied to the peace movement as a whole: "After two decades the name [Peace Now] seems to mock their concern. Peace has not come 'now,' and the present animosities between Israel and the Palestinians suggest peace may yet have a long wait."[50] In a press interview, Meron Benvenisti, one of the most prominent analysts of Israeli-Palestinian relations, also asserted that the peace movement had had almost no influence and that this reflected a lack of clearly defined goals. Moreover, the peace movement had ignored the real sources of the conflict and hence could not recognize that the only feasible solution was a binational state. He also claimed that the peace activists had never understood the Palestinian side, nor had they genuinely wanted to cooperate with it. When breakthroughs in the negotiations with the Palestinians were achieved, the various peace groups immediately claimed full credit; but when the process stalled, they failed to take responsibility and argued that it was a result of doing too little, too late. According to Benvenisti, the peace movement preferred to remain in a protective bubble: "The movement actually preaches to the converted. Further, quite often it creates resentment on the part of those who do not belong to the 'Left camp.' The outcome is of course the opposite of the one desired. The public in the Center and moderate Right resents what the peace movement symbolizes and therefore will never embrace its message, even when the message is close to mainstream beliefs, such as the 'two states for two peoples' idea."[51]

Arie Rotenberg, director of a large advertising agency and a public relations consultant who was responsible for large parts of the Labor Party's 1992 election campaign, believes that the peace movement was unsuccessful in "selling" its message to the Israeli public for the following reasons:

> The peace camp lives under the impression that the entire truth is on its side, that it really knows which is the right way to go, that Netanyahu leads the entire nation to a disaster, perhaps even to a catastrophe. . . . Whenever it lost the elections the peace camp asked itself whether the public was really stupid or was the Right simply successful in leading the people astray. In any case, however, the option that the peace camp offered the public was something it didn't want and immediately rejected. The time has come to sober up from the belief that because we are right we are going to win. Likewise we should reject the patronizing idea that we can "educate" the people, that we will make them see the light. Reality is going to educate the people and shape its beliefs. The daily political encounter plays an important role in this process—political views and ideas shape the normal political arena. They are the ones that shape public opinion in the long run. And precisely here it is where the peace camp has had significant achievements, the most important of which are creating a national consensus in support of the Oslo process and recognition of the PLO as a partner for the peace process. . . . The majority of the peace camp should get used to the idea that "peace now" is a nice product but doesn't have much selling potential. . . . This is true everywhere—peripheral groups produce novel ideas, and the large corporations then smooth the edges and make them useful for everyone.[52]

Yet, contrary to Rotenberg's argument, when judged by the criterion of whether they produced a change in public attitudes about the Israeli-Palestinian conflict, it seems the peace movement's efforts were effective. Despite the difficulties involved in establishing indisputable causality, there are various circumstantial indications that the peace movement successfully introduced new and innovative ideas about security matters into the public discourse. For example, in the past the peace movement was the only Israeli political body to view the Intifada as a legitimate national struggle of liberation and to acknowledge the Palestinians' right to self-determination and, thus, to a state. However, public opinion surveys conducted in recent years suggest that today more than half of the Israeli population believe that the Palestinians are a nation, and about the same number accept and even justify the establishment of an independent Palestinian state.[53] Another indication of the movement's success in changing public attitudes is the growing readiness among Israelis to support significant territorial concessions in return for peace.[54] Although the Oslo process altered the political environment, making the use of these terms and ideas more acceptable, these shifts in attitude suggest that the peace movement's continuous presence had some impact. Indeed, Uri Avneri, one of Israel's most experienced and prominent peace activists, dismisses disparaging assessments of the movement's impact:

> Political influence is a prolonged and complicated process. On the one side stands direct influence, which is seen in the newspapers' headlines, and on the other side stands long-term influence, which is manifested by the step-by-step changing of public opinion, which in its turn influences the decision-makers. . . . Yitzhak Rabin would never have taken the Oslo course unless the majority of the Israeli public was ready to recognize the existence of a Palestinian nation and to negotiate with the PLO. This readiness did not come out of the blue. It was made possible by long years of information dissemination and the activity of a small group of Israelis.[55]

Many peace movement activists therefore stressed that its most significant accomplishment was:

> to influence public opinion by broadening the scope of public debate. The insistent advocacy of the peace movement gradually led many people, both in the center and on the left, to modify their views and accept the need for mutual recognition and compromise. The idea that the occupation is a political, financial, and moral liability rather than a strategic asset, and that Palestinian self-determination is inevitable, gradually gained greater currency. . . . Recent opinion surveys . . . strongly suggest that the movement was successful in gradually moving the "middle" toward compromise and reconciliation.[56]

Further evidence of the peace movement's success is the influence it had on Israel's Arab neighbors. In an interview with the Israeli daily *Ha'aretz*, Dr. Amer el-Janet, a young Egyptian physicist who is the son of a prominent retired diplomat and one of the founders of the Egyptian peace movement, openly attributed the establishment of the Egyptian peace movement in 1998 to the Israeli peace movement's activities:

> I witnessed the process that people like el-Huli, and my father as well, had undergone. At a certain point [those formerly opposed to the idea of peace with Israel] started to say that certain members of the half of the Israeli public [that wants peace] contributed much to peace-making in the framework of Peace Now or the other peace movements while we, the Egyptian

people, did almost nothing in this direction. The bottom line is that Israeli peace movements exerted much practical influence not only on Rabin and Peres's political moves, but also on Egyptian society.[57]

In summary, it is evident that perceptual and organizational/functional factors impeded the peace movement's direct influence over the formal policy-making process that led to the signing of the Oslo Accords. The movement also was ineffectual in gaining comprehensive public recognition as a responsible and thoughtful participant in the national security debate, and had difficulty ridding itself of the stigma that it was naive and unpatriotic. Its ongoing attempts to expand its membership to include diverse sectors of Israeli society proved futile, as well. However, notwithstanding these important shortcomings, the Israeli peace movement as a whole had considerable success in weakening the prevailing zero-sum interpretation of Israeli-Arab relations. It also quite successfully challenged the mainstream perception that the conflict was inevitable, instead introducing the notion that a political solution could be found and implemented once Israel acknowledged the Palestinians' right to self-determination. Therefore, it is clear that the Israeli peace movement achieved the following indicators of a social movement's success, as defined by Thomas Rochon and Daniel Mazmanian: it helped to redefine the political agenda, changed social values, and expanded the range of ideas about what is possible.[58] Without these contributions, the dramatic policy change that included the signing of a peace agreement to end the protracted Israeli-Palestinian conflict might not have been possible.

Notes

1. The full text of this speech, made on July 26, 1994, can be found in the collection of Rabin's speeches: *Peace Seeker—The Speeches of Prime Minister Yitzhak Rabin* (Tel Aviv: Zmora-Bitan, 1995), pp. 35–39 [Hebrew].

2. It should be noted that in the specific Israeli context, the terms "peace movement" and "political Left" are closely associated and are sometimes even identified with one another. In the European context, and to a lesser extent in the American one, the term "political Left" pertains to certain sociopolitical ideologies—communist, socialist, or socio-democratic—that advocate the unqualified equality of all people, as well as the state's social responsibility to its citizens. In Israel today, however, members of the "political Left" are first and foremost understood to be advocates of a political solution to the Israeli-Arab conflict and/or considerable territorial compromises in return for peace.

3. Israeli team composition: Dr. Tamar Hermann (Tel Aviv University and the Open University of Israel), a political scientist specializing in extra-parliamentary politics and peace activism, as well as the influence of public opinion on foreign policy (team leader); Dr. Peter Lemish, Ph.D. in education (Bet Berl Art College), specializes in social critique; Yuval Lebel, MA (Political Science Dept.,

Tel Aviv University); Assaf Matzkin, MA candidate (Political Science Dept., Tel Aviv University). A third research assistant, Ms. Daniella Yifrah, MA candidate (Political Science Dept., Tel Aviv University) was a team member for a few weeks during the first stage of the study.

4. The full findings on the Israeli case study and their analysis are found in the final report the research team submitted to the Aspen Institute in October 1998. The report can be obtained upon request from the author of this chapter.

5. David Newman and Ghazi Falah, "Writing Together Separately: Critical Discourse and the Problems of Cross-Ethnic Coauthorship," *Area* 28 (1998): 1–12.

6. The sample included the following bodies: Alternative Information Center (Ha'merkaz L'informatzia Alternativit)*; Bat Shalom of the Jerusalem Link*; Clergymen for Peace (Rabbis for Human Rights—Rabanim L'maan Zehuyot Ha'adam); Committee for Israeli-Palestinian Dialogue (H'a'vaad Le'dialogue Israeli-Falestini, Mizrachiim); Council for Peace and Security (Ha'moetza Le'shalom U'bitachon)*; East for Peace (Hamizrach L'shalom); Hebron Solidarity Committee (Ha'vaad L'solidariyut im Hevron); Israelis and Palestinians for Non-Violence (Israelim V'Falestinim L'maan Ei Alimut); Israeli Council for Israel-Palestine Peace (Ha'moetza Ha'Israelit L'shalom Israel-Falastin); Mental Health Workers for Peace (Imut); Neve Wolfson Israeli-Arab Project Acre; Oasis of Peace (Newe Shalom); Strength and Peace/Paths to Peace (Oz V'shalom/ Netivot Shalom)*; Peace Bloc (Gush Shalom); Peace Movement Coordinating Committee—Haifa and the North; Peace Now (Shalom Achshav)*; Physicians for Human Rights (Rof'im L'ma'an Zehuyot Ha'adam)*; Rapprochement*; There is a Limit (Yesh Gvul)*; Women in Black (Nashim B'shachor)*.

7. These organizations are marked by an asterisk in the list above.

8. Bernard Reich correctly observes that a list of the vast literature on this conflict would fill several volumes. See Bernard Reich, ed., *A Historical Encyclopedia of the Arab-Israeli Conflict* (Westport, Conn.: Greenwood Press, 1996), p. 629.

9. For the development, features, and status of Palestinian peace activism, see chapter 6 in this volume.

10. For a detailed history of Israeli peace activism, see Tamar Hermann, "Between the Peace Covenant and Peace Now: The Pragmatic Pacifism of the Israeli Peace Movement in a Comparative Perspective" (Ph.D diss., Tel Aviv University, 1989) [Hebrew]; Mordechai Bar On, *In Pursuit of Peace: A History of the Israeli Peace Movement* (Washington, D.C.: U.S. Institute of Peace, 1996).

11. For a comparison of the two movements, see Rael Isaac, *Israel Divided: Ideological Politics in the Jewish State* (Baltimore, Md.: Johns Hopkins University Press, 1976).

12. In early 1970, President Sadat of Egypt responded positively to the basic premises of the peace initiative launched by Dr. Gunnar Yarring, the UN special emissary to the Middle East. However, to the frustration and anger of the Movement for Peace and Security, the Israeli government—led by Prime Minister Golda Meir—rejected Sadat's response as a potential beginning for peace talks, convincing most Israelis that it was nothing more than a hot-air balloon.

13. Uri Avneri, *My Friend the Enemy* (London: Zed Books, 1986).

14. For a typical example of the marginalization and scorn Mizrachi peace

activists felt from their Ashkenazi colleagues, see the interview with filmmaker Simon Bitton by Daliya Karpel. Simon Bitton, "The Symmetry of Bereavement," interview by Daliya Karpel, *Haaretz*, Weekend Supplement, April 23, 1999, pp. 35–37 [Hebrew].

15. For a detailed account of Israeli peace activism during the Intifada, see Reuven Kaminer, *The Politics of Protest* (Sussex: Polity Press, 1996).

16. Sara Helman and Tamar Rapoport, "Women in Black and the Challenging of the Social Order," *Theory and Criticism* 10 (1997): 175–192 [Hebrew].

17. Tracking the establishment of new groups is not necessarily the only or best way to measure the intensity of peace activity during different periods. Other criteria, such as the number of demonstrations, the volume of activists, etc., are equally operable. However, these indicators also have shortcomings. For example, no one—not even the police, who are only interested in large gatherings—keeps combined records of all the peace groups' demonstrations. Furthermore, the records of defunct groups often are dispersed. The number of activists also is difficult to accurately assess since in the past most Israeli peace groups did not institute formal member status or keep orderly membership lists.

18. For a short but representative "new historian" type analysis, see Ilan Pappe, "The New History and Sociology of Israel: A Challenge to the Old Version," *Palestine-Israel Journal* II (1995): 70–76. For a critical view of the "new historians" school, see Ephraim Karsh, *Fabricating Israeli History* (London: Frank Cass, 1997). For a more balanced view, see Mordechai Bar On, "The Historians' Debate in Israel and the Middle East Peace Process," in *The Middle East Peace Process: Interdisciplinary Perspectives*, ed. Ilan Peleg (Albany, N.Y.: SUNY Press, 1998), pp. 21–40.

19. The Alternative Information Center was established in 1984. It is a small, well-organized, mixed-gender, Israeli-Palestinian, service-oriented organization that supplies the media with alternative information about the occupation. The Center's radical form of peace advocacy places it on the fringe of the Israeli peace camp.

20. This viewpoint recently was expressed by Miri Ben-David, a social activist from Jerusalem who decided that peace activism was of secondary importance to the disadvantaged groups she wanted to assist: "I suddenly realized that it is not enough to make peace. That perhaps many people feel that . . . everyone tries to appease the Arabs and does not care about them." Nurit Vorgeft, "Messiah Ben-David," *Kol Ha'ir*, April 10, 1998 [Hebrew]. It should be noted that Ben-David refers to the government as Labor even though she was interviewed two years after the Likud Party had won the 1996 elections. Since 1977, the Labor Party has only been in power from 1992 to 1996. However, it and other old Ashkenazi elites are associated with the peace movement and are still identified as the real power holders in Israeli society. Chaim Baram, a well-known radical peace activist, made a similar critical remark: "Perhaps we will live and see the day when we will get rid of the Peace Now-style bourgeois alienation, and learn to join the struggle of the emotionally and culturally deprived sectors." Chaim Baram, "The Strike and Us," *Mitzad Sheni*, February 1998, p. 3 [Hebrew].

21. For example, Yoash Tzidon, "Peace Now or a Stable Peace," *Nativ*, April 1994, pp. 21–25 [Hebrew].

22. Mordechai Nissan, "The PLO and the Israeli Left: The Common Aim," *Nativ*, February 1994, pp. 5–11 [Hebrew].

23. Yuval Steinitz was a professor of philosophy and is now a Likud member of the Knesset. Previously affiliated with the peace camp, he moved several years ago to the Right following what he calls "an intellectual sobering."

24. Yuval Steinitz, "Peace as a Messianic Illusion," *Panim*, October 1997, pp. 32–34 [Hebrew].

25. Tamar Hermann, "Do They Have a Chance? Protest and Political Structure of Opportunities in Israel," *Israel Studies* 1 (1996): 144–170.

26. Benjamin Gidron and Hagai Katz, "Defining the Nonprofit Sector: Israel," working paper no. 26, The Johns Hopkins University Press, Baltimore, Md., 1998.

27. This attitude is exemplified in a letter written by Dr. Daphna Golan, a veteran peace activist and the former director general of Bat Shalom of the Jerusalem Link. Daphna Golan, "Letter to Deena," in *Walking the Red Line—Israelis in Search of Justice For Palestine*, ed. Deena Hurwitz (Philadelphia: New Society Publishers, 1992), pp. 102, 105.

28. One of the unplanned results of this activity was the 1986 enactment of a law prohibiting meetings between Israeli citizens and PLO representatives and/ or officials. Because of the vast number of grassroots dialogue groups, it was practically impossible for the government to ban them, as well, but policymakers clearly regarded them with disdain. (This law was overturned in 1993, soon after the Labor Party returned to power.)

29. Kaminer, *The Politics of Protest*, p. 217.

30. See, for example, Bert Klandermans, "The Peace Movement and Social Movement Theory," in *Peace Movements in Western Europe and the United States*, ed. Bert Klandermands, *International Social Movement Research* 3 (1991), pp. 1–42; Klaus Eder, *The New Politics of Class* (New York: Sage, 1993); James Downton and Paul Wehr, *The Persistent Activist—How Peace Commitment Develops and Survives* (Boulder: Westview Press, 1997).

31. See, for example, Tzaly Reshef, *Peace Now: From the Officers Letter to Peace Now* (Jerusalem: Keter, 1996), pp. 118–126 [Hebrew].

32. Imra@netvision.net.il, June 7, 1998.

33. Relatively few academics in the exact or life sciences participated in or identified with the peace movement, whereas a large number of them participated in extra-parliamentary movements of the Right—for example, Professors for Political Strength. Paradoxically, those academics of the exact and life sciences who were politically active in the peace movement often were members of the more radical groups. For example, several mathematicians played central roles in the radical Matzpen group, which as early as the 1960s demanded that Israel make far-reaching territorial concessions and other compromises to achieve peace with the Palestinians.

34. It should be noted that although kibbutz members are part of rural or agricultural communities, they always have been deeply involved in Israeli left-wing politics. In this respect, they never have demonstrated the classical politi-

cal features of farmers—political apathy or an identification with the conservative Right—which are seen among European farmers, for example.

35. A public opinion survey conducted by a commercial survey institute for *Dor Shalom* in May 1997 provided empirical proof that the peace movement's image remained unchanged. We cannot present the data, however, since the client has kept it confidential.

36. Tamar Hermann, "Through the Back Door: Israeli Women and Foreign and Security Policy-Making," in *Women and Politics in the Middle East*, ed. Mary Ann Tetreault (London: Routledge Books, forthcoming).

37. Simona Sharoni, *Gender and the Israeli-Palestinian Conflict* (Syracuse: Syracuse University Press, 1995).

38. This perception, however, is not substantiated by public opinion surveys conducted in Israel, which mostly indicate that men and women share similar attitudes regarding peace and war. See, for example, Tamar Hermann and Ephraim Yuchtman-Yaar, "Peace Index—March," *Haaretz*, April 4, 1998.

39. For example, Bat Shalom's web site gives this description: "Bat Shalom—a feminist center for peace and social justice. Our aim is to work towards a democratic and pluralistic society in Israel, where women will be of more influence. By bringing together women peace activists, women educators, and women community leaders, we are striving to raise one's consciousness, and to create together a culture of peace and social justice." Batshalom@nif.org, March 29, 1998. The disparity between rhetoric and practice in the mixed-gender peace organizations is best analyzed (and exposed) in a monograph written by a female activist of the 21 Years group, one of the most elitist and intellectual bodies of the Israeli peace movement. The writer maintains that such discrimination is a widespread phenomenon: "The division of labor within the movement followed gender lines, according to which men took over the more prestigious roles, such as the theoretical formulation of the movement's ideas and representing it in the mass media. Women, on the other hand, were in charge of the administrative assignments. Thus, the movement practically reproduced the traditional sexist work patterns that characterize Israeli society at large, and those in many other societies." Orna Sasson-Levi, "Radical Rhetoric, Conformist Practices: Theory and Practice in an Israeli Protest Movement," Shaine working paper no. 1, The Hebrew University, Jerusalem, 1995, p. 127 [Hebrew].

40. The recognition of this problem was clearly manifested when Mothers against Silence changed its name to Parents against Silence, in order to gain a stronger voice and wider public appeal.

41. Helman and Rapoport, "Women in Black and the Challenging of the Social Order."

42. On the attitudes of the Ultra-Orthodox and Orthodox communities regarding these matters see, for example, Tamar Hermann and Ephraim Yaar-Yuchtman, "On the Road to Peace? The Dynamics and Political Implications of Israeli-Jewish Attitudes towards the Oslo Process" (Paper presented at the American Political Science Association annual meeting, Atlanta, September 1999).

43. For example, William Gamson, *The Strategy of Social Protest* (Belmont, Calif.: Wadsworth, 1990), chapter 3.

44. Thomas Rochon and Daniel Mazmanian, "Social Movements and the Policy Process," *Annals of the American Academy of Political and Social Science* (1993): 75–87.

45. Shimon Peres, *The New Middle East* (Shaftsbury, UK: Element, 1993).

46. Such an argument was presented for example by Yoash Tzidon, an MK of the right-wing Tzomet Party, who in 1994 analyzed the destructive impact of the peace movement as follows: "The term 'peace now' is being translated at the present into the language of policy as 'territories for peace.' The aim of these who demand 'peace now' is to disengage themselves from the control over (a part of) another people, as soon as possible, even if this is paid for in the form of certain Zionist values, national assets, and a significant deterioration of the state's security and economic potential. . . . It is two years now since the 'peace now' policy was adopted by the Israeli government." Yoash Tzidon, "Peace Now or a Stable Peace."

47. For example, Tzaly, *Peace Now*, p. 10.

48. Victor Cygielman, "No, Oslo Is Not Dead," *Palestine-Israel Journal* II (Winter 1995): 3.

49. It should be noted that in 1996 Netanyahu won 11% more of the Jewish votes than Peres did.

50. Doug Struck, "At 20, Israel's 'Peace Now' Movement Idles in Dismay," *International Herald Tribune*, April 16, 1998, p. 6.

51. Meron Benvenisti, "Belfast, and Jerusalem," *Ha'aretz*, May 7, 1998 [Hebrew].

52. Arie Rotenberg, "Peace as a Mitsubishi Car," *Panim*, October 1997, pp. 71–74 [Hebrew].

53. For empirical evidence that Israelis now acknowledge Palestinian national aspirations, see Ephraim Yaar and Tamar Hermann, "Peace Index—March," *Ha'aretz*, April 4, 1999.

54. Yaakov Shamir and Michal Shamir, *The Dynamics of Israeli Public Opinion on Issues of Peace and Territories* (Tel Aviv: Tel Aviv University, The Tami Steinmetz Center for Peace Research, 1993).

55. Uri Avneri, "What is Political Influence?" *Ha'aretz*, April 3, 1998.

56. Bar On, *In Pursuit of Peace*, pp. 223–224.

57. Rami Rosen, "Our Paranoia, Your Fatigue," *Ha'aretz*, Weekend Magazine, May 15, 1998, p. 58 [Hebrew].

58. Rochon and Mazmanian, "Social Movements and Policy Process," p. 77.

6

NGOS IN THE CONTEXT OF NATIONAL STRUGGLE

MANUEL HASSASSIAN

The Palestinian people are currently in the midst of a long and hard-fought national struggle that has spanned the greater part of this century. In this struggle, nongovernmental organizations (NGOs) have played a protean role that has fluctuated with the political climate. Before the Zionist conquest of Palestine, NGOs were little more than small groups of city-based individuals who came together out of mutual interest in a particular issue—women's associations, literary groups, and religious formations all have a history in Palestine that dates back to the 1920s. At that time, civil institutions were limited to the middle and upper classes, which constituted only about 20 percent of the entire Palestinian population. The remaining 80 percent of Palestinian society was spread out in peasant land-owning communities without any major form of formal organization. For similar reasons, the Palestinian nationalist movement existed in a nebulous state, varying across communities according to their political hardships, educational levels, and basic needs. The formation of Israel in 1948 had a shattering effect upon all Palestinians, from the ruling elite to the poorest of peasants. The Palestinian community existed thereafter in diaspora and the hardships that they endured, whether in refugee camps, their West Bank and Gazan towns, or the newly created state of Israel, had a profound impact on their political consciousness, which in turn directly affected the groups that expressed Palestinian political thought, including both political organizations and NGOs.

This research project focuses on the years after the beginning of the Israeli occupation of the West Bank and Gaza Strip, in 1967. It is in these formative years, and thereafter, that the embryonic roots of modern Palestinian NGO formation can be traced. During these years, the Palestine Liberation Organization (PLO) was formed and attempted to liberate Palestine with varying degrees of success and failure. However, because these efforts were waged outside the Occupied Territories, the West Bank and Gazan populations were implicitly alienated or ignored, and their role in the national struggle minimized. Furthermore, the Israeli occupation severely restricted the potential activity of these communities and limited their development, while at the same time it encouraged people to leave. In the absence of a representative government, the communities of the Gaza Strip and West Bank began to focus their efforts internally, hoping to maintain and solidify a network of organizations that could provide for their needs. Slowly, but surely, a network of NGOs emerged that worked on a variety of issues and services.

Context

Paralleling the larger and more media-friendly Arab-Israeli conflict is a much less celebrated, less well-known dynamic—the emergence of an NGO sector. Comprehending this phenomenon for the Palestinians is difficult. In particular, defining the limits and scope of Palestinian NGOs is a great challenge. The confluence of political and social interaction within Palestinian society has overlapped to such an extent over the last century that it is difficult to clearly differentiate between the two. Moreover, the existence of Palestinian third-sector and nongovernmental organizations has been limited, since to date Palestinians have never had a sovereign or democratic government, and therefore cannot have organizations that exist outside of it. Furthermore, the PLO, as the Palestinian representative structure, has incorporated both strong political and socio-ideological goals. That is, in contrast to other organizations whose primary raison d'être is the liberation of a given homeland, the PLO acts as an umbrella organization that shoulders responsibility for political articulation, as well as the protection and sustenance of Palestinian nationalism and, very possibly, Palestinian national identity. Thus, although Palestinian civil society always has existed in a nascent form, consistently shadowing the development of national consciousness, it has failed to take a leading role in the national struggle because no clear and discernable lines exist between nationalism and societal development.

In addition, it is difficult to specifically analyze the effects of peace and conflict-resolution organizations (P/CROs) when, for the most part, there are no P/CROs in Palestine, very little peace-building is being done, and no imminent Palestinian-Israeli peace initiative exists. It is clear that the Oslo Accords were an attempt to resolve the conflict in a political, negotiated, and nonviolent manner, but they have failed to solve any of the major or even minor problems of the conflict. The Oslo process was designed to defer the solution of the "real" issues until later: land jurisdiction, sovereignty, borders, refugees, control of Jerusalem, settlements, and water. For a variety of reasons, including the progress of Israeli politics, it is unlikely that the Oslo track will ever reach this stage. Thus, since the political momentum in the region appears to be moving away from a peaceful resolution to the conflict, we can only assess how this situation has affected the nascent development of a Palestinian "peace and conflict-resolution" sector.

One factor that has impeded the growth of such a sector in Palestinian society is that the Palestinian people have never properly considered the development of a culture of peaceful coexistence with the Zionist movement. This emanates in part from a failure of the educational system, which, instead of developing its own agenda, has adopted a political ideology that demonizes the Zionist movement. In addition, after arriving in the Occupied Territories, the Palestinian Authority failed to focus adequate attention on societal development, concentrating on politics rather than community development. This has created a vacuum, wherein both the Palestinian population and civil society institutions have lacked guidance as to their role in the national struggle; they only understand that crossing certain lines elicits the Palestinian Authority's wrath.

Ironically, the Palestinian Authority claims to be acting in the name of national unity, arguing that the efforts of individuals and organizations compromise the unity of the Palestinian people, even though the Authority has not outlined a plan other than its own narrow political aims. As a result, relations between the Palestinian Authority, civil society, and the Palestinian people are strained. In fact, the Palestinian Authority came into the Occupied Territories attempting to act as the sole representative of the Palestinian people, when all along such representation already existed in the form of a nascent civil society. Thus, there is a struggle for power over who best represents the will of the people. This is markedly different from the other countries in this study, which have already achieved their independence, since at times the entire legitimacy of the Palestinian Authority has been questioned.

In addition, the neo-patriarchal structure of Palestinian society and its cultural resistance to Western-style institutions of democracy have affected the development of P/CROs and other civil society institutions. Such organizations are considered suspect if they do not adequately reflect the history, culture, and traditions of Palestinian society. Despite the tensions that exist between the Palestinian Authority and the Palestinian people, Palestinian society has resisted Western institutions of peace and democracy since these do not properly embody Palestinian customs and values.

Finally, any discussion of such matters would be incomplete without considering the role that Israel's occupation has played in impeding the development of Palestinian civil society institutions. For the last thirty years, Palestinians have existed under an extremely repressive occupational system without any direct representational government, while their need for national unity and steadfastness (*sumoud*) has intensified. Economic repression, the high costs of political participation (including imprisonment, torture, and death), and the Israeli occupying forces' deliberate efforts to infiltrate, root out, and thwart any attempts at national or collective unity—be it political, cultural, or social—have hindered the growth and power of Palestinian civil society institutions. Palestinian society has sustained an assault on its national, traditional, cultural, intellectual, societal, and political development, and this helps to explain the imbalance between Palestinian representational institutions and their Israeli counterparts.

Thus, many politically conscious Palestinians have found it more appropriate to oppose the occupation through armed resistance rather than through participation in NGOs. Although this situation is beginning to change—in part because armed resistance has failed to end the occupation—at this point NGOs are not likely to be at the forefront of Palestinian resistance. NGOs must first prove that they can achieve clear and sustainable ends. Although they were somewhat effectual during the period of the Intifada, it is unclear whether they will continue to be attractive to Palestinians and effective in realizing Palestinian national interests in the post-Oslo period.

Despite all of these factors, over the last thirty years the Palestinians clearly have attempted to build civil society institutions and organizations in the Occupied Territories, including an array of political parties, municipal service organizations, cooperatives, educational institutions, student senates, women's organizations, health care associations, charitable organizations, trade unions, business associations, child-care facilities, religious groups (including welfare and social service organization run by these groups), "think tanks," professional unions and syndicates (e.g., lawyers' guilds and medical associations), and chambers of commerce.[1] These various organizations and groups have been responsive to the social needs of the Palestinians in the absence of any indigenous government and have enabled them to survive under Israeli military occupation. In addition, the formation of these civil society organizations has bolstered the process of democratization and peace in Palestine since many of them (1) have laid the groundwork for grassroots training in pluralism and democratic behavior; (2) serve to counterpoise the autocracy of the Palestinian Authority; and (3) recognize that peace with Israel is absolutely essential for a prosperous Palestinian society. Ideally, these diverse groups will come to form an infrastructure of civil and political institutions—a prelude to an independent Palestinian state.

In addition, several other significant factors have developed within Palestinian society that are conducive to the growth of democratization and civil society. First, a tolerance for divergent opinions has evolved into an intrinsic value and tradition among Palestinians. This is particularly true within the political infrastructure of the PLO where the existence of pluralism among its various factions is widely acknowledged. Thus, today the mainstream respects and tolerates oppositional forces within the political spectrum. Undoubtedly, such opposing groups act as a check on the Palestine Authority's performance.

Another major factor is the development of a participatory political culture in which elections and popular consent are considered to be legitimate. A good example is the active political participation of women, which is an essential part of Palestinian civil society today and has had a crucial impact on the establishment and consolidation of pluralist thinking and democratic rule.

Thus, with such elements already operating within Palestinian society, it seems that the Palestinian Authority needs only to bolster and legitimize them in order to foster the nascent civil society that exists despite Israel's military occupation. In fact, social science observers have noted that Palestinian society is transitioning from a traditional/rural to an urban/neo-patriarchal society. Unfortunately, the subject of civil society in the Middle East, in general, and in Palestinian society, in particular, is a very new focus for scholarly research. But it appears clear that the future of Palestinian civil society and its impact on the process of democratization is organically intertwined with the political developments of the region.

Methods

Definition of a Palestinian P/CRO

Owing to the national struggle in which Palestinians were engaged at the time that this study was conducted, we did not consider the term "peace and conflict-resolution organization" to be applicable to the Palestinian context. Before the Oslo Accords, Palestinian society existed more or less in a constant state of war with the occupying Israeli Authority, especially during the Intifada, and most NGOs tended to have specialized goals. Therefore, there were few organizations that fit the project's definition of a P/CRO (Rapprochment Centre-Beit Sahour was perhaps closest to this definition, though their numbers increased after the signing of the Oslo Accords).

In addition, historically many Palestinian NGOs affiliated themselves with and received money from Palestinian political parties, even though few NGOs were willing to admit openly to such allegiances. It was a tactical advantage for the political parties to have representatives locally, as it gave reality to a national movement that otherwise was based abroad. Furthermore, the NGO presence gave unity to the external and internal struggle. It is important to note, however, that not all NGOs were affiliated directly with a particular political party. Independent organizations with their own funding sources certainly existed prior to the onset of the Palestinian Intifada (December 1987) and very much so after the signing of the Peace Agreements (September 1993).

However, it was only after 1993 that organizations that talked openly of peace—a peace based on the Oslo track—began to emerge. While such organizations existed to support the Oslo process, they represented a minority sentiment since most of the population was awaiting the outcome of the negotiation process. Because the Palestinians were still in the midst of a national struggle, the overall objective of most Palestinian organizations was the success of that movement. "Peace" generally was articulated only as a strategy to secure this larger objective. "Peace for peace's sake," as Israeli Prime Minister Binyamin Netanyahu envisioned it, generally was considered undesirable because it did not address questions of national injustice.

Thus, the Palestinian team developed and utilized an alternative definition of P/CROs for the organizations we studied. We used this definition flexibly, since the organizations we studied spanned considerable political/ organizational/societal breadth:

> A peace/conflict resolution organization in the Palestinian context is any voluntary non-governmental body or groups of individuals who conducted activity within the post-1967 time period (occupation) within the Occupied Territories and had as its agenda a nonviolent resolution of the conflict. Such groups therefore sought understanding both within Israel and abroad of the social, political, historical, and cultural context of the Palestinian people, often involving consciousness-raising activity, human rights advocacy, dialogue, and the provision of services intended to familiarize others to the Palestinian concern for justice, thereby finding partners who could be mobilized to end the source of Palestinian grievances.[2]

Methodology

Our study examined several Palestinian P/CROs—including the Palestinian Center for Human Rights (PCHR), Children of Abraham, and the Committee for Dialogue of Peace Forces—as well as some joint Palestinian-Israeli P/CROs, including the Alternative Information Center (AIC), Rapprochement Center-Beit Sahour, and the Jerusalem Center for Women. Our approach included interviews with representatives from these organizations and reviews of organizational literature and programs.

We investigated the efficacy of these organizations through two basic means: (1) interviews with people of varying occupational and personal views; and (2) an analysis of P/CROs in relation to the historical struggle between Palestine and Israel. All interviewees were asked to respond to questions based upon personal knowledge of verifiable facts, as well as their own opinions and interpretations of certain trends or dynamics. Interviewees were selected from six major categories: (1) representatives from Palestinian P/CROs; (2) representatives from the Palestinian Authority whose work in some way depended upon a relationship between P/CROs and the Palestinian Authority; (3) international representatives who dealt with Palestinian P/CROs, largely in the funding domain but also on a sociopolitical level; (4) representatives of the mass media; (5) academics and intellectuals; and (6) political leaders (both formal and informal) who were identified with the conflict and who represented the various factions involved in the conflict.

Some of the interviewees cut across categories: Ziad Abu Zayyad is both a member of the Palestinian Legislative Council and an historic and present leader of a P/CRO; likewise, Dr. Sari Nusseibeh is a professor, as well as a founder of a P/CRO, however he also comes from a politically powerful family, has dabbled in political negotiations, and may move into the formal political arena again. Of all of the interviewees, the representatives from international governments and organizations were categorized most easily. As outsiders to the conflict, their specific agendas were defined by the specialized work they performed with the Palestinian P/CRO sector. It is also worth mentioning that although each of the interviewees responded according to his or her own perspective and function(s), sentiments sometimes carried across categories. For instance, while Palestinian interviewees generally displayed common nationalistic sentiments, they often revealed differing individual ideologies.

The study also took into account changes in the conflict over time and how interviewees' perceptions of the past differed from those of the present. For purposes of the study, the signing of the Oslo Accords on September 13, 1993, was construed as the "breakthrough" point, even though this was a controversial topic for our interviewees. Questions tended to focus upon the P/CROs' impact in terms of: (1) influencing key events, developments, or negotiations that contributed to resolution of the conflict and in which the P/CRO sector played a role; (2) gaining recognition from the mass media, the parties to the conflict, and government officials, as well as forging links that helped to influence or generate political change; (3) defining the conflict and its resolution in new and different ways—that is, facilitating changes in public perception regarding the conflict and its resolution, including new ways (or new vocabulary) to define or describe the conflict, and promoting new strategies or activities for dealing with the conflict. Although the study as a whole adopted this same framework, the particularities of the Palestinian experience added a unique perspective to our investigation.

It is also important to consider the particular time frame in which the interviews were conducted (March and April 1998). During this time, the political situation was looking very bleak. That is, it was a particularly easy time to be critical of the peace process and, perhaps, to underestimate its promise in terms of fulfilling Palestinian national aspirations. This is reflected in the helplessness and often anger we witnessed during some of the interviews. Additionally, owing to political stagnation, interviewees clearly were also reevaluating the utility of the Palestinian Authority, the P/CRO sector's potential to mobilize any form of political activity or support from an exasperated Palestinian populace, the adequacy of remaining in political negotiations, and the necessity of some groups to remain in operation.

Initially we sought to assess the efficacy of the P/CROs according to the following five categories employed by the other research teams in the study: (1) access to governing elites; (2) impact on significant policies; (3) impact upon public opinion/culture; (4) potential to create political space for positive action; and (5) impact upon political and social processes. Although an evaluation according to these categories would have provided a comprehensive assessment of the P/CRO movement, such an assessment lacked applicability to the Palestinian context. For example, in terms of access to governing elites, the PLO was in exile for the majority of the conflict and therefore was inaccessible to routine lobbying. Furthermore, aside from the fact that the Israeli occupying authorities would have considered such lobbying a criminal activity, access to governing officials was better achieved through secret local activists representing each political faction. However, we did not have access to this information since it is confidential, even to this day. (It was not, for instance, within our power to ask a P/CRO representative if he or she worked or had worked as an operational activist for the PLO.) Likewise, in terms of the P/CROs' impact on significant policies, the PLO and subsequently the Palestinian Authority were organized in a way that limited effective influence of any kind outside the sphere of the Fatah Executive Committee under the leadership of Chairman Yasser Arafat. Furthermore, for much of the conflict, the PLO was not even in a position to initiate significant change.

Palestinian P/CROs only demonstrated quantifiable influence in the public opinion/cultural arenas and perhaps the political/social processes after the signing of the Oslo Accords. Therefore, for our purposes we expanded these spheres. For example, we found it more helpful to consider the overall efficacy of human rights advocacy in the Occupied Territories rather than to examine the efficacy of a certain human rights group upon a specific audience. Thus, we determined efficacy based upon the P/CROs' impacts on: (1) human rights advocacy; (2) consciousness-raising activities at the foreign level; and (3) consciousness-raising activities internally within Israeli and Palestinian societies. We also considered how the efficacy of these activities changed before and after the initiation of the Oslo process.

It must be noted that in evaluating the efficacy of Palestinian P/CROs, we encountered several impediments and flaws both at the theoretical and at more specific levels. First, it was difficult to determine how to measure efficacy at the movement or organizational level. Most organizations had more than one goal that they hoped to achieve. Therefore, it was necessary to evaluate the organization's efficacy in achieving each particular goal it had set for itself. Hence, efficacy varied among the organizations studied (given their variegated goals), as well as within each individual organization (given its particular agenda).

Second, evaluating the efficacy of P/CROs raised specific questions when it was considered within the larger context of the Palestinian nationalist struggle. Were we to examine efficacy in relation to the organizations' capacity to effect change for purposes of peace and conflict resolution, or were we to evaluate whether the organizations were effective in creating change for their own purposes? The two goals were not necessarily the same. Once again, this was due to conflicts between the nationalist struggle, the desire for a just peace, and the role the P/CROs played as partners in both of these struggles. Of the organizations examined in this study, it was evident that most, if not all, were committed to the national struggle before the peace process.

This certainly does not mean that the P/CROs we studied were in any way less committed to the concept of peace than nonnationalist P/CROs. It merely means that they were committed to a different form of peace. For instance, one of the leaders of a joint organization openly supported the idea of abandoning the Oslo peace process. It may appear to some that this leader was against the idea of peace and in no position to be running a joint Palestinian-Israeli "reconciliation" organization; however, he defended his beliefs stating that he was in favor of a comprehensive and just solution to the plight and injustices of the Palestinian people and felt that the Oslo channel was insufficient and unjust and would not achieve this goal.

Although some of these ideas may seem foreign to the reader, in fact they are quite common to many Palestinians. After the Oslo Accords were signed, many Palestinian thinkers, as well as the general public, felt uncertain about how to articulate a position somewhere between open support and open rejection of the peace agreements, a sentiment that gained significance with the subsequent failures of the Oslo process. These ideas were antithetical to the Israeli peace camp activists, most of whom perceived the Oslo process, despite its flaws, as a panacea to the problems of the conflict.

Findings

Overview

Typically, NGOs do not represent the official establishment but reflect grassroots values with a high level of accuracy since these organizations are directly in touch with the people. This discrepancy was evident in the results from our interviews. Particularly pertinent to our findings was the overall effect of the Palestinian Authority's arrival in the Occupied Territories in 1994. As noted earlier, during the years of occupation (although the occupation still exists, we defined it as those years before the Palestinian Authority's arrival), the NGO sector in the West Bank and Gaza acted as a shadow government, attempting to provide the basic necessities of education, health, agriculture, and social initiatives. After the arrival of the Palestinian Authority, the NGOs' role became unclear as national ministries began to claim responsibility for the services NGOs had once provided. Further friction arose when the third sector began to question the Palestinian Authority's efficacy and efficiency. These tensions resulted in a polarization between the NGOs and the Palestinian Authority, as both claimed to represent the best interests of the Palestinian people.

To date, this conflict has not been resolved, in large part because of the continuation of two dynamics: (1) the Palestinian Authority's negotiation in a paralyzed peace process, which has raised further questions about the Authority's respect for political accountability, human rights, the rule of law, and the process of state building (particularly with regards to democracy); and (2) the NGOs' criticism of and intransigence toward the Palestinian Authority's political approach. These factors, together with the NGOs' unwillingness to let go of basic principles of the national struggle, continue to cause friction between the NGOs and the Palestinian Authority. Our findings tended to reflect these factors, given the failure of the peace process at the time we conducted the study.

In the end, our findings showed that the contribution of third-sector activity to "peace-building" was largely insignificant. Those connections that did exist were largely dependent on the overall momentum of the political process. The handful of dialogue sessions or binational activities that were started after the signing of the Oslo Accords seemed only to be sustained by the friendships that were forged when the activities had been more successful or even by the inability of both sides to acknowledge the total inefficacy of their activities on a larger scale. The dispiriting reality was that Palestinians and Israelis maintained a comfortable distance from each other in the five years after the Accords were signed. However well intentioned the P/CROs were, they tended to reflect this political dynamic. Those who wish in the future to talk seriously about the problems that divide the two communities will need to acknowledge this factor.

We noted that third-sector organizations generally could be divided into two categories: those that were started before or during the Intifada, and those that began after it ended, often corresponding with the signing of the Oslo Accords. Organizations in the first category tended to be characterized by a strong sense of ideology and activism. Although it is difficult to make generalizations about the group of organizations we studied, it is clear that, given the political realities and the political affiliations of these groups (which were largely center/leftist in orientation), they sought to facilitate change by working within the confines of the occupation. Working within the system, pushing its limits, and getting Israelis and the outside world to see the conditions of Palestinians' daily lives were large motivating factors. In addition, two other elements tended to motivate these organizations: the activists' own personal experiences with politics and their ability to communicate their experiences to an Israeli audience that was just waking up to the question of Palestinian nationalism.

Those organizations that were initiated to fight for Palestinian rights and convey this message to foreign audiences, regardless of the political climate (typically these groups were started prior to or during the Intifada), contrasted with those organizations that began as a result of a specific political process (typically these groups were initiated in response to the Oslo Accords). Because those organizations started after the Oslo process tended to be less self-motivated, their activities and popular appeal were more susceptible to the political climate. Thus, the impasses in the peace process had severely reduced the levels of activity in these organizations, and subsequently affected their potential efficacy. On the other hand, those organizations that began prior to the Oslo Accords tended to continue their work despite the bitterness of the political climate.

Primary P/CRO Characteristics

We found that most of the Palestinian P/CROs were established in order to overcome various aspects of the Israeli occupation: to prevent Israeli human rights violations; to facilitate the peace process after the Oslo Accords; to promote self-reliance and rebuild Palestine during the Intifada; and to raise public awareness of women's rights, democracy, or the functions of government. None of the P/CROs we studied was established explicitly for the purpose of conflict resolution. P/CRO founders came from both intellectual circles and grassroots movements. Strong individual or group leadership, motivated by a defined political agenda or vision, characterized those organizations created before the Oslo Accords. Those that came afterwards also had strong individual leadership, but seemed unable to command any popular support for their cause; despite their well-intentioned efforts and leadership, their work seemed to be ineffective.

Participants in the P/CROs varied according to age, sex, class, education, religion, and nationality. Of all the organizations we studied, only one had a limitation to its constituency: the Jerusalem Center for Women recruited women participants exclusively. However, many of the P/CROs believed in equality of the sexes and consequently promoted women's rights, with the aim of raising awareness. Accordingly, the P/CROs included women as members of their governing boards and staff. The goal was to empower women and incorporate their advocacy into civic education, as well as to provide training programs on gender and equality. The P/CROs viewed this type of activity as a human rights issue. Among the various organizations studied, there were also differences in the roles that participants played. Some organizations were composed of a group of participants/activists who did the majority of the work. Others were led by a group of activists who in turn hoped to recruit additional participants. Finally, there were those organizations that were led by activists, and sought participants only for a specific event without any follow-up.

The interviews did not reveal clear details about the internal structures of the Palestinian P/CROs. All of the organizations were supervised by general assemblies with varying numbers of representatives. These assemblies acted as governing bodies that oversaw the work of the executive boards and staff. In some cases the employees themselves selected the members of their general assemblies, but we were unable to discern any other clear patterns. In general, most of the organizations studied tended to espouse a strong sense of democratic procedure, despite the educational, religious, and sexual variations among their participants, activists, and leaders. Organizations reached collective consensus through open discussions with their constituencies and generally by voting on final decisions. An open and dynamic decision-making process that was receptive to change for all of the organizations' activities seemed to be optimal in terms of maintaining participant involvement and interest.

Without describing the particulars of each organization, certain general elements were apparent in the ideologies of the organizations studied. Indeed, ideology seemed to have a powerful effect upon the organizations' stability, stamina, and longevity. Those organizations that were motivated by a strong sense of ideology tended to survive longer and to be more effective than those that were dependent upon a political process, such as the Oslo Accords. For example, organizations that dealt with human rights issues were not reliant on the Palestinian political leadership; therefore, they were committed to maintaining their operations regardless of fluctuations in Palestinian leadership or political authority. Similarly, organizations like the Alternative Information Center, which offered a critical perspective of the political leadership and the media, defined tasks and an agenda that were continuous and illimitable.

In contrast, those organizations that tended to be based on more elusive goals, such as changing Palestinians' and Israelis' opinions of one another, seemed to be inflexible and more likely to fail over time. The stalling of the peace process had all but paralyzed moderate forces in both camps and this subsequently affected the overall efficacy of such groups. Those loyal and dedicated activists from both sides who came to activities, such as joint discussion groups, were unable to mobilize others outside of their group. Consequently, their well-intentioned work became a case of "preaching to the converted." Even an organization like the Rapprochement Center, which had historic success with joint discussions, began to ignore the importance of publicizing these meetings, focusing its energy on building strength within the Palestinian community rather than trying to build bridges with the "other side." Thus, organizations that were based on political realities (i.e., the Oslo process) tended to be vulnerable to the turbulent elements of the struggle, thereby loosing internal strength, as well as their ability to change others.

Therefore, ideology seemed to play an important part in the success or failure of the organizations studied. On the one hand, it motivated activists and contributed to the stamina of the organization. On the other hand, if the activists were drawn to an organization only through a vague interest, their commitment was far more ephemeral and subject to the vagaries of politics and popular opinion. In addition, a solid sense of ideology tended to create a strong foundation of funding. Once the organization had proved itself and shown its ideology in an uncompromising fashion, funders tended to be attracted to the organization's dependability and commitment.

Although it is difficult to draw general conclusions about the financial workings of the organizations studied, several additional patterns emerged. Some of the organizations (particularly those with NGO experience and a history that predated the Oslo process) developed complex and variegated donor bodies, while others had very little and in fact sometimes no official fund-raising capacities. Many of the organizations with strong funder relations were very selective about their funding sources. For instance, various organizations refused money from government sources, especially those from America (i.e., USAID, etc.). Furthermore, these organizations generally declined money from funders who required that certain conditions be met. In providing funds to these NGOs, the funder had to trust that the money would be used for the organization's preestablished goals and not for those the funder specified. Some Palestinian P/CROs developed extensive links abroad in order to advocate for major sources of funding and to collaborate on training projects. Various European funders, particularly those associated with Christian organizations, were particularly helpful to Palestinian NGOs. Only one of the organizations studied, AIC, actually generated funds from its own activities.

The P/CROs we studied perceived their relations with the National Authority in one of two ways. Some saw themselves playing a role complementary to the National Authority. The P/CROs in this category offered training courses that provided the Authority with personnel equipped with the managerial and competitive skills necessary for a modern and efficient administration. Other P/CROs saw themselves as bodies that monitored the National Authority. Their work focused on tracking the National Authority's adherence to human rights and democratic principles. Those NGOs that had gained experience resisting the Israeli occupation utilized these same skills to monitor the Palestinian Authority and considered their work to be a contribution to peace building in the region. The Palestinian NGOs that maintained relations with Israeli NGOs did not actually perceive their work as a mechanism for resolving the conflict directly but as a means for normalizing relations prior to solving the outstanding political issues. At the same time, however, there were other P/CROs that were completely comfortable with Israel's cooperation, which they even utilized to help defend Palestinian human rights.

Primary P/CRO Activities

HUMAN RIGHTS ADVOCACY.   The issue of human rights had a popular and firm foundation in many of the organizations we surveyed. Organizations of both national and binational constituencies tried to popularize this issue, which shows that for this activity an opportunity existed to work toward a mutual end. This also explains the general efficacy of the P/CROs that promoted this type of work.

Prior to the signing of the Oslo Accords, human rights organizations played a crucial role in trying to publicize the abuses of the Israeli government and army during the Intifada. Of the organizations examined, some showed remarkable sophistication and experience in collecting and publishing data, and in defending political prisoners. They became warehouses of important information on human rights abuses by the Israeli army, and these efforts gradually helped to erode the existing international public opinion that Israel was a "benign occupier" of the Territories. For this same reason, many human rights activists (both Israeli and Palestinian) were forced to serve prison sentences in Israeli jails, often having their references and data confiscated.

In addition, a strong international media presence reinforced the P/CROs' human rights work, producing television images that confirmed many of the startling figures the P/CROs had documented. For example, both the Palestinian Center for Human Rights (and its predecessor the Gaza Center for Human Rights) and the Alternative Information Center played important roles in producing high-quality information that was distributed widely to a large foreign audience. Their success spawned a series of smaller organizations that adopted their models. Although we studied the PCHR and the AIC in-depth, there were other organizations that also were able to produce change. In particular, Al-Haq, the notable West Bank human rights group, often was noted as working tirelessly and effectively for its cause.

Nevertheless, there were limitations in pursuing human rights work. As Raji Sourani, the leader of the PCHR, pointed out, human rights activists always hoped that their work would end such violations, but that clearly was not a realistic goal. The most that they could hope for was that the number of violations committed would be reduced and that the abusing authorities would think twice before deciding to commit further violations. Although there was always more work that could be done, ultimately the information about human rights abuses was available and those who could end the violations had to decide to act. Sourani acknowledged that if his organization had not been there, the number of violations the Israeli army and government committed against Palestinians would have been much higher. Thus, the efficacy of Palestinian human rights organizations clearly was evident, yet nonetheless difficult to measure precisely.

With the signing of the Oslo Accords, basic rules outlined in the Fourth Geneva Convention specifically defined international human rights violations, and this enabled people from differing backgrounds to concentrate their efforts around a clear issue. In addition, when the Palestinian Authority arrived in parts of the West Bank and Gaza, organizations that had previously focused their attention solely on violations by the Israeli army and government had no reservations about criticizing the Authority. Not surprisingly, all of the human rights organizations we studied were ideologically affiliated with those who openly derided the Oslo Accords.

As with the Israeli occupation, protesting the human rights violations of the Palestinian Authority often led to imprisonment and harassment. Various notable human rights figures butted heads with the Palestinian Authority and consequently served prison terms. Human rights workers found this reality deeply disheartening since the same advocates whom the Palestinian Authority imprisoned had earlier publicized the atrocities of the Israeli occupying forces. To see the Authority adopt the oppressor's ways and abuse the human rights of the very people they had sought to help and defend particularly demoralized human rights workers. According to one organization, the coverage of human rights violations was divided 80 percent–20 percent between the Israeli and Palestinian authorities, respectively.

Most of the notable figures we interviewed on the question of human rights work, including PLO members (elected government officials), felt that the Palestinian P/CROs were of high quality and demonstrated good standards of moral decency. They praised the work these organizations had done under the occupation and also after the arrival of the Authority. Nevertheless, several general criticisms were raised about the movement. Dr. Sari Nusseibeh noted that the human rights organizations tended to create awareness on an elitist level. For instance, if the Palestinian Authority had decided to imprison the well-known human rights advocate Iyad Sarraj, it would have caused an international stir and elicited criticism. Therefore, it was much easier for both the Palestinian Authority and the Israeli authorities to arrest unknown persons upon suspicion of associating with the Islamic Resistance Movement (Hamas). Even when there was no evidence against such persons, there was no warrant for their arrests, they were not given access to a lawyer, and they were tortured and placed as "administrative detainees" for a renewable six-month cycle, fewer people, both locally and internationally, would have been willing to speak out against the illegal imprisonment of such lesser-known political prisoners, whose rights were violated with far greater frequency than those of the better-known activists. To this extent, human rights consciousness and advocacy, both locally and internationally, had failed.

Another criticism was that the definition of human rights was too narrow. Gross violations of human rights are media-friendly: torture, death, imprisonment, and so on. However, human right violations rarely included the basic difficulties and injustices that many Palestinians experienced in their daily lives. For example, when Israel closed the Occupied Territories as a form of collective punishment, there was little international interest (if any), despite the fact that it continued to affect Palestinians' living conditions. In addition, neither the Palestinian Authority, the Israeli government, nor the international community were willing to address other human rights violations, including the availability of adequate health and educational services, the banning of child labor, the right to one's own water.

Finally, there was criticism regarding the P/CROs' ability to make both Palestinians and Israelis aware of human rights abuses among certain populations. There were latent hypocrisies among the masses of both populations, who seemed willing to ignore human rights abuses if those with the "wrong" ideologies committed them. While riots were sure to follow news of a Palestinian who had been tortured to death in an Israeli prison, the Palestinian population did not demonstrate a similar sensitivity to comparable abuses by the Palestinian Authority. Some form of a "blind spot" clearly existed in the campaign for human rights. It was not that the majority of Palestinians did not realize that the Authority abused their rights; in fact, they knew it only too well. But they kept silent because they felt the need to show national unity behind the Palestinian Authority, they genuinely feared reprisal from the Authority, they had very few supporters who were willing to stand up for them, and/or they were generally unaware of human rights. These factors complicated the issue of human rights advocacy among the Palestinian P/CROs we studied and certainly raised questions about their efficacy.

CONSCIOUSNESS-RAISING ACTIVITY AT THE FOREIGN LEVEL. We considered the various Palestinian and joint P/CROs to be involved in consciousness raising activity if they engaged in efforts to convey the Palestinian experience to an external audience, including reporting human rights abuses, communicating the Palestinians' desire for peace, or recognizing the Palestinians' history of injustice. The P/CROs were not especially successful at executing such activity, since it was difficult to get others to recognize the depth and scale of the Palestinian plight. Although there were basic issues for which all Palestinians were fighting—including an admission of historic and present injustices, an end to the occupation, a freeze on the building of settlements, and the return of Palestinian refugees—the question of how to express these problems plagued the P/CROs we studied, as well as those who were working toward the national struggle as a whole, since communicating these issues was a multiple task that was difficult to execute collectively.

All of the P/CROs we studied that were established prior to the Oslo Accords tended to convey a nostalgic longing for the years of the *Intifada*. It was during this time that many of the organizations were formed, experienced incredible growth and efficacy, and found it much easier to identify people with similar ideological beliefs who would work tirelessly to achieve their aims. Indeed, during the Intifada, activists of all kinds produced remarkable achievements working toward a collective goal. But it is important to note that it was the unity of the goal—that is, ending the Israeli occupation—that produced so much collective energy and, in so doing, attracted the attention of the international audiences and Israeli audiences, in particular.

Determining the efficacy of these organizations was difficult for several reasons. First, the NGOs were not fighting for peace but for the end of the occupation. Furthermore, the Oslo Accords, which some considered a victory but others deemed a failure, brought about the end of the Intifada. Lastly, events seemed to take on a new light when considered from an historical perspective. For instance, during the Intifada one of the organizations we studied conducted wide-scale forms of civil disobedience that attracted international attention, even gaining an editorial in the *New York Times*. The organization was able to achieve worldwide recognition for its activities, and foreign readers heard about events of which they were previously unaware. Consequently, international audiences were perhaps more inclined to favor the Palestinians in their struggle and to bring international pressure on Israel to end the occupation and its human rights abuses. In these respects, the organization was extremely effective.

However, in other ways, the activists' activities failed to achieve the organization's goals. First, although the activists had hoped that mass civil disobedience would spread across the West Bank, it did not extend outside of the territory in which the activists resided. Second, their activities did not stop the Israeli occupation. Third, their work helped to facilitate the Oslo Accords, which the international community supported but which the activists were against and considered a complete failure. Fourth, although the activists have largely disappeared, the Israeli occupation still exists. Therefore, from this perspective, the organization's efforts failed.

This example illustrates the relativity of the concept of efficacy, particularly as it applies to the Palestinian context. Overall, the P/CROs were limited in their ability to communicate the Palestinian problems to foreign audiences. Prior to the Oslo Accords, the P/CROs effectively created international public awareness in favor of the Palestinians' struggle and against the Israeli occupation. They were able to mobilize a dedicated international audience with worldwide networks that came to support the Palestinian cause. However, their efforts led to the Oslo process, which many viewed as a failure.

Once the Oslo Accords were signed, the unity the activists had experienced during the Intifada was shattered, along with the unanimity of the international alliances that had been created during those years. Much of this discord had to do with the unpopularity of openly rejecting the Oslo track after it had been developed. International supporters often criticized those Palestinian organizations that chose to stick to their principles and reject the Oslo process, and sometimes withdrew their donations. When the Oslo Accords failed to solve the problems of the occupation, it was largely too late for the P/CROs since the Palestinian Authority quickly moved in and claimed to represent the Palestinian people and their struggle. Furthermore, the resulting tension between the P/CROs and the Palestinian Authority after the Oslo Accords led to problems, such as financial competition, impaired freedom of expression, and restrictions on the right to obtain licenses. In particular, since the NGOs had acted as a service-oriented government under the Israeli occupation and the Palestinian Authority assumed that responsibility, difficulties arose when the P/CROs and the Palestinian Authority adopted differing political positions.

In addition, the P/CROs' efficacy in promoting consciousness-raising activity in the years after the Oslo Accords was marred by division among the organizations and the lack of a clear voice. Some P/CROs tried to convince their audiences that the Oslo Accords and the Palestinian Authority had not changed the realities of the occupation and the historical injustices that the Palestinians had experienced. Others accepted the agreements and supported international lobbying on their behalf. But several fissures divided the P/CROs as a group, and some of the organizations even split internally. The organizations were divided over whether they should support the Palestinian Authority against the Israeli intransigence exhibited in Oslo or whether they should oppose the Palestinian Authority, which they considered incompetent and insufficient representation of Palestinian needs. These issues seriously divided and in many ways neutralized the organizations, especially the joint organizations, since the Israeli peace activists did not know how to react to these questions. On the whole, the lack of clear consensus among the P/CROs and their failure to specify viable alternatives created confusion within the international community, which tentatively supported the Palestinian Authority.

CONSCIOUSNESS-RAISING ACTIVITY AT THE INTERNAL LEVEL.   The Intifada became a phenomenon that neither the Israeli government nor the Israeli public could ignore, and during this time Palestinian activists displayed creativity in reaching out to the peace-oriented members of the Israeli community. The Israeli peace camp had its own reasons for seeking a peaceful solution to the conflict and Palestinian activists hoped to capitalize on this energy to counteract the Zionist propaganda of a "benign occupation." They also sought to take advantage of Israeli contacts and experience, and to legitimize their work by showing the international community that they had no reservations about working with Israelis as long as they were treated as equal partners and worked toward collective goals of justice.

As was the case with consciousness-raising activity within the international community, the "purity of cause" of the Intifada simplified the activists' work at the internal level. As Palestinians saw that there were Israeli peace forces and activists who were willing to work for their cause, they also began to distinguish between Israelis as people and Israelis as oppressors dressed in army uniforms. Likewise, Israelis came to see the Palestinians as a people who were fighting for their national rights and not just a people who were predisposed to "killing Jews" or "the destruction of the state of Israel."

As a movement, however, the joint Palestinian and Israeli organizations were ineffective at identifying and achieving one common, specific goal. Nevertheless, individual efforts in each community had limited efficacy. Although it is difficult for us to measure the effects of Palestinian organizations on Israeli society since our research did not extend to Israeli P/CROs, there is some evidence of success; for instance, the Rapprochement Center-Beit Sahour was able to mobilize the Palestinian community to fight the occupation with the support of some Israeli activist friends who publicized their events in the Israeli media. Among Palestinians, P/CROs generally were considered effective at producing creative avenues for the national struggle and raising the sophistication of the fight from rock throwing in the streets to using the written word and other alternative means to change public opinion. Overall, it was clear that Palestinians at least came to recognize that there were two groups in Israeli society that held differing opinions about the Palestinians and their territorial rights.

Although the NGOs came to oppose the totalitarianism of the Palestinian Authority after the Oslo Accords were signed, and this further contributed to Palestinian discontent, this was not the case initially. The international donor community seemed quite willing to support a whole new genre of organizations that popularized the ideas of coexistence and mutual acceptance. Though a number of these P/CROs were established during the first two years after the signing of the Oslo Accords, many complained that there was little momentum from either community in support of their causes. Even the election of Binyamin Netanyahu—whose policies regarding the occupation were objectionable to members of both peace camps—did not lead to a Palestinian-Israeli alliance or a strong network in support of peace. The Israeli peace activists and the Palestinian populations disapproved of Netanyahu's government individually rather than collectively. On the Palestinian street much of the rancor stemmed from the fact that Netanyahu tended to reinforce old fears about the Zionist conquerors of Palestine. However, the Palestinian P/CROs were unable to harness this energy and collective anger, and use it toward constructive ends.

Furthermore, the Palestinian populace was unsure of where to direct its emotions: in support of the Authority, toward the NGOs, or against the Israelis. The lack of consensus, the stalling of the Oslo peace process, the naïve hope that a positive step would occur at some point, compounded with an overall exhaustion of the struggle, caused the political demobilization of large sectors of Palestinian society. Thus, P/CROs were unable to make large inroads since the Palestinian people were uninterested, fatigued, or imbued with a sense of futility about their efforts. Furthermore, since their collective initiatives had led to the Oslo Accords—which many Palestinians considered a "rotten egg"—individual contributions toward the peace process became an unreasonable option. P/CROs were unable to make any serious dents in this sense of apathy and despair; in fact at times the P/CROs came to disparage the peace process. Their feeling that the Palestinian Authority would challenge anyone who opposed its policies only worsened the situation.

Conclusion

In light of the findings outlined above, one may wonder whether a Palestinian "peace camp" exists. The answer is that it most certainly does. This camp is represented by the Palestinian Authority: a group of people who for the last twenty-five years or so have sought a political compromise with Israel for the plight of the Palestinian people. The Oslo Accords are the result of this long and hard-fought struggle to gain acknowledgement from Israel and the international community that the Palestinian people exist and have a national right to self-determination and territorial rights to Palestine. Unfortunately, for reasons not entirely their own, the political leadership failed to arrive at a solution corresponding with the national aspirations of the Palestinian people: they did not end the occupation, the human rights abuses, or the theft of land and resources, nor did they create a state, a democracy, or any type of sovereignty that would convince the Palestinian public that their best interests and natural rights were protected or secured.

This political failure subsequently affected those working in the third sector. NGO activists abandoned much of their work supporting the peace process when they came to perceive the Oslo Accords as an agreement that legitimized the Israeli occupation, the corruption and self-aggrandizement of the Palestinian Authority, and Israel's control over fundamental Palestinian rights, resources, and properties. Although the third sector fought to hold onto the support of the people, only those organizations whose work had principled outlooks based on a realist perspective of the Palestinian predicament remained.

These remaining NGOs continue to work, and have perhaps gained some prestige by predicting that the Oslo process would fail. Nevertheless, for reasons that are not entirely clear, these organizations are less effective at the grassroots level than they were historically. This may be due to an overall depoliticization of the Palestinian public, which has grown tired of the struggle, and the pervasive political disillusionment that the Oslo process and the Palestinian Authority have created. Given their current status, it seems unlikely that these P/CROs will be leading movements of popular mobilization either for or against the stagnation of the Oslo process. This is because the Palestinian public feels trapped by the Israeli occupation, the inefficiency of the Palestinian Authority, the rhetoric of political action as a whole, and a lack of international support.

Notes

1. Shukri Abed, unpublished article on Palestinian civil society.

2. The following was the study's original operational definition of peace and conflict resolution organizations: "Peace and conflict resolution organizations refer to non-governmental, citizen initiated organizations advocating peace, reconciliation, and coexistence between Israel/Palestine on the basis of mutual recognition and/or the use of dispute-resolution strategies as a means of addressing the Palestinian-Israeli conflict."

7

PEACE AND CONFLICT-RESOLUTION ORGANIZATIONS IN NORTHERN IRELAND

FEARGAL COCHRANE & SEAMUS DUNN

B y the early 1970s, Northern Ireland's "troubles" gave rise to a polity in which normal democratic politics scarcely existed: the "national" government at Westminster was disinterested, the regional government at Stormont was partisan, and the organs of local government had little responsibility and less power. Most of the day-to-day policymaking was in the hands of powerful civil servants and quangos. The resulting "democratic deficit"[1] meant that a voluntary sector came to occupy much of the public space in which the formal political structure otherwise would have existed. This sector grew consistently in size, influence, and the scope of its responsibilities.[2] The reasons for this are complex, and many of them are particular to Northern Ireland; however, it is possible to make a general argument that as opportunities for participation in conventional political structures decline, the voluntary sector emerges as an alternative site for democracy and citizen activism, and there is a consequent shifting of human resources and energies away from party politics and into the civil society.

Given the incentives and opportunities for voluntary action in Northern Ireland, it is not surprising that the sector is extremely large in comparative terms. A recent survey by the Northern Ireland Council for Voluntary Action (NICVA) estimated that there were over 5,000 active voluntary organizations, absorbing more than £400 million annually—this in a small region with a total population of only one and a half million people.[3]

Within the voluntary sector is a highly diverse subset of peace and conflict-resolution organizations (P/CROs). This diversity is largely a result of the fact that the sector is unregulated and unstructured; consequently, a wide variety of individuals and community groups are fairly free to begin work as activists and practitioners—and even as trainers—in areas such as community development, mediation, reconciliation, intergroup contact, and human rights activism. Furthermore, funding from the European Union, the United States, and the British Government (its Northern Ireland Office, in particular) has facilitated development and growth in the nongovernmental organization (NGO) sector. This monetary support is evidence of the general concern to promote good social, cultural, and community relations between Northern Ireland's two communities, and to encourage reconciliation and conflict-resolution activity.

The complexity and diversity of P/CROs in Northern Ireland points to a difference between Northern Ireland and the other regions within this comparative study: the Northern Ireland P/CROs did not have the coherent political objectives that their counterparts had in South Africa ("end apartheid") or Israel ("end the occupation"). While some P/CROs in Northern Ireland worked to erode or transform traditional unionist and nationalist socio-political identities, just as many—if not more—were committed to accommodating these identities and establishing political and social structures that would allow for their peaceful coexistence. To reflect this diversity, it was important that the sample of Northern Ireland P/CROs include not only cross-community peace organizations with an explicit focus on the political conflict but also single-identity groups from both sides of Northern Ireland's divided society with a more implicit and complex conflict resolution agenda.

Unionist and Nationalist Perspectives

To carry out this study of NGOs in the voluntary sector of Northern Ireland, it was first necessary to consider the different development of NGO cultures within the unionist and nationalist communities, respectively. For many years, the Northern Ireland government was dominated by the unionist community, which consequently regarded the government, in a general sense, as a competent deliverer of social services and indeed as something of a large-scale "community development" organization. Protestants, on the whole, saw a direct and usually positive correlation between their concerns and votes, and the activities and social programs that the government undertook.

The nationalist community's experience was rather different. Nationalists felt little allegiance to the postpartition state and felt excluded from it. While many nationalists deliberately opted out of the state and its structures for ideological reasons, the unionist government did little to persuade nationalists that they were part of the political community of Northern Ireland. Unionists often treated nationalists with suspicion and contempt, and excluded them from both the political process and the workplace. As a result of this sectarian bias, the nationalist community could not rely on the state to satisfy all of its needs and soon developed its own "third sector," based on community cooperation but nonetheless infused by a sense of injustice and the political desire to reform the postpartition polity.

By the early 1970s it had become difficult to disentangle the socioeconomic and the political grievances that lay behind both nationalist and unionist community action. A nonviolent "civil rights" campaign involving public marches and demonstrations developed in an effort to achieve political reforms. While nationalists felt that their complaints concerning poor housing, unemployment, and political discrimination were legitimate, the unionist perception was that these protests were designed as an attack upon the political regime. As this disagreement became increasingly violent and the central government's reach and authority decreased, unionists and nationalists alike had to rely on their own resources to fulfill some of the services the state had once provided and to satisfy newly emerging needs. Relief centers and transport systems were established to assist people who had been forced to leave their homes, while vigilante groups, such as the Shankill Defence Association, were formed in Belfast.

Selecting Organizations for the P/CRO Study

The central problem in conducting the research for this study was the heterogeneity of the voluntary sector in Northern Ireland. Whatever their particular focus, almost all of the voluntary groups would argue that they had a role to play in the creation of a peaceful and progressive society; at the same time, very few of them would describe themselves as being exclusively concerned with conflict-resolution and the promotion of peace. Accordingly, some of the organizations chosen for the study included peace and conflict-resolution activities as part—or even only as incidental consequences—of their work, rather than as its central focus.

P/CROs in Northern Ireland can be divided into three groups according to whether they work with both unionist and nationalist communities and, if so, how they conduct their work. "Cross-community" groups work simultaneously with unionists and nationalists in joint activities; "inter-community" groups work with both communities at the same time, but separately from one another; and "single-identity" groups work with only one community, arguing that preparing that community for later dialogue with "the other side" is the first phase of a conflict-resolution strategy. We included organizations of each type in our study.

In the first stage of the research, we selected seventy NGOs for preliminary study. In the second phase, we chose thirty-six NGOs that exhibited either an explicit or implicit focus on peace and conflict-resolution activities. After each of the thirty-six organizations had completed a detailed questionnaire, we chose a final subset of ten organizations for intensive study. We gathered information about these organizations through semi-structured interviews with their members, and by analyzing their public statements, manifestos, and internal documents. The ten organizations we studied in depth are listed below in alphabetical order:

- *The Clogher Valley Rural Development Centre (CVRDC)* was formed in 1993 as a cross-community center for Catholic and Protestant residents within the Clogher Valley region.
- *The Committee on the Administration of Justice (CAJ)* was formed by concerned legal professionals in 1981 as a nonpartisan civil rights organization focusing on emergency legislation and its application.
- *Dove House Resource Centre* is a registered charity that was formed in 1984. It is a single-identity community development organization that provides a variety of services to the Catholic community in the Derry area.
- *Families Against Intimidation and Terror (FAIT)*, formed in 1990, was a single-issue organization that directed its energies into campaigning against paramilitary intimidation and violence.
- *The Peace Train* was formed in 1989 to protest against the Irish Republican Army's (IRA) bombing of the Belfast-Dublin railroad.
- *Quaker House*, formed in 1982, is a religious cross-community dialogue-promotion organization.
- *The Springfield Inter-Community Development Project (SICDP)* is an inter-community group formed in 1990 to provide development assistance to both Catholics and Protestants within interface areas of North Belfast.
- *Ulster Community Action Network (UCAN Londonderry)* is a single-identity organization formed in 1995 that is dedicated to reviving and nourishing the working-class loyalist community within the Waterside area of Londonderry.
- *Ulster People's College (UPC)*, a registered charity, was formed in 1982 as a cross-community educational resource with a particular focus on disadvantaged and excluded sections of the community, such as the unemployed, urban working class, and women's organizations.
- *Women Together for Peace*, a registered charity, was formed in 1970 to encourage dialogue between Northern Ireland's communities, and in particular to provide women with the opportunity to demonstrate their opposition to politically motivated violence.

Although we do not provide extensive details here about the characteristics of each organization so as to justify its inclusion in our sample, we hope that this information will emerge as we present the results of the study. It is important to emphasize that the study was not intended to evaluate the "worth" of the ten organizations, and although we record and examine the groups' value judgments and ideological focuses, we have attempted to remain objective.

Group Origins

We began our study by examining how and why the various groups originated, trying to identify the issues that stimulated their formation. On the whole, we found that the P/CROs had emerged in order to deal with the symptoms of the conflict in Northern Ireland, rather than its real or perceived causes. Attempts to understand fundamental causes were infrequent, and instead organizations stressed obvious, day-to-day manifestations of the conflict, such as incidents of politically motivated violence, perceptions of communal deprivation, or beliefs that one community was losing out, politically, socially, culturally, or economically.

UCAN (Londonderry) was formed as a result of unionist resentment at the dearth of funding available for grassroots socioeconomic development projects and initiatives in and around the Waterside area of Londonderry. The organization was grounded in this perception of deprivation and also in a strong sense of alienation and injustice, fueled by a belief that the nationalist community was being far better served. UCAN also reflected a general concern that the unionist community was losing the struggle to sustain and advance its culture. UCAN's focus was on the impact of the conflict on a particular community, and in this respect it bore some resemblance to other organizations from which it was otherwise almost totally dissimilar. For instance, like UCAN, Women Together was concerned with the effects of the conflict on the lives and experiences of a specific community—that is, women—in Northern Ireland. The CAJ is another organization that responded initially to the symptoms and consequences of the conflict, rather than its underlying causes. What precipitated the CAJ's formation was mounting evidence that the British government was experiencing difficulty devising and operating legislative procedures to curb and punish politically motivated violence while simultaneously respecting human rights.

Sometimes the impetus for the formation of an organization was very specific. The Peace Train, which held its first meeting at the Stormont Hotel in Belfast in 1989, was formed in direct response to the IRA's bombing of the Belfast-to-Dublin railway line. When one of the organization's former activists was asked what factors motivated the Peace Train's diverse membership to rally as and when it did, his reply was that the group was established to vent an emotional gut feeling, rather than to give voice to an analysis of the situation and its problems. People from a wide variety of political and cultural persuasions assembled simply because "there was something inherently appalling" about the IRA (which espoused Irish unity) repeatedly blowing up a prominent physical link between Northern Ireland and the Irish Republic.[4] Thus, once again the organization's genesis had more to do with the symptoms than the causes of Northern Ireland's conflict.

Some groups had more complex formation patterns, developing from organizations that already existed or on the basis of preexisting community experiences and initiatives. For example, SICDP was officially founded in 1990 (although it had existed informally since 1988) as the result of strategic rethinking about antecedent NGO activities in a particular area of North Belfast. There had been a tradition of community relations work in the area, but local activists became disillusioned with its ineffectiveness and increasingly convinced that in order to achieve lasting and sustainable change it was essential that the promotion of community development be more deliberate and coordinated. Thus, unlike groups such as FAIT and the Peace Train, SICDP was not founded in reaction to a specific event, such as a "punishment attack" or a bombing; instead, it was based on an assessment of the best long-term means for addressing a community's social, economic, and political concerns. It also appears that the thoughtfulness that characterized SICDP's formation continued as the group grew. Documentary sources from 1996 to 1999, such as the organization's most recent operational plan, together with evidence from interviews, suggest that the organization underwent an incremental evolution using trial and error and accumulated experience, instead of taking abrupt shape as an expression of moral indignation.

For example, SICDP developed in reaction to a perceived failure of previous community relations work, involving cross-community contact through children's holidays and "ghettoway days," in which adults and children from both communities were taken away for a day to give them a break from the pressures of living under high stress. The hope was that this would give each community's members the opportunity to discuss issues of common concern with people from the "other side." Although these activities helped to establish some cross-community friendships, it seems that, despite all the efforts and considerable expenditure over the years, the distance between the two communities grew and intercommunity tensions worsened daily. SICDP was an attempt to engage in more practical activities that would produce longer-lasting results:

> I suppose people were frustrated that no matter what they did, things remained the same. . . . They'd been doing all this work with these kids, taking them away and then they brought them back, and as soon as they brought them back and let them go, it was like letting animals go out of a cage, they went back into the wild and they weren't changed in any way. They were changed for the days that they were away and made friends and all of this, but their understanding soon went away when they came home.[5]

Organizational Focuses, Aims, and Aspirations

The Northern Ireland NGOs aimed to achieve a variety of different ends. For example, UCAN, a single-identity group, was constituted in the mid-1990s, but its emergence gave form and a name to a low-profile but province-wide alliance of working-class unionist organizations that had existed since the early 1970s (including the Ulster Defence Association, the largest unionist paramilitary organization in Northern Ireland). The alliance's general aim was to revive the cultural and economic heritage of Ulster unionism in Northern Ireland's urban centers. The alliance did not call itself UCAN, and its member groups operated under their own names. Since the alliance had no funding, its members used their own resources when joint programs were mounted. When UCAN (Londonderry) emerged out of this umbrella group in 1995, it added an economic critique to its heritage-reviving brief, and began to lobby for improvements in the socioeconomic conditions of unionist working-class members in the Waterside area of Londonderry. Therefore, UCAN was primarily about community development, improvement, and regeneration, and did not focus directly on peace and conflict resolution.

Some ostensibly single-issue human rights groups, such as FAIT and the Peace Train, used the issues on which they focused to make broader points. Although the Peace Train was formed to protest against the IRA bombing of the Belfast-to-Dublin railway line, some former Peace Train activists believe that this specific concern served as a vehicle to expose the flawed logic of paramilitary violence. As one former member noted: "Yes . . . I think most people, myself included, would have seen it as an effective way of focusing attention on the costs which the IRA were imposing. . . . I don't think there were any railway enthusiasts!"[6] Thus, this group capitalized upon the irony that a republican movement, which aspired to a united Ireland, was at the same time destroying one of the few geographical and infrastructural links between the island's two political regimes.

While groups such as the Peace Train or FAIT clearly—if at times somewhat indirectly—opposed paramilitary organizations, other groups, such as the SICDP, adopted a more conciliatory and inclusive approach. This was perhaps more pragmatic given the group's desire to work within working-class urban areas and win at least the acquiescence of paramilitaries who lived within (and to some extent controlled) such areas. According to one activist, the SICDP's argument was:

> If you wanted to have a community development strategy which went across the two communities, what you really needed to be doing was involving those people who were involved in the conflict, and using ex-prisoners as a type of local-hero and . . . saying to [those] people, "This is the way we should be working." [People with] street cred. Also, [we had

to be] prepared to talk to people in paramilitary organizations, not to ask for their permission to do particular things, but to say to them, "What do you think of this idea?" That doesn't mean to say if they say "No, it's a totally bad idea," that you walked away and didn't do it, but at least you spoke to them, you've found out. . . . The point about it was that paramilitaries needed to be involved . . . they needed to see that inter-community work wasn't a threat to them.[7]

The aims and objectives of single-issue and single-identity groups, and those of some inter- and cross-community groups, were fairly clear and focused. However, other organizations, such as Quaker House and the UPC, formulated looser, more general, and more flexible aims intended to respond to changing community needs, and to avoid straitjacketing their organizations into dealing with pre-identified and possibly misidentified grievances. Quaker House is possibly the best example of an organization with a fluid and adaptable focus, which was facilitated by the group's small size and the large degree of autonomy it had from its governing body. The two people who ran Quaker House were free to follow where their work led them or where they felt morally compelled to go. Unlike a single-issue human rights group, or even most community development organizations, Quaker House's scope of action was encompassing. Oversight from the organization's governing body normally came retrospectively, following reports on work that already had been done. It was implicitly assumed that the Quaker House staff was best equipped to decide what the organization should do and that the staff's "local knowledge" was a valuable resource. As the staff noted: "We don't have to, like so many bodies do, simply give a report on what's been achieved against money spent. There is a certain amount of faith that, we're here, and being part of the community, that things will evolve, and we will be led to find the right thing to do."[8]

Participants and Members

A wide variety of factors influenced members' decisions to join a P/CRO. In the case of UCAN, the network from which it emerged played a large role in determining its initial membership. This network included the UDA and other working-class unionist groupings; therefore, almost by default, a large proportion of its initial membership had urban, working-class backgrounds. More often, though, the issue(s) on which an organization focused determined its membership. For example, FAIT's opposition to paramilitary violence appealed to people concerned with that issue. As one activist commented: "The sort of people involved in FAIT when it was originally founded were people who had been involved [in], or had suffered from, paramilitary activity."[9] Moreover, because one of FAIT's special considerations was punishment beatings, and the vast majority of these happened to young, working-class, urban males, it attracted a membership with links to—or simply from—this constituency.

In contrast, the Peace Train focused on an issue that, symbolically at least, resonated with a wide cross-section of Northern Ireland inhabitants, including the middle class. However, it was not just the issue's intrinsically widespread appeal that accounted for the varied background of the group's participants. The Peace Train deliberately endeavored to interest high-profile public figures in its work; the resulting media attention increased the organization's visibility and capacity to promote itself to a wide variety of potential members. Furthermore, the Peace Train believed that it could sway public opinion through a media-driven publicity campaign.

The SICDP, on the other hand, deliberately eschewed a heterogeneous activist base. The SICDP focused on promoting socioeconomic regeneration and community development—objectives that it regarded as contingent upon gaining access to and credibility within working-class communities. Accordingly, it sought to recruit a very specific kind of activist, as a founding member of the SICDP noted: "Well, they would all have been people who were working-class. They would have had twenty years of community development and community work."[10] Indeed, at one point, the SICDP actively resisted pressure from a funder to appoint well-known political figures to its management committee because it believed that this would have sent the wrong message to the communities it was seeking to work with and influence.

Thus, the participants' social, political, and economic profiles were directly related to the P/CROs' organizational characteristics, although clearly those characteristics that were most pertinent varied among the organizations. As a whole, the organizations' members were an eclectic mix of people. They ranged from middle-class individuals, whose motives were general altruism and philanthropy, to individuals with more immediate reasons for activism, such as living in areas affected by political violence. These varied motives make it difficult to generalize about the P/CRO activists and sympathizers; however, most indicated some similar considerations for their involvement in P/CROs. They evinced concern about the deteriorating political situation in Northern Ireland and the accompanying rise in sectarianism; a sense of responsibility to the community, both parochially and nationally; and optimism and self-confidence that action in concert with others would "make a difference," even if only a small one. This sort of optimistic, "can-do" spirit was evident across most of the organizations.

Political Perspectives and Sympathies

The political perspectives of Northern Ireland's P/CROs were often complex and multilayered, reflecting the heterogeneity of their memberships; and the perspectives of individual members spanned the political spectrum. But the salience of political perspectives and sympathies differed among the organizations. Several P/CROs claimed that political perspectives played no role in the ethos and operation of their groups. For example, the CVRDC and SICDP denied that politics was important in their activities. Perhaps more surprisingly, Dove House, a single-identity group, also claimed that the organization took no account in its community development work of its members' political perspectives, despite the fact that almost all of them were from a nationalist/republican background.

For a cross-community reconciliation group like Women Together what was most important was that its official perspective tread a fine line between nationalism and unionism. Women Together attempted to attract as many women opposed to violence as possible, regardless of whether they were nationalist or unionist sympathizers; therefore, the group was careful to avoid stepping on any ideological toes by leaning in either direction. The essential feature of its position was that violence was not a legitimate means to achieve any political objective. United on this one point, the political perspectives of the participants in Women Together activities were otherwise very varied.

One of the few generalizations that can be made about the political perspectives of P/CROs in Northern Ireland is that the vast majority of the organizations, and the people who became involved in them, had broadly left sympathies. This is the one similarity that was evident across the whole sample, regardless of the group type, function, or socioeconomic profile of its members.

Joining and Leading P/CROs

Northern Ireland's P/CROs established varyingly rigorous regulations to govern their functioning. Single-issue campaigning groups with poorer resources, such as the Peace Train, typically operated in a less formalized and more ad hoc manner than did well-funded, relatively large-scale community development organizations, such as SICDP. Groups such as the Peace Train often afforded gifted amateurs some latitude to play with ideas, while larger and more stable groups had to establish clear procedures to ensure accountability, especially if they were responsible for delivering community services. Furthermore, the Peace Train's founders did not expect that it would be a permanent organization. Many people gravitated toward the events it sponsored precisely because it had a clearly defined, short-term purpose; saw itself as a loose and temporary coalition of concerned groups and individuals; and directed its energies into activities and programs rather than structure-building. No resources were allocated for the development of an elaborate chain-of-command or bureaucracy.

This pattern contrasts sharply with the formalized mechanisms within Women Together, for example. Women Together's institutionalization was a consequence—at least in part—of the fact that its leaders came from the trade union movement and brought with them both a culture of accountability and the mechanisms to enforce it. The group was never ad hoc or informal, and its transactions were always highly structured and transparent. Financial accounts were maintained from the first day of its formation, and minutes of its meetings were kept and written up assiduously.

At the other extreme lies Quaker House, which is composed of a Quaker couple, who work as partners. As has been noted already, Quaker House enjoyed substantial freedom, was implicitly trusted by its funders, and brought to its P/CRO work the consensus-building tradition of Quakerism. As a result, few procedures were established for transacting the organization's business: "It's very participative . . . we don't vote to make decisions. The theory behind that is that if the meeting is trying to make a decision about something there is a correct decision to be found, God's will if you like, and it's up to us to find it. So there's no point in voting, and if you do, you just exclude the people who lose the vote."[11] In its extremely laissez-faire approach to self-regulation, Quaker House incarnated an atypical organizational ethos and internal structure.

The Target Audiences

Some P/CROs targeted specific communities, while others sought to influence a broader public audience; at least one organization, FAIT, did both. On the one hand, FAIT directed its message at the paramilitary organizations involved in intimidation and punishment attacks. FAIT picketed the offices and leaders of political parties—such as Sinn Fein and the Progressive Unionist Party—that many associate with the paramilitaries. On the other hand, FAIT regarded as its audience the broad community within which the paramilitary organizations operated, and it used the media to make its case to the general public.

The Peace Train also used the media to reach a broad audience: "We saw the media as enormously important in terms of radiating our message [and] amplifying it, and I think the whole campaign was quite media oriented, not least I think because the Peace Train idea was a fairly imaginative one and had visual [impact] . . . I think initially the target audience was the general public. . . . The rail-line being blown up regularly just becomes like part of the weather as it were . . . so I think it was to jolt people out of that apathy."[12] By contrast, Quaker House did not target any specific groups. Indeed, one of its key functions was to provide a neutral meeting place for groups that might otherwise "have difficulty in meeting other groups of people, who might find the use of neutral space helpful. Usually this would have a political edge to it. It could be [paramilitary groups], yes, or people close to them. People who wanted neutral space which wasn't made public."[13]

The UPC, like FAIT, targeted different audiences depending upon which of its various activities it was pursuing. The organization was established as a community education resource and residential facility, but regarded its mandate as fairly wide-ranging. Its core clients were members of socially and economically disadvantaged communities—the poor; the ill-housed; the disabled; women; and the working class, in general—and the bulk of its energy went into serving these constituencies. But it also attempted to reach other sectors of the population. For instance, part of the organization's agenda was to change the way in which the community within Northern Ireland as a whole thought about social policy and the conflict in the region. The organization also aimed to exert pressure on policymakers and thus devoted resources to building influence within this community. Thus, the UPC maintained a dual focus: delivering a range of services to a relatively focused group of clients, and campaigning and lobbying to diverse groups and individuals about a variety of social and political issues.

Some groups targeted more specific audiences. Women Together's membership was clearly demarcated: its target audience was women who were interested in ending the violence. On the other hand, Women Together also hoped to reach the paramilitary organizations, politicians, and the media, all of which had a role in ending the paramilitary violence.

Similarly, the CVRDC was founded to serve a discrete, distinct constituency: the rural farming community in the Clogher Valley area. To adequately achieve its mission, it was vital that the CVRDC quickly fulfill the needs the community articulated. Therefore, the organization was highly responsive and, as a member suggested, less inclined than other groups to impose its own solutions: "We were starting from a blank page. So, we didn't turn up and say 'right—we'd better do something to do with farming,' although the reason why it keeps coming up is because it is the key employer in the area. It was more a matter of trying to sit down and see what could be done from scratch with a blank page."[14]

Like the CVRDC, the SICDP's core client group also was determined geographically, although its clients were socioeconomically quite different from those of the CVRDC: "It was from Divis Street up to the corner of the Whiterock [Road]. It was very much [aimed at] people who were alienated, marginalised, whatever [term] you want to use. Very much people who were 'under the cosh' in terms of being politically excluded and socially excluded."[15]

Funding the Peace Sector in Northern Ireland

Funding is almost always a central problem for the voluntary sector, and in this regard the Northern Ireland P/CROs studied generally were representative of the sector as a whole. Our sample included small groups, such as UCAN (Londonderry) and the Peace Train, which operated on extremely small budgets; but it also included larger organizations with six-figure annual incomes. Given these figures, we attempted to determine what type of funding the P/CROs sought, the methods they used to attain that funding, and whether or not their efforts were successful.

Organizations that were able to operate on very limited budgets were mainly campaigning and pressure groups, which tended to enjoy a large degree of organizational autonomy. Funders had little capacity to impose restrictions (because the punitive withdrawal of funding had minimal consequences), and in some cases these organizations simply ran programs as and when their resources allowed. Organizations that required substantial funding were primarily those involved in community development or significant and regular service-delivery programs. Although their access to resources enabled these organizations to undertake such activities, it also threatened the occurrence of "mission drift"—whereby organizations gradually fall into following the priorities of the funding community, rather than those of their constituents. Thus, in a sense, the larger and better-funded organizations can be viewed as "prisoners" of their own success—they were constantly in search of resources to preserve jobs and maintain services, but perhaps had to make concessions in the process.

There was little long-term funding available for P/CROs; grants for periods longer than three years were uncommon (the exceptions are noted in the next section). Six- to twelve-month grants for specific projects were relatively easy to obtain, but more difficult to get renewed, which meant that many P/CROs struggled with project and program continuity. Because most funders specified that their funds only were to be used to support the project for which they were granted (a practice known as "ring-fencing"), many organizations faced difficulties in building and maintaining a general administrative infrastructure.

Some groups faced greater funding challenges than others did. A number of P/CROs had difficulty obtaining funding because of the types of activities in which they engaged. For example, according to British law, a campaigning group with an overtly political focus cannot apply for charitable status and is thus ineligible for funding from sources such as trusts and foundations. Some organizations were more cautious than others about the sources from which they received funding. Typically, community development organizations were less nervous than human rights groups because the latter often dealt with issues that were divisive and sensitive, and therefore could not appear to have sympathy for one community over another. There also was a difference in the way the organizations approached their fund-raising activities. The smaller groups adopted a minimalist approach and a reactive strategy; the larger ones engaged in social networking with the funders, and pursued a much more proactive and coordinated funding strategy.

Stability of Funding

A variety of sources funded the P/CROs and provided them with varying amounts of money, disbursed over different periods of time, for a variety of purposes. This funding ranged from small three-month project-related grants to three-year contributions for core funding. It is also important to note that nearly all of these groups could obtain some funding from the British government.

For some organizations the pursuit of funding was a relatively low priority. First, some organizations neither had (nor needed) much conventional funding, especially if they ran their programs exclusively in and for either the nationalist or the unionist communities. For instance, UCAN (Londonderry) had no core funding from any source (nor did it have any employees). Local community assistance (sympathetic businesses provided furniture, paint, labor, and other material resources) made UCAN's activities possible. The organization did receive money from the Northern Ireland Voluntary Trust to manage conferences, but this money was normally ring-fenced and could not be used to defray operating costs. Second, parent organizations funded some groups on a secure and ongoing basis. For example, Quaker House's parent organization in Britain paid the salaries of the two staff members that Quaker House employed. Assured of this support, Quaker House spent no time looking for money from other funders.

This sort of indifference to funding, however, was the exception rather than the rule, and most organizations spent significant amounts of time and much organizational energy in finding, maintaining, and developing funding sources, sometimes diverting the group away from its original purpose. The attention that most organizations devoted to funding meant that their membership profiles changed—a common result of the processes of institutionalization. As funding considerations grew in importance for the organizations, the original members (sometimes referred to as the "gifted amateurs") often were forced out or alienated. These people had joined the P/CROs because they believed in their original focus or radical agendas and wanted to make a difference, but they lacked the interest and time to develop the formal organizational structures or financial strategies that their organizations needed as they began to professionalize. Consequently, the "gifted amateurs" frequently were replaced by professional administrators, who, while just as committed to the organizations' goals, placed more emphasis on institutional development, and were better equipped to protect and expand the organizations' resource bases. Almost inevitably, the result was increased bureaucracy and more formal relationships between the organizations' members. This process also led to resentment between P/CRO members and resignations from the organizations.

The Ethics of Funding

The organizations in the study faced two broad ethical questions with regard to securing their revenue sources. The first was whether they should accept funding from sources whose general political orientations were manifestly at odds with their own. The second question was whether they should accept funding from sources that might attempt to influence the organization's perspective or agenda, such as a party to the conflict, even if the sources were fairly distant from the P/CRO.

P/CROs within Northern Ireland were particularly unaffected by general ideological differences between themselves and potential funders. In response to a question about whether one community development organization would accept funding from a tobacco company, a representative replied: "I'd take anybody's money . . . well anybody's money within reason, I suppose, but when you're trying to promote economic development and community relations and community development, it doesn't matter a damn to me who pays for the photocopier, you know?"[16]

The question about whether a P/CRO would accept funding from a source that would try to influence its political agenda provoked more concern among the P/CROs, although it did not really affect organizational behavior. However, the organizations at least thought about how it might damage their public profiles if they accepted funding from sources that could be perceived as politically interested. For example, some unionists suspected that the International Fund for Ireland was designed to help entrench the Anglo-Irish Agreement of 1985 (which most of the unionist community opposed) and regarded its funding as conscience money for acquiescence with a policy they rejected. Accordingly, many unionist politicians encouraged NGOs to shun the fund. However, even for a unionist group as radical as UCAN (Londonderry), this injunction was not enough to outweigh the practical benefits the funding could bring to the community it served: " To tell you the honest truth, the job is more important. I think it's very hypocritical of these churches who say, 'Oh we wouldn't take money from the National Lottery,' but then they plough money into fucking arms companies. But then that is churches. . . . If there is a need and there is money, take it."[17] From the time of its inception, the SICDP, which also had strong links to the unionist community, accepted funding from the International Fund for Ireland, as well.

It is also worth noting that almost all P/CROs in Northern Ireland, whether unionist or nationalist, accepted funding directly or indirectly from the British government, which some consider to be one of the parties to the conflict in Northern Ireland. The CAJ was atypical of the groups studied in that it explicitly refused to accept funds from British government sources. Its reluctance was based on a concern to protect the independence and integrity of the organization since these were essential for the conduct of its human rights work.

Thus, in general, P/CROs in Northern Ireland were more likely to ask themselves the pragmatic question as to how they could secure the resources to maintain existing work and develop new projects without hurting their credibility and impairing their ability to achieve their objectives. Generally, they did not have explicit policies about which sources of funding were "forbidden," largely because such policies were unnecessary. Most groups concentrated on well-known and established local, European, and international funders, rather than more exotic sources, and as a result rarely encountered funders of dubious repute.

Relationships with Funders

Most of the P/CROs had fairly relaxed relationships with their primary funders. Formal reporting procedures ordinarily were required, but informal communication between the P/CROs and their funders also was common, so that funders served in advisory capacities, if necessary, and became familiar with the grantees and their activities beyond the infrequent reports the P/CROs submitted. Reporting requirements varied according to the funder and the nature and size of the grants involved. Some funders required quarterly reports, while others expected only an annual report, sometimes supplemented by a report midway through the grant cycle. Some funders visited the groups to talk about grant applications or to oversee the progress of work that already was funded, while others insisted on seeing the minutes of committee meetings to determine whether the organizations were being run efficiently.

Few of the organizations we studied had poor relationships with the funding community, apart from feeling that they generally were under-funded or being annoyed when funders interpreted their funding mandates in ways that disqualified a project from being funded. One exception was Dove House, which believed that it was the victim of political discrimination when the British government ceased its funding in 1986.[18,19] The organization maintained that it suffered from the Hurd Principles (named after former British foreign secretary, Douglas Hurd), which state that the government should not fund organizations in Northern Ireland that are "fronts" for or that give support to "terrorist" groups. Typically, and understandably, concern over political vetting was highest within single-identity working-class organizations primarily engaged in community development activity and less prevalent in cross-community groups with a more obvious peace and reconciliation focus.

Almost all of the P/CROs emphasized *trust* as the crucial ingredient in the partnership between themselves and the funders. If trust was broken—as a result of inadequate auditing arrangements, financial irregularities, unsatisfactory project progress, or a funder's belief that resources were being used for unauthorized activities—then the relationship between the P/CRO and the funder was seriously damaged. Therefore, gaining and maintaining the trust of funders was crucial to an effective fund-raising strategy. Several factors contributed to the P/CROs' ability to build trusting relationships with their funders: a history of financial accountability; a track-record for stability and delivering services efficiently, or for campaigning energetically and effectively; personnel whom the funders respected and knew to be competent; and a reputation for delivering promised products.

It can be argued that focusing on protecting the funding relationship and the funder's trust was not altogether beneficial: in doing so, emphasis shifted from ideas for peace and conflict-resolution initiatives to the organizations that promoted them (albeit indirectly). Therefore, there might have been a bias among the funders toward funding "moderate," "safe," middle-class, established groups, whose interests matched their own but whose agendas did not confront the really difficult and controversial issues at the heart of the political conflict in Northern Ireland. Therefore, because the funding community was concerned with supporting more traditional and experienced organizations, groups were excluded that were considered more risky to fund, had no connection to the funders through a social network, had no track-record, and took a more critical approach to peace/conflict resolution activity.

The Dangers of Involvement

Few of the P/CRO members surveyed in Northern Ireland regarded the risks they faced as being very great, and groups that might have expected to encounter significant danger did not. For example, FAIT sought publicity for the victims of punishment beatings, intimidation, and feuds, and also was involved in collecting interview and video evidence of threats and intimidation. Its members were prepared to name names, to appear at public meetings where those deemed guilty of violence were present, to picket offices and meetings, to appear on television and accuse and denounce the groups involved, and generally put themselves in dangerous public situations to promote their agenda. Presumably, the paramilitary groups perceived these actions as threatening or at least extremely negative. But FAIT encountered very little intimidation. The assumption must be then that the paramilitary groups decided that any form of retaliation would be counterproductive and perhaps would substantiate FAIT's claims.

Likewise, and somewhat surprisingly, there is no evidence that the Peace Train, which challenged the paramilitaries about their repeated attacks on the Belfast-to-Dublin train, or its members experienced any actual attacks. In addition, only individual members of UCAN (Londonderry), which had strong links to the UDA, a paramilitary organization, experienced any harassment, and even this was not predicated on their membership. The slight harassment P/CRO members faced took the form of threatening phone calls, which organizations suspected came more often from disgruntled or politically opposed individuals rather than from paramilitary groups.

Organizations that faced less risk were those involved in less political activities, such as community development or economic regeneration (CVRDC, Dove House, or the SICDP), adult or community education (UPC), or community relations work (Quaker House), all of which were very unlikely to be directly, immediately, or publicly at odds with "the men of violence."

The Question of Efficacy

Given the energy and resources that the P/CROs devoted to dealing with aspects of the conflict in Northern Ireland, an assessment of their overall impact on the "peace process" is valuable. However, impact is very difficult to measure. Much of the most useful and potent activity in this field took place continuously, incrementally, and all but invisibly, and can be identified only retrospectively. Consequently, it is only possible to give an impressionistic and qualitative assessment of the P/CRO sector's impact on the political conflict in Northern Ireland over the last thirty years.

The significant progress Northern Ireland has made toward peace in the last five years culminated on April 10, 1998, when unionists and nationalists reached a historic political agreement. Did the P/CRO sector's activity affect the peace process, and if so, how? Would the peace process have happened anyway, regardless of the work of these organizations over the last thirty years? What is quite clear is that the P/CRO sector did not have a *direct* impact on the peace process in Northern Ireland. The impetus toward negotiation often was violent acts rather than peaceful events. For instance, the signing of the Downing Street Declaration in 1993 had everything to do with the terrifying prospect of descent into civil war after the Shankill Road bombing of 1993 and virtually nothing to do with any specific activities within the P/CRO sector.

The P/CRO sector's collective achievement was the introduction of an inclusivist NGO philosophy into the political arena. However, it is very difficult to point to a single organization that had a significant impact on the direction of the peace process. Some argue that the most effective P/CROs were not those with the highest public profiles, but instead the small-scale local initiatives that strove to make a more enduring contribution. For instance, the large demonstrations and public vigils that groups such as the Peace People organized in the late 1970s failed to sustain momentum because they lacked a sense of strategic purpose or direction. However, such groups did serve a valuable purpose as emotional safety valves for the expression of community opposition to violence.

In addition, the activity of P/CROs over the last thirty years encouraged political debate and allowed community activists to constitute an extra tier of progressive leadership within civil society, generally, and in the political process, particularly. The P/CROs provided a means to incorporate both nationalist and unionist former paramilitary members into the political process, afforded space for such people to develop competence within more conventional politics, and saw some of these people graduate to mainstream political party membership.

Conclusions

The voluntary sector in Northern Ireland is healthy and diverse and those organizations within it that are involved with peace and conflict resolution (however peripherally) are varied, complex, and multifaceted. Therefore, it is extremely difficult to formulate general descriptive or analytical propositions about P/CROs within Northern Ireland. However, a number of issues and themes recurred in this study, from which some general conclusions can be drawn about the social and cultural features of the P/CRO sector.

The P/CROs rarely presented an analysis of the causes of the conflict in Northern Ireland, and so, necessarily, they responded to issues and problems that were consequences and symptoms of the conflict. These included social alienation, group marginalization, a perception of relative deprivation and skewed funding patterns, the threat of cultural loss and dilution, and the dearth of planned community regeneration.

Although the people involved with the P/CROs had varying backgrounds, sometimes an organization's activists were somewhat homogeneous—this can be attributed in part to a P/CRO's particular geographical focus or the issues with which it dealt. Almost all P/CRO activists shared a desire to contribute to and bring about a more unified and more civilized society where violence would not be used to secure political ends. "Politics with a capital P" played a fairly small role in most P/CROs, despite the fact that many of the P/CROs were used as a substitute for formal politics after 1972. The peculiar tension within Northern Ireland between unionists and nationalists was probably less prevalent in the P/CROs and in their way of thinking than in any other area of life in Northern Ireland. Even if this tension sometimes played a role in small and almost unnoticed ways, only rarely did it seriously or dramatically impinge on the work of these organizations.

Some P/CROs had short existences, others lasted longer (although usually precariously so); some were conspicuously energetic, proactive, and unconventional in their thinking, others were significantly less so. As voluntary organizations, nearly all of the P/CROs depended on the public sector, government, and charitable bodies for funding. The anxiety that these supporting bodies felt over the conflictual and destabilizing nature of Northern Irish society meant that they made considerable funding available to the P/CROs. Of course, there were hidden agendas, eligibility constraints, and, to a lesser extent, rules about the accountable use of funding. But the voluntary sector would not have survived in the form it has without this funding. Although questions might have been raised about the ethics of funding-related issues, on the whole it appears that such issues did not trouble the P/CROs, which generally were unconcerned about the sources from which their money came.

Finally, the work of the P/CRO sector had a significant "slow-burning" effect on the political process during the last thirty years and made an important, if indirect, contribution to the wider civil society within which the P/CROs were located. The NGO ethos of inclusiveness, dialogue, and consensus slowly percolated upward into the party-political debate and eventually became a feature of the talks that culminated in the Good Friday Agreement. In addition, personnel from the P/CRO sector—who were put off from political involvement for many years because of the post-1972 "democratic deficit"—brought the knowledge and skills they garnered from their work in the P/CRO sector to the negotiating process in the 1990s and played a major role in the political settlement reached on April 10, 1998. Whether or not the Good Friday Agreement survives, the contribution the P/CRO sector made to it has been significant and is deserving of recognition.

Notes

We would like to thank the following members of the Northern Ireland ISPO Steering Group for their invaluable guidance during the project: Professor Ed Cairns, University of Ulster; Professor Adrian Guelke, Queen's University of Belfast; Dr. Deirdre Heenan, University of Ulster; Professor Sally McClean, University of Ulster; and Mr. Quintin Oliver, Director of Stratagem. We would also like to express our gratitude to everyone else who cooperated with the research, especially the P/CRO groups themselves who gave very generously of their time.

1. For a fuller discussion of this term, see A. Pollak, ed., *A Citizen's Inquiry: The Opsahl Report on Northern Ireland* (Dublin: The Lilliput Press, 1993).

2. The language used in Northern Ireland to describe what we have called "the voluntary sector" is varied and inexact, and includes the following: volun-

tary sector, nongovernmental sector, community sector, third sector, not-for-profit sector, and independent sector.

3. Northern Ireland Council for Voluntary Action, *The State of the Sector* (Belfast: NICVA, 1997).

4. Dr. Liam Kennedy (Peace Train activist), interview with Dr. Feargal Cochrane, June 17, 1997.

5. Billy Hutchinson (SICDP activist), interview with Dr. Feargal Cochrane, August 13, 1997.

6. Dr. Liam Kennedy interview, June 17, 1997.

7. Billy Hutchinson interview, August 13, 1997.

8. Alan Quilley and Janet Quilley (Quaker House activists), interview with Dr. Feargal Cochrane, March 26, 1997.

9. Sam Cushnahan (FAIT activist), interview with Dr. Feargal Cochrane, March 14, 1997.

10. Billy Hutchinson interview, August 13, 1997.

11. Alan Quilley and Janet Quilley interview, March 26, 1997.

12. Dr. Liam Kennedy interview, June 17, 1997.

13. Ibid.

14. Sean Kelly (CVRDC activist), interview with Dr. Feargal Cochrane, June 16, 1997.

15. Billy Hutchinson interview, August 13, 1997.

16. Sean Kelly interview, June 16, 1997.

17. Lexie McFetters (UCAN activist), interview with Dr. Feargal Cochrane, March 10, 1997.

18. Donnacha MacNeillais (Dove House activist), interview with Dr. Feargal Cochrane, September 17, 1997.

19. Michael Heggerty (Dove House activist), interview with Dr. Feargal Cochrane, October 9, 1997.

Part IV

Comparative Analysis of P/CROs

8

A COMPARATIVE VIEW: PEACE AND CONFLICT-RESOLUTION ORGANIZATIONS IN THREE PROTRACTED CONFLICTS

MEGAN MEYER

A glance at the regional conflicts in Israel/Palestine, Northern Ireland, and South Africa reveals striking differences in their sociopolitical histories, bases of contention, and journeys toward peace. Yet, even the most disinterested observer is likely to associate these conflicts with one another owing to the historic level of violence in each region. Not surprisingly, previous studies have compared the three regions.[1] However, no previous work has aimed to examine and compare across these three regions a sample of nongovernmental organizations (NGOs) that have struggled to foster peace—what we call peace and conflict-resolution organizations (P/CROs). This study takes a first step toward documenting such organizations and this chapter examines them in a comparative fashion.

Comparative studies of complex societies and their organizations naturally face significant empirical challenges, and this study has been no exception. Given the differing conceptions of peace among the protagonists within and between each of the three regions, simply defining a P/CRO was a seriously debated issue from the start (see chapter 1). Nevertheless, a multiple-case cross-region comparison of P/CROs offers immense advantages over single-case or single-region studies. Not only can it document a broader spectrum of organizations and highlight regional differences, but ideally it can capture consistent patterns of organizational behavior that transcend regional variations. Recognizing the advantages of such an approach, scholars studying NGOs and social movements have called for greater comparative research, especially for regions outside of the United States and Europe.[2]

The first aim of this chapter is to describe the general features (leaders, resources, strategies, and structures) of a sample of twenty-seven P/CROs, irrespective of their regional affiliation.[3] In doing so, the chapter illustrates the similar ways in which the P/CRO leaders and members in each region mobilized resources and mounted significant organizational efforts to foster peace despite the hostile environments in which they operated. The chapter's second aim is to compare the way in which each region's unique political context influenced the ideological frames, financial resources, and strategies the P/CROs adopted.

General Attributes of the P/CROs

Formation

While a handful of the P/CROs in the sample were established before 1980 and a few emerged in the early 1990s, as table 8.1 illustrates, most (67 percent) were founded in the 1980s during periods of heightened conflict and violence in each region. In discussions of organizational formation, members frequently cited a violent event or a general increase in violence as the main stimulus for action. Such events included the Lebanon War and the Intifada in Israel/Palestine, increasing violence between the state and resistance movements in South Africa, and escalating paramilitary violence and intimidation in Northern Ireland. However, the proliferation of P/CROs during the 1980s was also a response to expanding political opportunities. In South Africa, for instance, P. W. Botha instituted several reforms during the mid-1980s that facilitated the establishment of many NGOs that were explicitly anti-apartheid. Northern Irish P/CROs arose partly in response to increasing encouragement from the U.K. government, which subsidized the development of NGOs engaged in "cross-community" work. So too in Israel, the third sector blossomed in the 1980s when a new political and social atmosphere encouraged such activity and the 1980 Law of Associations (Amutot)—which created a simpler and more open procedure for forming and registering nonprofit associations—increased nonprofit activity overall.

Founders/Leaders

Although escalating violence and political opportunities were critical to the formation of the P/CROs in each region, the courage, initiative, and commit-

TABLE 8.1.   Date of P/CRO Formation

Years	N	Percent
Before 1970	5	19
1971–1980	2	7
1981–1990	18	67
After 1990	2	7

ment of charismatic leaders cannot be overlooked. A prime example is Ruth Agnew, a cleaner in the Gas Works in Northern Ireland, who had a series of three distressing dreams about increasing violence that stimulated her to organize a women's community meeting at which the P/CRO, Women Together, was founded. Similarly, in South Africa Dr. Frederick van Zyl Slabbert and Dr. Alex Boraine, both Members of Parliament (MPs) in the Progressive Federal Party, walked out of Parliament in protest over the political deadlock of the time and founded the Institute for a Democratic Alternative for South Africa (Idasa). This organization would later orchestrate the groundbreaking meeting in Dakar between representatives of the African National Congress (ANC) and Afrikaner elites. Likewise, in Israel Dr. Ruchama Merton inspired a group of physicians to provide free medical services to Palestinians in the Occupied Territories, establishing what is now called Physicians for Human Rights.

Although a few P/CRO leaders, like Ruth Agnew, had little political experience, most were highly educated and had substantial experience in and connections with existing activist and NGO networks, including the women's movement, trade unions, leftist political parties, universities, religious institutions, and other NGOs. These connections were invaluable because they gave leaders access to the financial and membership resources necessary to build and sustain organizations.

Resources: Members and Money

Just as scholars studying organizational behavior would predict,[4] leaders' personal and professional connections to networks were fundamental to the formation, growth, and survival of most of the P/CROs. Eight organizations grew directly out of established religious institutions, universities, or other NGOs and therefore had few funding concerns. For instance, Quaker House (QH) in Northern Ireland and Quaker Peace Center in South Africa developed under the auspices of the international Quaker movement. A comment from the case report on Quaker House reveals the security that its connection to the British Quaker Peace and Service Committee afforded: "There was no financial dilemma therefore or spontaneous activity leading to the setting up of the group followed by a concern about how they would sustain their activity . . . QH began as a very clearly defined stand-alone project."[5]

Other organizations like the Center for Conflict Resolution and the Center for the Study of Violence and Reconciliation in South Africa were established within and backed by South African universities and benefited from the resources, legitimacy, and protection that these institutions conferred: "The Project [CSVR] was founded in this way mainly because it was hoped that if it was perceived by the apartheid state as an ivory tower research institution (which it never was, being from the start involved mainly in activist research), it would be ignored and allowed to function free of constraints. . . . The other reasons for the university linkage were the credibility the affiliation provided, and the anticipation that it would lend an analytical rigour to the organisation's research."[6]

Still other P/CROs like the Springfield Inter-Community Development Project in Northern Ireland and Bat Shalom (BS) in Israel evolved out of existing NGOs. In such instances, the existing organizations provided both funding and familiar forms of organization, as reflected in the report on Bat Shalom: "BS particularly enjoyed the benefits of the well-developed organizational substructure, as well as the connections it had inherited immediately at birth from the Women's Peace Network (Reshet), out of which BS had virtually emerged."[7]

Preexisting social and professional networks also provided the P/CROs with the critical resources of members and staff. Indeed, those interviewed stated that the most common method of recruitment was through word of mouth. Members and staff in virtually every organization also reported a high degree of affiliation with or formal memberships in other NGOs and P/CROs in their regions. This finding further illustrates that the types of individuals drawn to such activities typically are well integrated into social and activist networks, as other scholars studying social movement recruitment generally have found.[8] These scholars suggest that targeting such preexisting networks is not only a common recruitment strategy among leaders, but is likely to be the most effective method of stimulating and maintaining commitment to collective action:

> The most effective organization of collective action draws on social networks in which people normally live and work, because their mutual trust and interdependence can easily be turned into solidarity. . . . Social networks are sometimes created in the course of collective action. But they endure longer and are more likely to produce an ongoing social movement when they are rooted in pre-existing social ties, habits of collaboration and the zest for planning and carrying out collective action that comes from a common life.[9]

This tendency to draw members and staff from personal and professional networks is reflected in the fairly homogeneous demographics of the P/CROs' memberships in each region. In all cases, middle-aged, middle-class, and highly educated individuals clearly predominated. The Israeli P/CROs comprised predominantly Jews from middle- and upper-class Ashkenazi/European origins. The South African P/CROs consisted primarily of white, middle-class, English-speaking staff and members (although reports have noted increasing black representation during the 1990s). Only the Northern Irish P/CROs displayed significant membership from groups on both sides of the conflict, drawing from both the Protestant and Catholic communities.

Clearly, local networks were critical to the P/CROs' formation and growth over time, but remarkably the bulk of the P/CROs' funding came from foreign sources. Table 8.2 shows the number of P/CROs that drew over 50 percent of their funding from foreign sources during the last few years of their existence, and lists the names of the most significant international funders, including European churches, American foundations, and various foreign governments.

This reliance on international funding is understandable considering the highly contentious and risky environments in which the P/CROs operated. In particular, the oppositional stances that the Israeli and South African P/CROs adopted toward their respective governments made it impossible for them to appeal for government funding. This was less of a problem in Northern Ireland since the P/CROs' "foreign" funding came predominately from the U.K. government, which heavily subsidized the Northern Irish NGO sector and strongly supported the intercommunity dialogue that most of the P/CROs promoted.

The P/CROs in all three regions were considerably restricted in their ability to obtain private local support, as well. For instance, much of the Israeli public viewed the territorial compromises that the P/CROs proposed as a serious threat to Israel's security. Likewise, foreign funding was the only viable source of support for the South African P/CROs because of the risks inherent in associating with anti-apartheid groups in South Africa, which

TABLE 8.2. Number of Foreign vs. Domestic Funding Sources within Each Region

Funding sources	Israel	Northern Ireland	South Africa
Scope	6 international 3 mixed (national & international)	7 U.K. and/or European 1 mixed U.K. and Irish	9 international 1 national

Major sources	Foundations
	  Ford
	  Tides
	  Rich
	  People-to-People
	European churches
	  EZE
	  ICCO
	Foreign
	  Governments
	  Canadian Embassy
	  U.S. Embassy
	Private donors
	  Local and
	    International
		U.K. government
		  Community Relations
		  Council
		European Union and
		  U.K. Government
		Department of Education
		  for N. Ireland
		International Fund for
		  Ireland
		Belfast Action Teams
		Northern Ireland
		  Volunteer Trust
		Foundations
		  Ford Foundation
		Religious organizations
		  British Quaker and Peace
		    Service Committee
			Foundations
			  Ford
			  Rowntree Trust
			  Kellogg
			  Mott
			European churches
			  EZE
			  ICCO
			  Swiss church
			  Church of Sweden
			Foreign governments
			  USAID
			  Royal Danish Embassy
			  Royal Netherlands Embassy
			  Canadian government
			  Norwegian government

unfavorable tax legislation for charitable giving further compounded. Similarly, the British government's traditional subsidization of the Northern Irish civil and NGO sectors and the region's historically depressed economy resulted in low levels of local private support for the Northern Irish P/CROs. In addition, because all of the Northern Irish P/CROs condemned paramilitary violence, associating with them posed the threat of paramilitary backlash, as one member of Families Against Intimidation and Terror (FAIT) noted: "companies are very reluctant to be seen to be identified with FAIT. They will support us and they will praise us but they will not give us funding because perhaps they think that 'the paramilitaries will hear about this' [and burn their businesses down]."[10]

Foreign funding was also desirable as it came with minimal constraints. Members reported that donors granted them a high degree of autonomy in pursuing their missions and activities. In particular, the South African P/CROs appeared to have few constraints and very relaxed, if any, reporting requirements, as is evident from the report on the End Conscription Campaign (ECC), a coalition of organizations that opposed military conscription: "[The Director] notes that many overseas funding organisations were sensitive to the various constraints and restrictions under which the ECC and similar organisations operated, and so were prepared to make quite substantial auditing concessions."[11]

Tactics

Scholars studying the tactics of social movement organizations (SMOs) recognize that such organizations continually adapt their tactics according to political, resource, and membership shifts, and that they not only combine various tactics to pursue their goals, but doing so may be the most successful strategy.[12] An examination of the day-to-day activities of the P/CROs in this study revealed that their use of tactics was no less complex. Table 8.3 shows the six major types of tactics that the P/CROs employed most frequently and documents the number of organizations in our sample that used them at least once.

TABLE 8.3. Number of P/CROs That Used Particular Tactics

Tactic type	N	Percent
Public education	20	74
Service	18	67
Bridging	16	59
Protest	13	48
Lobbying	14	52
Research	4	15

As is evident from the table, most of the P/CROs adopted an eclectic tactical approach, utilizing more than one strategy. Over two-thirds of the sample engaged in some kind of *public education* effort (publications, classes, lectures, workshops, conferences, fairs, TV and radio appearances) or provided *services*, which we defined broadly to include both social services (typically counseling and support for victims of violence) and professional services (skills training classes, accumulation and dissemination of information, and advocacy on behalf of the victims of civil rights abuses). In addition, more than half of the sample organized *bridging* activities that included the facilitation of informal dialogues, formal mediations, the provision of "neutral" space for both inter- and intra-community dialogues, or the organization of social activities that included individuals from both sides of the conflict (sharing meals, tours of "others'" neighborhoods, or youth camps and trips). Fewer of the P/CROs, but still a considerable number, organized at least one *protest* activity, ranging from mass demonstrations to small vigils and public prayer. Protest activities also included acts of civil disobedience, like refusing to serve in the military (in Israel this was limited to refusing to serve in the Occupied Territories). A considerable number of the P/CROs also pursued change through the courts or by directly *lobbying* government officials. Only a few, however, conducted independent *research*, although, as indicated above, many engaged in the interpretation and dissemination of information through public education campaigns. In sum, the data in Table 8.3 illustrate the creativity and flexibility with which these P/CROs approached their missions.

Nevertheless, most of the P/CROs preferred a specific mix of tactics based upon the unique interests, skills, and beliefs of the P/CROs' leaders and members and the tactics that were known and available within each region. As scholars suggest is typical of social movements generally, a division of labor developed among the P/CROs within each region, whereby each P/CRO developed a niche based upon its specific "tastes in tactics."[13] For example, a P/CRO composed of lawyers in Northern Ireland primarily chose to litigate and lobby in pursuit of its policy reform agenda, and an Israeli P/CRO composed of physicians chose as its main activity to provide medical services to Palestinians. Likewise, a few organizations composed of academics typically chose to pursue change through some combination of public education and bridging activities. Generally all of these organizations refrained from protest, as this was not consistent with the "professional" identities of their memberships. Ultimately, the particular expertise and ideological preferences of their memberships led the P/CROs to pursue a specific mix of tactics and determined which were unacceptable for use. Therefore, although the organizations used a variety of tactics throughout their existence, generally they used, and became well known for using, one or two specific tactics—a phenomenon that has been described in other literature as a "dominant strategy of action."[14]

As table 8.4 illustrates, the dominant tactics the P/CROs used fall into one of four distinct categories: protest, advocacy, advocacy/service, and bridging. Only five of the P/CROs in the sample routinely and consistently chose protest as their main method of effecting change, using public political acts that ranged from small vigils or street theater to large marches, and sometimes activities that tested legal boundaries—such as the two organizations that advocated conscientious objection to compulsory military service. Although all five organizations occasionally combined protest with the less confrontational activities of public education campaigns and lobbying, protest was always their main priority, as was noted in the case report on a well-known Israeli organization: "The movement has always defined itself first and foremost as a protest movement. Even when it offered some services or lobbied, protest stood at the center of its self-image."[15]

Advocacy organizations were those that primarily lobbied and engaged in public education campaigns without organizing significant protest campaigns or providing substantial service or bridging activities. Although at times these P/CROs may have tested the boundaries of their institutional approach to action (by occasionally engaging in small protests, for instance), their primary identity was as public educators attempting to influence public opinion and government policy. A primary example is the Council on Peace and Security in Israel, which was composed of high-ranking, retired military officers: "the Council declared that it will support the policies of any government that acts in the spirit of the Council's principles. On the other hand, the Council will criticize any government which acts in opposition to those principles. However, the criticism would not be made in public, in order not to turn the decision makers into the public enemies."[16] The social and professional status of these members clearly provided them with access to the centers of policy decision making. However, while their social position enabled them to feel particularly comfortable and efficacious playing a lobbying role, it also made them uncomfortable about engaging in public acts of challenge. It is not surprising, therefore, that when the organization's staff attempted to mobilize the membership to protest at a time of political stalemate, few members were supportive and the activity never was repeated.

TABLE 8.4. Dominant Strategy of Action among P/CROs

Dominant strategy	N	Percent
Protest	5	19
Advocacy	3	11
Advocacy/service	11	41
Bridging	8	30

There were only three P/CROs that solely engaged in advocacy, a low number compared to the eleven organizations that combined advocacy with the provision of social services. This hybrid approach to action is common,[17] but this does not mean that it is easy to navigate. Indeed, internal conflict frequently resulted when members disagreed about which focus should take priority. Consequently, even though both strategies clearly were established within the P/CROs of this kind, one strategy frequently took priority over the other.

The P/CROs in the bridging category focused their energies primarily on activities aimed at increasing cross-cultural understanding and interaction among parties to the conflict. However, these P/CROs did vary from one another, as some wanted simply to foster interaction and dialogue among antagonists, others mainly to provide "neutral" space for dialogue, and still others to provide formal and professional conflict mediation and resolution services. Despite these differences, each P/CRO in the bridging category displayed a heightened concern about maintaining an objective or neutral image and therefore shied away from protest or pubic lobbying activities, as illustrated in the response from a member of a Northern Irish Quaker group when asked why she did not participate in a particular vigil: "We are always very conscious of this residue of goodwill so to speak, associated with the Quaker label. It is something that we must be very conscious of and not, by stupid action, just blow it all."[18]

Thus, although virtually all of the P/CROs in this sample could be classified as employing a variety of tactics, the characteristics of the P/CROs' leaders and members strongly determined which tactics were favored and avoided, thereby defining the unique character of each organization.

Structures

The most compelling question in the literature regarding organizational structures of P/CROs is how they change over time. Much research suggests that organizations have a natural tendency to formalize their structures over time and that this is done as a means to develop legitimacy, mobilize resources, and survive.[19] However, recent studies on the environmental and women's movements suggest that the personal composition and ideologies of an organization's membership will influence the degree to which it formalizes its structure.[20] We aimed to investigate these questions with regards to the P/CROs in our study.

One fundamental difference within the sample was between those P/CROs that aimed to develop formal memberships (sixteen) and those that intended from their founding to be professional organizations consisting only of paid staff (eleven). For instance, a report on the Institute for a Democratic Alternative in South Africa states: "From the outset there was no doubt among the founders that [the group] would have to be a formal organisation. This, of course, implied that it was not to be a membership-based organisation. Rather it was to rely on paid staff who would be recruited when the need for them arose."[21]

Despite these varying aspirations during their formative stages, it is remarkable that ultimately paid staff came to manage twenty-four of the twenty-seven P/CROs in the sample and that most developed formal structural characteristics. These changes were reflected in the P/CROs' structural features: over three-quarters of the sample had formally recognized leaders, executive or management committees, and formal/legal status as "nonprofit" or "voluntary" associations, as table 8.5 illustrates.

The level of formalization evident in most of the P/CROs contrasted with their structures during their formative stages. Most remained relatively small during the first several years of their existence, and many (virtually all in Northern Ireland and Israel) relied exclusively on the work of volunteer staff. However, as a quote from a member of a Northern Irish protest P/CRO illustrates, in many cases volunteers were unable to cope with organizational growth and maintenance over time: "I think one of the reasons the Northern Committee went down the road of a Constitution and funding was because I think everybody realized, after the first train, that the volume of work involved in organizing and planning couldn't be sustained by a voluntary committee. I mean, people were working from their own homes, in the evenings, at night, during the day and I mean it just was too much to be sustained on any long-term basis."[22]

The fact that most of the P/CROs developed formal structures is not surprising given that organizational theorists consistently have predicted and documented this pattern of organizational behavior for decades.[23] As these theorists would suggest, discussions with members revealed that they formalized either to manage effectively complicated and growing budgets or to cope with expansions in membership and activity levels. For instance, a member of a Northern Irish group indicated how financial management issues necessitated structural formalization: "Well, we had a structure, we had our meetings but it was more informal. There's an element of professionalization within the organisation now, which we had to do in terms of getting our finances right."[24] Similarly, the report on an Israeli protest organization, which initially had intended to remain all-volunteer, indicated that proce-

TABLE 8.5. Degree of Formalization

Structural characteristic	N	Percent
Paid staff	24	89
Formal leadership	22	81
Formal management committees	23	85
Formal incorporation	22	81

dures were formalized and the organization was registered legally in order to handle the regulatory rules that accompanied foreign funding: "at the late 1980s it became clear that the enlargement of the activities' scope required that paid staff would be hired. . . . A reorganization process was launched then [and] three paid positions were decided upon."[25]

Admittedly, the high level of formalization we found reflects the fact that most of the P/CROs in our sample had survived over time. Almost a third of the sample (eight organizations) had been in existence for twenty years or more, and the sample as a whole had a median age of fourteen years. Therefore, we may have missed groups that disbanded early or remained so small that the research teams did not identify them. This may have been particularly true in the South African sample, as the final report noted that those organizations chosen for the study represented the "core" of an anti-apartheid NGO network. Nonetheless, it is significant that the majority of the sample began as small organizations, and, over time, conformed to theorists' expectations.

Even though the level of formalization in the sample was consistent with our expectations, the case reports revealed that the adoption of formalized structures did not take place without concern or conflict among members. For instance, participants of several groups expressed concern over the loss of volunteers, as a member of a Northern Irish group noted: "It's just that the voluntary movement has always emphasized that it is a voluntary movement. It's people giving of their spare time, but there is a danger that it will become too professionalized. If it becomes too professionalized then there is a real issue there. What is the role of the volunteer then?"[26]

These fears reflect what Jo Freeman in her studies of women's social movement organizations in the United States refers to as the "classic dilemma of social movement organizations: the fact that the tightly organized, hierarchical structures necessary to change social institutions conflict directly with the participatory style necessary to maintain membership support and the democratic nature of the movement's goals."[27] Consequently, even those P/CROs that aimed to develop formal structures struggled to foster an open or democratic atmosphere internally. In some instances, decision makers consulted regularly with staff and put significant policy decisions to a member vote. Nevertheless, a single individual or small group ultimately dominated the decision making. Therefore, when attempting to classify organizations by their structural "type," as shown in table 8.6, we categorized most of the P/CROs in our sample as *moderate bureaucracies*. In addition to adopting the formal attributes shown in table 8.5, these organizations placed the decision-making authority in the hands of the officeholders, and had a moderate to high degree of job specialization and of formal rules and procedures for decision making.

Some of the P/CROs, however, significantly resisted the pressures to formalize and managed to maintain collectivist traits over time. Several of these

TABLE 8.6.   Structural Forms

Structural form	N	Percent
Moderate bureaucracy	19	70
Pragmatic collective	5	19
Collective	3	11

organizations adopted hybrid structures and were classified as *pragmatic collectives*.[28] Even though these organizations had paid staff, the number was very low (ranging from one to four), the division of labor was minimal, and they showed significant efforts to make decision making collective (although the thoroughgoing consensus characteristic of collectives was rarely sought). Only three organizations, all of which were in Israel, met the criteria for *collectives*. They had no paid staff, no formal leaders or committees, a low to nonexistent division of labor, and were managed by collective decision-making processes— that is, consensus among all members was actively sought.

Most of the *pragmatic collectives* and *collectives* differed from the *moderate bureaucracies* in one significant way: they believed that the manner in which they conducted their work was as important as the political objectives they sought to achieve, displaying what Jo Freeman refers to as an "ideology of structurelessness."[29] These beliefs were reflected most profoundly in the *collectives'* failure to formally recognize leaders and their consistent struggles to make decisions by consensus. This is revealed in the following excerpt from the report on Women in Black (WIB), an Israeli P/CRO that stood vigil against the occupation:

> An interesting case involving the making of a decision emerged after WIB won an award which brought with it a few thousand dollars prize. The movement had to decide how and when to use this money. WIB activists refused to nominate or elect for that purpose a committee. Therefore it was decided to publish an announcement about the prize in their newsletter and to ask all activists' advice what to do with the money. (The ad was phrased as follows: "Help! We have received unrequested money!"). The activists' response came to null. Therefore the editorial board tried once again to elicit a response. Eventually, after more than a year of hesitations, a non-decision was made to use some of the money to support the publication of the newsletter and some to support the publication of a book about Women in Black. The rest of the money was given to a woman's organization in Gaza.[30]

As frequently occurs in such structureless organizations, highly committed members occasionally made decisions when necessary, even though they were never formally recognized as leaders. This also was evident in the report on the collective Israeli group Yesh Gvul (YG) that encouraged conscripts to refuse to serve in the Occupied Territories:

> Being a non-hierarchical, informal organization based on the very individualistic idea of selective refusal, YG had no official leadership. However, there were people who were long-term activists in YG and essentially kept the organization alive. . . . The selection was not a formal one, as there were no elections. Rather, leaders emerged naturally, from among those who had the time and were committed to the organization. As there were no formal positions, there was no material compensation for leadership.[31]

In addition to a commitment to egalitarianism, most of the eight P/CROs that maintained collectivist traits also were strongly committed to maintaining a single focus. A comment from a member of Peace Train, a Northern Irish P/CRO that campaigned against the Irish Republican Army's (IRA) bombing of railway lines, illustrates this strong commitment to a single focus and to organizational dissolution upon accomplishing their single goal of putting an end to the bombing: "Even at the time when the constitution was drawn up, I remember there was a line put in at the end that, 'when this organisation ceases to exist,' it wasn't 'if,' 'when the organisation ceases to exist, any funds held in hand will be dispersed to like-minded organisations.'"[32]

Also evident in the reports was a strong determination not to mobilize large budgets. Indeed, in addition to egalitarianism and a single focus, five of the eight P/CROs with alternative forms either did not seek to develop a funding base or were adamant about keeping their budgets small. Ultimately, it was clear that the *collectives* and *pragmatic collectives* in the sample did not fully institutionalize because they did not *want* to do so. Therefore, we have concluded, as others have, that members' ideological preferences strongly influence the degree to which their organization will formalize.[33]

The P/CROs in Comparison

The preceding overview reveals that, across all three regions, the P/CROs in our sample reacted similarly to common organizational challenges. The P/CROs found it necessary to mobilize memberships and foreign funding, virtually all chose to use a variety of tactics to pursue their goals, and most developed formal structures as a means to manage growth in funding and activity levels over time. Further analysis, however, reveals some noteworthy cross-regional differences, which we had expected given other comparative research on social movement organizations.

Most of these comparative studies, for instance, have examined how the unique cultural and political context of a region influences the characteristics that its organizations adopt. Cultural studies suggest that an organization naturally will reflect political context conditions in its framing of a problem and also will attempt to resonate with the dominant beliefs of its society in order to maximize the mobilization of members and resources.[34] In addition, separate studies by Gelb; Kriesi, Koopmans, et al.; Kitschelt; and Rucht suggest that open democratic systems (decentralized with several points of access and a high degree of separation of power) are more likely to facilitate the development of formally structured and well-organized SMOs that tend to use conventional tactics; and, in contrast, more centralized and closed systems that have a tradition of repressing challenging groups tend to foster the development of poorly organized or decentralized SMOs that use unconventional or violent tactics.[35] In the following pages, variations in the dominant ideological frames, resources, and tactics among the P/CROs in our sample are identified and examined in light of the political contexts of each region.

Framing

Table 8.7 displays the types of "frames" (i.e., how the movement defined and viewed the nature of the conflict, its causes, and its remedies) the P/CROs adopted across the three regions. The P/CROs were classified according to the following four frames: (1) a *person* frame, in which the P/CROs identified personal attitudes and beliefs as the primary cause of the problem and changing them was the primary solution; (2) a *system-reforming* frame, in which the P/CROs identified government policy as the primary problem and policy reforms within the current system as the primary solution; (3) a *system-transforming* frame, in which the P/CROs viewed political, economic, and social structures as the primary problem and transformation of these structures as the primary solution; and (4) *mixed* frames, in which the P/CROs equally emphasized both personal attitudes and system failings as the roots of the problem.

The political and cultural contexts in Northern Ireland, Israel/Palestine, and South Africa clearly influenced the unique way in which the P/CROs in each region framed their missions. The Northern Irish P/CROs in our sample adopted a *person-oriented* frame in which the personal attitudes of the protagonists of the conflict were considered primarily responsible for Northern

TABLE 8.7. Frame Types by Country

Frame	Israel (9)	Northern Ireland (8)	South Africa (10)
Person	1	5	0
System reforming	7	1	0
System transforming	1	0	5
Mixed (person & system)	0	2	5

Ireland's situation and changing them was the basis of a solution. Accordingly, they emphasized processes of personal reflection and reconciliation as fundamental to creating peace, as illustrated in this quote from a member of the women's group, Women Together: "[We] think of the conflict as something which each and everyone of us has a part in . . . the conflict finds its sustenance because those who do not go so far as to pull the trigger, fail to accept a spirit of tolerance and conciliation in their own personal views."[36]

Generally, the Northern Irish frames contained three central assertions. First, leaders and members of the P/CROs expressed the belief that the attitudes of all Northern Irish citizens were to blame for the conflict, regardless of religion and class. Second, that reform of personal attitudes and reconciliation on an individual level were necessary to affect peace and political change; therefore, education and the impartial facilitation of dialogue without advocacy for a particular political solution were of critical importance. Third, that cultural diversity should be respected while a broader or common national identity or loyalty was fostered. Only one group veered from this orientation, primarily blaming British policies for the conflict and focusing its efforts on policy change.

This person orientation is understandable when we consider the political and cultural context within which the Northern Irish P/CROs were established. For instance, the P/CROs in this sample originated after the onset of the "troubles" and many arose later in the mid-1980s when the Irish and British states, both open democracies, increasingly were viewed as neutral mediators. John Whyte's exhaustive survey of literature on the Northern Irish conflict illustrates that up until the 1960s most explanations put the conflict in "exogenous" terms: they either blamed the British, the Irish, or the capitalists; but that "endogenous" interpretations, which focus on divisive identities and attitudes as the cause of the conflict, have dominated analyses of the last few decades. He explains that with the troubles, "the conflict so obviously was between two opposed communities with the British government trying more or less ineffectively to assuage it, that an internal-conflict approach became at once more plausible."[37]

More specifically, in his discussion of NGOs engaged in conflict resolution Fitzduff adds that this change in perspective was further strengthened with the Anglo-Irish Agreement of 1985 and the Downing Street Declaration in 1993 because both signaled the British government's willingness to withdraw sovereignty if and when a majority wished.[38] The British government and its involvement in Northern Irish affairs, which included significant financial investments in the region's voluntary and public sectors, could no longer plausibly be identified as the problem; rather, relations between communities had to be addressed. Heavy financial subsidization of the voluntary sector—including the P/CROs in this sample—also implied that the P/CROs were particularly likely to reflect British positions toward the conflict, which since the late 1960s have emphasized intercommunity relationships and the building of what Duncan Morrow describes as "common ground."[39]

In contrast to the Northern Irish P/CROs, those in the other two regions advanced *system-oriented* frames. However, the Israeli groups pressed only for reform of the political system while the South African groups insisted that transformations of the political and economic systems were necessary. For instance, the Israeli P/CROs consistently exhibited a frame that targeted government policy as the locus of change. The frame clearly placed the heaviest blame for the continuing conflict on the Israeli government and its occupation of Palestinian territories, and considered the occupation to be both morally wrong and a threat to the future security of the Israeli state. A written statement from the Council on Peace and Security illustrates this perspective: "Continued control of another nation involves negation of civic and political rights, use of force and power, which over time harm the moral and security foundations of the state."[40] Therefore, the solution that most Israeli P/CROs proposed included withdrawal from the Occupied Territories and the self-determination of the Palestinian people, including the right to create a separate Palestinian state.

As with Northern Ireland, the dominant orientation of the Israeli P/CROs is understandable given the political history and context of the region. For instance, the political context that created the state of Israel and international attitudes toward the conflict ever since explain the orientation toward the continued separation of Israelis and Palestinians. Originally, the British government and the UN preferred to divide the land and separate the Jews and Palestinians—a tactic that to an extent validated and perhaps even strengthened the divisive identities. Additionally, there was no need for the P/CROs to try to transform the political system because its democratic structures offered formal access to all citizens equally and provided extra-parliamentary groups with an informal forum through which they could press for change. The Israeli government's policies of occupation after the 1967 War (the establishment of settlements, the retention of territories, and the violation of Palestinians' civil and human rights), however, increasingly were viewed, within Israel as well as in the international community, as aggressive and repressive. Naturally, therefore, most of the P/CROs—all of which arose after the 1967 War and many in direct response to the Lebanon War and the Intifada, advocated for policy reform rather than transformation of the system. Only two organizations in the Israeli sample diverged from this dominant framing of the conflict—a dialogue P/CRO and an organization that opposed political separation and promoted socioeconomic equity.

Finally, the South African P/CROs exhibited a *system-transforming* frame that advocated an end to apartheid and the creation of a democratic state. Beyond this broad framework, the conflict was seen as multidimensional. Peace required not just the effective nonviolent management of conflict but also the transformation of both political and economic inequalities. As the Center for Conflict Resolution stated: "The causes of violence in South Africa are complex and deep-rooted. Their elimination requires a substantial transformation of the state and its institutions, as well as the introduction of democracy, respect for human rights and social and economic justice."[41] In addition, the South African P/CROs believed that these changes should be affected in an environment of reconciliation in which diversity was respected but, ultimately, a unified national identity was sought. Those that varied from this dominant frame did so only in that they emphasized a need for changes in personal attitudes, in addition to structural changes.

The highly closed and repressive nature of the South African political system, which denied formal and informal political access to the majority of its population and more or less violently repressed all challenging groups, explains why the P/CROs exhibited system-transforming frames. Additionally, most of the South African P/CROs arose during the 1980s in an environment of growing domestic and international pressure to dismantle apartheid. It was agreed that the regime was illegitimate and had to be abolished. In addition, the centrality of economic reform among the P/CROs also is understandable given that years of repressive laws had generated a level of socioeconomic inequality unparalleled in Israel and Northern Ireland. Furthermore, because the P/CROs were established to challenge the apartheid regime directly, their vision for peace was in direct contrast to apartheid ideology. In response to apartheid's program of complete racial segregation (which included efforts to strengthen or create tribal identities and divide the population accordingly), the P/CRO sector proposed the creation of a unified South Africa based on a system of nonracial democracy. This democratic vision also is understandable since most of the P/CROs' leaders and members were of English descent and had strongly held beliefs rooted in British liberalism and democracy.

Resources

As mentioned previously, the P/CROs in our sample drew funding from a variety of sources, many of which were foreign, including foundations, governments, religious institutions, private donors, membership dues, and fees for service. However, as table 8.8 shows, the P/CROs in each region varied according to the funding sources upon which they relied most heavily.

The unique political history and context of each region explains these variations. For instance, although all of the P/CROs relied heavily on foreign money, the type of international funding the P/CROs had available and used varied by region and reflected the unique political conditions surrounding each conflict. Reliance upon foreign funding was most dramatic in South Africa, where nine out of ten organizations benefited heavily from foreign governments and international agencies that desired to support NGOs

TABLE 8.8. Number of Organizations Funded in Whole or in Part by Funding Source

Source	Northern Ireland	Israel	South Africa
Foreign foundations	2	7	9
Foreign government	6	3	7
Foreign religious	1	2	8
Foreign private/corporate donors	0	8	3
Local private/corporate donors	1	4	3
Self-generated (member & service)	4	4	5

challenging the apartheid government. The importance of this international funding to the South African P/CROs is reflected in the research team's final report: "It is clear that without overseas funding peace/conflict resolution organizations simply would not have found sufficient resources to exist or survive."[42] Thus, foreign foundations, foreign governments, and foreign religious groups all were important sources of funding for the South African sample.

However, as the political context of South Africa changed, so too did the funding that the P/CROs used or had available to them. With the recent transition to an open democracy in 1994, the P/CROs came to perceive domestic government funding as not only more acceptable but also necessary for survival. In the postapartheid era, foreign funders were not only channeling their support directly to the democratic government (as they have done traditionally in Israel) but also requiring more accountability from the P/CROs they continued to fund. Consequently, the P/CROs looked increasingly toward procuring government contracts as well as finding ways to increase efficiency and self-generated income. One P/CRO member described the shift to democracy as stimulating "a transition from creative opposition to positive cooperation."[43] As a result of this cooperation, several of the P/CRO leaders moved into government positions. Such a change illustrates, first, how the P/CRO sector served as a training ground for future leaders, and second, how political changes can threaten the survival of an a sector of organizations once their main goal—in this case the end of apartheid—is accomplished.

The Israeli organizations also relied heavily on international sources but drew more funding from foreign private donors and foundations than from foreign governments or religious institutions. This difference between South African and Israeli P/CROs is understandable given the political structures in each country. For example, since foreign governments considered the closed and repressive South African system illegitimate, it is not surprising that they channeled funding directly to P/CROs demanding change. In contrast, rather than support Israeli P/CROs directly, foreign governments, such as the United States, were more likely to direct their support to the open and democratic Israeli government and make that support contingent upon negotiation and policy changes within that system. A particularly striking example of this was U.S. President George Bush's denial of $10 billion in loans to Israel when the Israeli government refused to halt the rapid expansion of settlements in the West Bank and Golan Heights.[44] This pressure led to the 1991 Madrid Conference where talks between Israel, a Jordanian-Palestinian delegation, Lebanon, and Syria set the stage for future negotiations. In Israel, therefore, foreign foundations and private donations from Jews in the Diaspora played the most significant role in supporting the P/CROs. Indeed, the high level of foreign private donations reflects Diaspora Jews' long history of significant support for Jewish causes in the Land of Israel.

In contrast to both Israel and South Africa, the "international" funding of Northern Irish P/CROs came predominantly from the United Kingdom and European Union, as stated earlier. All but two organizations (one Quaker organization solely funded by the British Quaker Peace and Service and another funded by local and foreign foundations) received government funds either directly from the British government through the Community Relations Council or indirectly from British and European Union funds channeled through the Northern Irish Department of Education, the Northern Irish Voluntary Trust, or the Belfast Action Teams program.

Support for the Northern Irish P/CROs from foreign foundations and other countries was remarkably minimal compared to the other two regions. This lack of international involvement, especially from the United States with its large Irish American population, is surprising until one considers the reluctance of most countries to interfere in what have been considered "British affairs." Discussing the level of U.S. involvement during the 1980s when most of the P/CROs arose, Jonathan Tonge notes, "A reassertion of the special relationship between Britain and America during the Thatcher premiership and Reagan presidency during the 1980s ensured that American involvement was kept to the minimum necessary to proceed without alienating Irish America."[45]

Tactics

The question of why certain movements or SMOs employ the strategies and tactics that they do has long intrigued social movement scholars. Charles Tilly made a significant contribution to this area of inquiry two decades ago when he suggested that groups typically draw upon a limited, but familiar, "tactical repertoire." [46] In his work, he stated that: "Within any particular time and place, the array of collective actions that people employ is (1) well defined and (2) quite limited in comparison to the range of actions that are theoretically available to them. In that sense, particular times, places, and populations have their own repertoires of collective action."[47] Tilly drew his conclusions from a comparison of American and British movements across "eras" (he focused on the period from 1750 to 1830 and demonstrated that the strike only became a common means of protest in the nineteenth century). According to Tilly's claim that "repertoires of collective action" are context-specific, one would expect to find cross-country variation in the tactics the P/CROs in our sample employed. However, because all of the P/CROs existed during the same era—in which increasing globalization led to widespread international diffusion of protest and tactics—our investigation revealed negligible cross-national variations.

Indeed, table 8.4 shows that variations in the dominant strategy of action (protest, advocacy, advocacy/service, and bridging) across regions were minimal and that groups within each region employed all of these strategies. Still, some small differences are worth noting: the Israeli groups were more likely to engage in protest activities than were both the Northern Irish and South African P/CROs, and the Northern Irish P/CROs engaged in minimal lobbying activities compared to the other two regions. These differences are illustrated in table 8.9, which breaks down table 8.3 by region.

As the table shows, all but two of the Israeli advocacy/service P/CROs engaged in some form of protest activity, even if this amounted simply to small actions, such as public prayer or a one-time vigil or demonstration. In contrast, only three P/CROs in both Northern Ireland and South Africa engaged in such activities. Membership resources, political context, and framing factors explain these cross-country variations. First, and most important, Israel had a higher number of groups with formal memberships that could be mobilized for protest (eight) compared to Northern Ireland (three) and South Africa (five). Second, although protest had become a legally sanctioned and publicly accepted form of political expression in Israel during the 1970s, limiting laws and repressive state response to protest in South Africa made this form of activity less appealing. Specifically, during the 1960s the Apartheid government enacted, among other repressive laws, legislation outlawing freedom of assembly and demonstration. Although some organizations clearly ignored this law, most avoided protest activities for fear of state reprisal. The lack of protest among the mostly white South African P/CROs in our sample also reflects the division of labor that developed within the anti-apartheid movement as a whole. While explicit protest and resistance were associated

TABLE 8.9. Number of P/CROs Using Particular Tactics by Region

Tactics	Israel (9)	Northern Ireland (8)	South Africa (10)
Public education	7	5	8
Service	4	6	8
Bridging	4	5	7
Protest	7	3	3
Lobbying	4	2	8
Research	1	0	3

with radical movements, such as the ANC, "white" groups tended to work largely within the system, where they had access to political decision makers. Even the few organizations that did protest separated themselves from those that engaged in *violent* resistance to apartheid:

> The presence of groups committed to this latter option of violent resistance within the UDF coalition, posed a threat to the Black Sash's liberal principle of the "end not justifying the means." And shying away from endorsing such insurgency or being actively drawn into violent protest, the Sash membership resolved to co-operate with, rather than to affiliate with, the new democratic alliance of the UDF. . . . The Sash chose rather to play the role of "Honest Broker" negotiating for change from both within the ambit of government-created structures and outside of such government aligned forums, as suited its own ideology and perspective on the most appropriate means and method of lobbying for peace, justice and change.[48]

Yet there is a different explanation for the minimal use of protest activities in Northern Ireland. During the 1960s, when Catholics began pushing for change, protest became an accepted and common form of action there. Thus, the small number of P/CROs that engaged in protest is more likely a reflection of the person-orientation and networking goals of most of the Northern Irish P/CROs. Members of virtually every P/CRO, for instance, expressed concern about one of the contesting communities viewing them negatively and therefore several refrained from protest actions. In explaining why they did not participate in a particular vigil, a member of a Quaker group stated:

> We are held in high respect by both sides and we have to be careful not to blow that credit by foolish action. I suppose we made a conscious decision that we would not go up and demonstrate in Harryville [in support of churchgoers being picketed by loyalist Orangemen] although our sympathy is very much on the side of supporting the Catholic congregation . . . we thought if we were there and seen there by some of our loyalist friends, they would have immediately assumed that we were taking sides.[49]

The person-orientation of the Northern Irish P/CROs—which led them to target individuals rather than pressure political leaders in order to change public opinion—also explains why they were less likely than both South African and Israeli P/CROs to engage in lobbying. For instance, almost half of the Israeli and almost all of the South African P/CROs lobbied government officials, while only two Northern Irish organizations did so. The "democratic deficit" that existed in Northern Ireland under British direct rule, which limited the level of influence and access citizens had to those responsible for making policy, also accounts for this difference. Lobbying, therefore, was seen as less feasible and effective. In contrast, lobbying was a natural choice for several groups in Israel and South Africa, where P/CROs had access to the political system through voting and personal and professional networks, and where P/CROs had clear aims to influence the government to adopt particular positions (end the occupation and end apartheid, respectively).

Despite these small differences in the frequency with which certain tactics were used in each region, cross-country variation was negligible and there was no substantial difference in the broad repertoire of tactics known and available to the P/CROs in each region. This lack of variation, despite political and cultural differences, is understandable given that all of the organizations in the sample existed during the same period in which technology facilitated the rapid international diffusion of social movement ideas and tactics. Some of the case reports from within this small sample provide evidence of such diffusion. For example, the actions of Americans during the Vietnam War appeared to have inspired the idea for Israeli soldiers to refuse to serve in the Occupied Territories: "This kind of moral decision was part of the sixties protest repertoire (against Vietnam war and other occasions). Although it was not a very common action [in] Israel, it was known and appreciated by some."[50] Similarly, a founder of an adult college in Northern Ireland mentioned that the inspiration for the college and the philosophy behind it came from the example of "folk high schools" in Scandinavia and the "Highlander" model in the United States. These models emphasize education as a means to stimulate social action among low-income populations. Relatedly, NGOs in other countries imitated the innovative tactics of at least one of the P/CROs in our sample. The report on Women in Black, whose members dressed in black and held silent vigils against the occupation, notes that groups in parts of Europe, as well as in Northern and Southern America, adopted this symbolic and novel form of protest by dressing in black and simply broadening the message from "women against the occupation" to "women against war."

Conclusion

The broad view of P/CROs presented here demonstrates that the P/CROs across the three regions in our sample shared similar characteristics and conformed to certain patterns of organizational behavior found among social movement and third-sector organizations generally. First, the pressure to adopt formal organizational structures was clearly strong, as most of the P/CROs in each region did so over time. The lack of appreciable cross-regional variation in this respect points to the immense pressure organizations experience to adopt familiar and successful structural forms.

Second, adopting formal structures also enabled the P/CROs to mobilize critically important foreign funding. Virtually every organization relied heavily on funding from foreign governments and foundations, and members frequently reported that formal organizational structures were necessary to manage the institutional rules and regulations that accompanied such funding. Although local networks were crucial to the P/CROs' mobilization of human resources, foreign funding ultimately encouraged and enabled the P/CROs to grow, formalize, and survive in the midst of hostile local environments characterized not only by violent conflict but also by political volatility and fluctuating public and membership support.

Third, the P/CROs across the sample had a tendency to use an eclectic mix of tactics. The P/CROs demonstrated overwhelmingly a proclivity to use the broadest tactical repertoire possible given their organizational resources and members' moral preferences. Not only were the P/CROs in every region likely to use a mix of tactics, but a similar tactical repertoire was known and available to the P/CROs across the three regions, providing evidence of increasing globalization. The high number of P/CROs that mixed strategies, combined with the fact that almost half engaged in protest activities, also supports other scholars' observations that protest is becoming a common part of everyday politics, as noted in Meyer and Tarrow's recent book in which they discuss this trend toward the creation of a *movement society*: "We have observed that one of the characteristics of the movement society is that social movements can combine disruptive and conventional activities and forms of organization, while institutional actors like interest groups and parties increasingly engage in contentious behavior."[51]

Although the P/CROs displayed a strong tendency to mobilize foreign funding, adopt formal structures, and use an eclectic mix of tactics drawn from a globally familiar tactical repertoire, the findings also revealed powerful niche development within each region. Therefore, the study provides strong support for those scholars who claim that members' ideologies must be considered in any analysis of organizational behavior. For instance, ideological commitments to egalitarianism, single goals, and small budgets influenced the degree to which the P/CROs formalized their structures, and members' professional expertise and moral beliefs clearly determined the dominant strategy of action that each P/CRO pursued. Scholars also suggest that niche development is not only common in social movements but may be advantageous to their success, as different types of organizations can fill needed roles.[52] Therefore, as Jasper recently suggested, to understand the nature of organizational behavior future studies of P/CROs and NGOs generally must examine more fully the lives, expertise, and beliefs of members and especially of charismatic founders and leaders.[53]

Documenting the organizational experiences and attributes of P/CROs is an important first step to an enhanced understanding of such organizations. Arguably, however, the most compelling question remains: what impact do P/CROs have on the public attitudes, political decisions, and overall level of violence in unstable or violent regions? The chapter on efficacy in this book describes this study's findings in this regard. But determining the effectiveness of certain ideological, resource, structural, and tactical attributes is extremely difficult to conclusively ascertain. P/CROs are but one set of actors—politicians and the media being among the others—shaping public attitudes and setting the political agenda. Nonetheless, if we aim to understand the roles that such organizations play in preventing and resolving conflicts around the globe, future studies will need to devise innovative ways to assess the efficacy of such organizations.

Notes

1. Donald H. Akenson, *God's Peoples: Covenant and Land in South Africa, Israel and Ulster* (Ithaca, N.Y.: Cornell University Press, 1992); H. Giliomee and J. Gagiano, J., eds., *The Elusive Search for Peace* (Cape Town, South Africa: Oxford University Press, 1990).

2. R. Pagnucco, J. Smith, et al., "Social Movement Theory and the Comparative Study of Nonviolent Collective Action," The Joan B. Kroc Institute for International Peace Studies Working Paper Series, 1992.

3. For several reasons detailed in the Israeli chapter, two autonomous teams—Israeli and Palestinian—independently conducted the data collection for the Israeli/Palestinian sample. Owing to numerous difficulties the Palestinian team faced in collecting data, only the nine Israeli cases have been used in this comparative analysis. In addition, the comparative team determined that two cases in the Northern Irish sample did not adequately meet the definition of a P/CRO, and therefore, only eight of the ten cases have been included here.

4. J. McCarthy and M. Zald, "Resource Mobilization and Social Movement: A Partial Theory," *American Journal of Sociology* 82 (1977): 1212–1241; Y. Hasenfeld, *Human Service Organizations* (Englewood Cliffs, N.J.: Prentice-Hall, 1983).

5. S. Dunn and F. Cochrane, Quaker House case report for ISPO study, 1998, p. 9.

6. S. Stacey, Center for the Study of Violence and Reconciliation case report for ISPO study, 1998, p. 3.

7. T. Hermann, Bat Shalom case report for ISPO study, 1998, p. 2.

8. D. McAdam, "Micromobilization Contexts and Recruitment to Activism," *International Social Movement Research* 1 (1988): 125–154; D. Della Porta, "Recruitment Processes in Clandestine Political Organizations: Italian Left-Wing Terrorism," *International Social Movement Research* 1 (1988): 155–169; R. J. Kendrick, "Meaning and Participation: Perspectives of Peace Movement Participants," *Research in Social Movements, Conflicts and Change* 13 (1991): 91–111.

9. S. Tarrow, *Power in Movement: Social Movements, Collective Action and Politics* (Cambridge, Mass.: Cambridge University Press, 1994), pp. 136, 150.

10. S. Dunn and F. Cochrane, Families Against Intimidation and Terror case report for ISPO study, 1998, p. 35.

11. S. Stacey, the End Conscription Campaign case report for the ISPO study, 1998, p. 33.

12. R. Dalton, *The Green Rainbow: Environmental Groups in Western Europe* (New Haven, Conn.: Yale University Press, 1994); D. McAdam, "Tactical Inno-

vation and the Pace of Insurgency," *American Sociological Review* 48 (1983): 735–754; D. Minkoff, *Organizing for Equality: The Evolution of Women's and Racial-Ethnic Organizations in America, 1955–1985* (New Brunswick, N.J.: Rutgers University Press, 1995).

13. R. Dalton, *The Green Rainbow*; J. Ennis, "Fields of Action: Structure in Movements' Tactical Repertoires," *Sociological Forum* 2 (1987): 520–533; J. Jasper, *The Art of Moral Protest* (Chicago: University of Chicago Press, 1997).

14. D. Minkoff, "Bending with the Wind: Strategic Change and Adaptation by Women's and Racial Minority Organizations," *American Journal of Sociology* 104 (1999): 1666–1073.

15. T. Hermann, Peace Now case report for ISPO study, 1998, p. 6.

16. T. Hermann, Council on Peace and Security case report for ISPO study, 1998, p. 12.

17. Minkoff, *Organizing for Equality*; Minkoff, "Bending with the Wind."

18. S. Dunn and F. Cochrane, Quaker House case report, p. 40.

19. P. DiMaggio and W. Powell, *The New Institutionalism in Organizational Analysis* (Chicago: University of Chicago Press, 1991), pp. 63–82; J. McCarthy and M. Zald, "Resource Mobilization and Social Movement"; M. Zald and J. McCarthy, *Social Movements in an Organizational Society* (New Brunswick, N.J.: Transaction Books, 1987), pp. 161–180.

20. R. Dalton, *The Green Rainbow*; C. Hyde, "Feminist Social Movement Organizations Survive the New Right," in *Feminist Organization*, ed. M. M. Ferree and P. Y. Martin (Philadelphia: Temple University Press, 1995), pp. 306–322; N. Mathews, "Feminist Clashes with the State: Tactical Choices by State-Funded Rape Crisis Centers," in *Feminist Organization*, ed. M. M. Ferree and P. Y. Martin (Philadelphia: Temple University Press, 1995), pp. 291–305.

21. A. Lekwane, Institute for a Democratic Alternative in South Africa case report for ISPO study, 1998, p. 10.

22. S. Dunn and F. Cochrane, Peace Train case report for ISPO study, 1998, p. 51.

23. J. McCarthy and M. Zald, "Resource Mobilization and Social Movement"; R. Dalton, *The Green Rainbow*.

24. S. Dunn and F. Cochrane, Ulster Peoples College case report for ISPO study, 1998, p. 28.

25. T. Hermann, Peace Now case report, p. 21.

26. S. Dunn and F. Cochrane, Ulster Peoples College case report, p. 12.

27. J. Freeman, "Political Organization in the Feminist Movement," *Acta-Sociologica* 18 (1975): 233.

28. The term "pragmatic collectives" is borrowed from R. Bordt, *The Structure of Women's Nonprofit Organizations* (Indianapolis: Indiana University Press, 1997).

29. Freeman, "Political Organization in the Feminist Movement," p. 237.

30. T. Hermann, Women in Black case report for ISPO study, 1998, p. 18.

31. T. Hermann, Yesh Gvul case report for ISPO study, 1998, p. 25.

32. S. Dunn and F. Cochrane, Peace Train case report, p. 24.

33. Dalton, *The Green Rainbow*; C. Hyde, "Feminist Social Movement Organizations Survive the New Right"; N. Mathews, "Feminist Clashes with the State."

34. H. Johnston and B. Klandermans, *Social Movements and Culture* (Minneapolis: University of Minnesota Press, 1995), pp. 3–24; D. Snow and R. Benford, "Ideology, Frame Resonance, and Participant Mobilization," *International Social Movement Research* 1 (1988): 197–217; D. Snow and R. Benford, "Master Frames and Cycles of Protest," in *Frontiers in Social Movement Theory*, ed. A. Morris and C. M. Mueller (New Haven, Conn.: Yale University Press, 1992), pp. 133–155.

35. J. Gelb, "Social Movement 'Success': A Comprehensive Analysis of Feminism in the United States and the United Kingdom," in *The Women's Movements of the United States and Western Europe: Consciousness, Political Opportunity, and Public Policy*, ed. M. F. Katzenstein and C. Mueller (Philadelphia: Temple University Press, 1987), pp. 267–289; H. Kitschelt, "Political Opportunity Structures and Political Protest: Anti-Nuclear Movements in Four Democracies," *British Journal of Political Science* 16 (1986): 57–85; H. Kriesi, R. Koopmans, et al., *New Social Movements in Western Europe: A Comparative Analysis* (Minneapolis: University of Minnesota Press, 1995); D. Rucht, "The Impact of National Contexts on Social Movement Structures: A Cross-Movement and Cross-National Comparison," in *Comparative Perspectives on Social Movements*, ed. D. McAdam, J. McCarthy, and M. Zald (New York: Cambridge University Press, 1996), pp. 185–204.

36. S. Dunn and F. Cochrane, Women Together case report for ISPO study, 1998, p. 9.

37. J. Whyte, *Interpreting Northern Ireland* (Oxford: Clarendon Press, 1990), p. 195.

38. M. Fitzduff, "Managing Community Relations and Conflict: Voluntary Organizations and Government and the Search for Peace," in *Voluntary Action and Social Policy in Northern Ireland*, ed. N. Acheson and A. Williamson (Aldershot: Avebury, 1995), pp. 63–81.

39. D. Morrow, "In Search of Common Ground," in *Northern Ireland Politics*, ed. A. Aughey and D. Morrow (London: Longman, 1996), pp. 56–64.

40. T. Hermann, Council on Peace and Security case report, p. 2.

41. S. Stacey, the Center for Conflict Resolution case report for ISPO study, 1998, p. 16.

42. R. Taylor, Final Country Report, South Africa, 1998, Section 4.1.6.

43. P. Waugh, Quaker Peace Center case report for ISPO study, 1998, p. 60.

44. D. Gerner, "The Arab-Israeli Conflict," in *U.S. Foreign Policy in the Third World*, ed. P. Schraeder (Boulder: Lynne Reinner Publishers, 1992), pp. 361–382.

45. J. Tonge, *Northern Ireland* (London: Prentice Hall, 1998), p. 152.

46. C. Tilly, *From Mobilization to Revolution* (Reading, Pa.: Addison-Wesley Publishing Company, 1978).

47. C. Tilly, "Repertoires of Contention in America and Britain, 1750–1830," in *The Dynamics of Social Movements: Resource Mobilization, Social Control, and Tactics*, ed. M. Zald and J. McCarthy (Cambridge: Winthrop Publishers, 1979), p. 131.

48. C. Taylor, Black Sash case report for ISPO study, 1998, p. 29.

49. S. Dunn and F. Cochrane, Quaker House case report, 1998, p. 13.

50. T. Hermann, Yesh Gvul case report, p. 7.

51. D. Meyer and S. Tarrow, "A Movement Society: Contentious Politics for a New Century," in *The Social Movement Society*, ed. D. Meyer and S. Tarrow (New York: Rowman & Littlefield Publishers, 1998), p. 25.

52. R. Dalton, *The Green Rainbow*; Jasper, *The Art of Moral Protest*; M. Zald and J. McCarthy, *Social Movements in an Organizational Society*, pp. 161–180.

53. Jasper, *The Art of Moral Protest*.

9

THE EFFICACY OF THE PEACE AND CONFLICT-RESOLUTION ORGANIZATIONS: A COMPARATIVE PERSPECTIVE

Assessing the efficacy of peace and conflict-resolution organizations (P/CROs)—namely, the extent to which they contributed to the promotion of peace, the resolution of intergroup conflicts, or a just society—is a very vexing issue. Viewing P/CROs from the perspective of the third sector, we face the typical problems of measuring organizational effectiveness.[1] These organizations often confront diverse constituencies with different expectations, resulting in various and conflicting goals. As a result, they encounter multiple conceptions of effectiveness. As Au suggested in the case of nonprofit organizations, the definition of effectiveness is ultimately subjective and normative.[2] The problem is further confounded when we attempt to assess the impact of a network or a class of organizations, as this study does.

One possible approach is to focus primarily on the services that nonprofit organizations provided and evaluate their contributions to the welfare state.[3] Although some of the P/CROs did provide services, this was not their primary focus. Therefore, this method is less useful to our study. A broader approach is to assess the contributions of these organizations to the civil society, in terms of fostering civic participation, extending social networks, and contributing to democratic institutions. Whether or not these organizations have positively contributed to the civil society has certainly been a contentious issue.[4] While some see virtue in their very existence, scholars have also noted that the state can make sinister use of them.[5]

Undoubtedly the P/CROs in all three regions attempted to develop mediating structures between the state and the public, strengthen network relations and ties, and increase citizen participation in vital issues facing the society. In Palestine, for example, these and other nongovernmental agencies helped meet civic and social needs when no central authority existed. When the Palestinian Authority emerged, these organizations began to mediate between citizens and representatives of the Authority and to advocate on the citizens' behalf. In South Africa, these organizations represented important civic associations that gave citizens an opportunity to participate openly in anti-apartheid activities and to provide and receive services to counter the regime's effects. In Northern Ireland, many of these organizations engaged in community building and development with the explicit aim of empowering residents. Similarly, in Israel, several of these organizations offered citizens opposed to the occupation new channels, outside the political parties, to express their views and provided distinct educational and support services that would not have been available otherwise.

Assessing the contributions of these organizations to the civic society intersects with another view of the P/CROs as social movement organizations. There has been considerable research on the efficacy of social movements.[6] Yet evaluating the efficacy of the P/CROs from this perspective is no less difficult. As Klandermans writes, "The success and failure of movements are complicated to examine, if only because the answer to the question of whether the outcomes of a social movement organization's efforts to act upon its environment succeed or fail is a matter of interpretation which depends on the standards used and on who is making the judgement."[7]

This is clearly the case in our study. Not only did the concept of peace acquire a distinct local meaning in each region, but the organizations we studied did not necessarily coalesce around it. For example, in Northern Ireland the concept of peace generally meant achieving inter-community dialogue and collaboration; however, for some it meant the redress of ethnic inequality or the development of strong single-identity community institutions. In Israel, the concept of peace was fraught with ambiguous meanings: for some it simply represented an amorphous notion of ending the occupation; for others it signified granting the Palestinians their national aspirations and developing normal neighborly relations with them. The Palestinian situation was similar: while all agreed that "peace" meant the establishment of a Palestinian state, some also included democracy and social justice as their goals. In South Africa, too, there were different ideas about what "peace" meant: for most it implied not only ending apartheid but also the formation of a democratic society; others also included the reduction of social, economic, and ethnic inequalities. Thus, the different meanings of peace within and among the various regions make it difficult to assess the P/CROs' overall impact in each country, let alone across countries.

Moreover, in all three regions—especially Israel/Palestine and Northern Ireland—the outcomes are still unfolding, with ebbs and flows that evoke either optimism or pessimism depending on the particular time frame that is considered. As the peace and conflict-resolution processes take their twists and turns, what is viewed as success at one point in time may turn into perceived failure at another. For example, the efficacy of the Palestinian P/CROs is viewed very differently before and after the Oslo Accords. Likewise, many of the South African P/CROs radically shifted their objectives when apartheid ended. Therefore, timing is an important factor in assessing the success or failure of social movements. Periods of crisis may improve a movement's chances of success. Similarly, a movement may initially gain advantages, only to see them erode later on. Moreover, initial successes may provoke counter-movements, thereby creating a "backlash."[8] In other words, each major time period in the life cycle of a social movement is characterized by a particular political context that influences a movement's ability to succeed. For example, the Israeli P/CROs had appreciably more influence on government policies when the Labor Party was in power. After the assassination of Prime Minister Yitzhak Rabin and the rise to power of the Likud Party and its leader, Binyamin Netanyahu, the P/CROs lost this influence and even experienced considerable backlash.

There is also a fundamental problem in attributing causality. In all three regions many forces far more powerful than the P/CROs influenced the peace process. These, of course, included the state regime itself, the main protagonists in the conflict (e.g., the paramilitary organizations in Northern Ireland, the African National Congress (ANC) in South Africa, and the Palestine Liberation Organization (PLO) in Palestine), changes in local and global political alignments, foreign governments and international organizations, and public opinion. This makes it very difficult to isolate the contributions, if any, of the P/CROs. It is quite possible that the larger forces that made the peace process possible also facilitated the emergence of the P/CROs and made their agendas more receptive. Moreover, some studies that have attempted to measure the efficacy of social movement organizations in changing governmental policies suggest that their effectiveness is modest at best.[9] As Tamar Hermann states in the Israeli Final Country Report, "The accumulated body of research on the efficacy of social movements in general, and peace movements in particular, suggests that it is, in fact, minimal. This seems to be the case even when these political actors are highly active and well organized. Therefore, there may be little to measure."[10]

However, this view may be overly pessimistic. If we broaden our perspective to consider the P/CROs' impact not just on governmental policies but also on the broader collective good, then the efficacy of such organizations may become more substantial. Amenta and Young suggest that collective goods may be concrete—such as benefits to the constituencies of the movement—but also intangible, such as changes in mainstream cultural beliefs, images, and language.[11] From this perspective, the question is no longer simply whether the P/CROs met their stated goals, but rather whether their activities provided collective benefits to their constituencies. For example, when Bruce Kent, a major figure in the Campaign for Nuclear Disarmament, reflects back on the movement's achievements, he acknowledges that the peace movement did not stop the deployment of such weapons.[12] However, he points to broader collective benefits that resulted from the movement. These include breaking the secrecy about nuclear weapons and empowering citizens to openly debate and question the authority of military leaders on this issue, giving women a stronger voice on this and related issues about national security, and encouraging public demand for civil rights in Eastern Europe during the 1980s. Similarly, in this chapter we will not only ask whether these organizations influenced national policies, but also whether the regions would have fared worse without the P/CROs.

Theoretical Perspective

In this chapter, we adopt an approach developed more recently by social movement scholars, which recognizes that the P/CROs' contributions are multidimensional and more encompassing than the traditional measures of achieving public acceptance and recognition and changing policies.[13] In particular, we pay special attention to the cultural contributions of these organizations. We examine the extent to which the P/CROs contributed to their country's cultural repertoire, which Swidler defines as a "tool kit of symbols, stories, rituals, and world views . . . [as well as] culturally-shaped skills, habits, and styles" from which groups may draw to frame their grievances and develop innovative tactics.[14] Gamson proposes assessing a social movement's impact on cultural change through analysis of public discourse, particularly the mass media.[15] Building upon his previous work, Gamson suggests two measures of success: (1) the cultural acceptance of the social movement as indicated by its "gaining the status of a regular media source whose interpretations are directly quoted,"[16] and (2) new cultural advantages as indicated by the prominence given to the movement's preferred "frames" (i.e., how the movement defines and views the nature of the conflict, its causes, and its remedies) as compared to antagonistic frames.

We emphasize cultural impact because we recognize that the P/CROs may have had little direct political effect in light of the powerful political forces operating in each region. On the other hand, the P/CROs did adopt and pursue new frames to define the conflict and its solution.[17] They clearly hoped to influence the ways in which the public, in general, and political elites, in particular, viewed the conflict and entertained alternative nonviolent solutions. Therefore, it is important to assess the extent to which the P/CROs succeeded in institutionalizing these new frames in public discourse.

Synthesizing the various approaches to measuring the efficacy of social movements,[18] we developed the following dimensions for our study:

1. *Impact on the peace/conflict resolution*: the extent to which the P/CROs, in the aggregate, contributed to important events or developments in the peace process.
2. *Impact on the peace-making/conflict-resolution process*: the extent to which the P/CROs gained access to the parties involved in the conflict and government officials; brought about changes in the political processes (e.g., the rise of new political parties, changes in political coalitions, changes in governmental procedures) that contributed toward the peace/conflict resolution.
3. *Impact in defining the conflict and its resolution*: the extent to which the P/CROs brought about changes in public perceptions about the conflict and its resolution; created new ways to define and describe the conflict, including the parties involved in the conflict; introduced new norms of conduct or relations between people representing the various factions in the conflict (e.g., new images of the people involved in the conflict, new modes of dialogue); linked its ideas about peace/conflict-resolution to other values, such as democracy, human rights, and social justice; developed a new set of strategies or activities (e.g., public demonstrations, dialogue groups, educational materials, media events) to promote peace/conflict resolution.

By adopting a comparative perspective, we also explore the degree to which the regional differences in cultural, political, and organizational patterns may have played a role in affecting the P/CROs' efficacy in each country.

Methodology

Each country team was asked to interview three to five representatives of (1) the mass media (i.e., newspapers, radio, and television) who had covered the conflict; (2) political leaders (formal and informal) who were involved with the conflict, as well as those who represented the various factions involved in the conflict; (3) government officials who were responsible for the management and handling of the conflict; (4) academics and intellectuals who had studied and written about the conflict; and (5) recognized leaders of the P/CROs. The teams had various degrees of success in reaching all of these informants. The Israeli team, in particular, had to rely on secondary sources— that is, published books, articles, and newspaper accounts written by politicians, journalists, and leaders of the peace movement. On the basis of the interviews and reviews of available documents, each team prepared a report that presented and analyzed the data for each dimension. These reports form the basis of our comparative analysis. We quote from them extensively to illustrate and support our findings.

The reader should bear in mind the context and particularly the status of the peace process in each country when these interviews were conducted and how those factors might have affected the respondents' assessment of the P/CROs' impact. In South Africa, the assessment occurred during a period in which the apartheid regime had been successfully and peacefully terminated, and the country had experienced its first democratically elected government. In Israel and Palestine, on the other hand, the assessment took place after the assassination of Prime Minister Rabin and the ascendancy to power of the coalition under Prime Minister Netanyahu that brought the peace process to a grinding halt. These events had a profound effect on both the Israeli and the Palestinian peace organizations. In Northern Ireland, the Irish Republican Army (IRA) reinstated its cease-fire in 1997, the Good Friday Agreement was signed on April 10, 1998, and a majority of the population voted for a new Northern Irish Assembly. Nonetheless, considerable doubts existed about the willingness and ability of the contesting parties to actually implement the agreement.

Findings

Influence on Key Events in the Peace/Conflict-Resolution Process

Across the three regions, there was a general consensus among the respondents that the P/CROs had had limited, and possibly marginal, impact on the critical events that shaped the course of the peace process in each country. This was not unexpected since in each region critical events were influenced either by the main protagonists in the conflict or by external international events. Nonetheless, informants from all three regions could point to at least one critical event in which the P/CROs played a significant role, although often there was no consensus about the impact that role had had on the peace process.

In Israel, the most critical event was the Oslo process, culminating in the signing of the Accords in September 1993. Among the activists in the peace movement—especially the founders of Peace Now—there was a strongly held belief that the movement had laid the groundwork for the Accords through the many informal contacts and dialogues the movement had made with the Palestinians at a time when the state had outlawed such contacts. They believed that these contacts had provided the much-needed modicum of mutual trust that enabled the subsequent negotiations in Oslo. To quote from the Israeli Report, "Thus, not only did the peace movement openly and strongly support the launch of the Oslo Process, but perceived it to be a victory of its own making."[19] Reuben Kaminer, a peace activist, stated that, "From any point of view, the Declaration of Principles bore the deep imprint of the peace movement."[20]

On the other hand, the policymakers' assessments were quite mixed and contradictory. Politicians from the Labor Party tried to minimize the peace movement's influence on the Oslo process because they did not want the public and their opponents to perceive them as being unduly influenced by the movement. They wanted to portray the peace process as a "rational strategy," emanating from a careful consideration of geopolitical developments. Politicians from the Likud Party, who were opposed to the Oslo Agreement, took the opposite view, namely that the peace movement had co-opted the Labor Party. In doing so, they hoped to demonstrate that the Labor Party had succumbed to "radical" political pressures. That the major political parties—both those that supported and those that opposed the Accords—had to come to grips with and argue about the peace movement's role in and alleged contributions to the peace process is in itself a testimony to the fact that the movement played a role that neither party could ignore.

For the Palestinian P/CROs, the Intifada—the uprising of young Palestinians to challenge the Israeli occupation—was a critical event that had important implications. The P/CROs used the opportunity to influence not the event itself but its consequences, namely pushing toward the Oslo Accords. The P/CROs joined and supported the aims of the Intifada and capitalized on it to document and disseminate—especially in the international media—abuses by the Israeli army and human rights violations. Via their relations with international organizations and an effective international media campaign, they were able to mobilize international support for their cause. Many of the informants felt that these efforts brought considerable international pressure on Israel to enter into negotiations with the PLO and helped galvanize the peace movement in Israel itself.

In Northern Ireland, it was very difficult to discern whether the P/CROs had any impact on the critical events leading to the Good Friday Agreement. A few respondents suggested that the P/CROs had played some role in the work of the 1993 Opsahl Commission, which was one of the earliest efforts to establish a dialogue between the protagonists. The Northern Ireland Report quotes one respondent as saying, "I think the Opsahl Commission created a climate in terms of people saying that groups must engage and we must be actually looking at some level of compromise and that the absolutes must be broken down. I think Opsahl was also important for very clearly reaching out in terms of speaking to republicans and loyalists and trying to break down some of the stereotypes."[21] Still, several respondents argued that the events leading to the IRA cease-fire and the Good Friday Agreement actually resulted from the escalation of violence, which finally pushed the parties into negotiations. There was an overwhelming agreement among respondents that the P/CROs had no direct impact on any of the key events leading to the Good Friday Agreement.

In South Africa, the July 1987 Dakar meeting between reform-minded members of the Afrikaner elite and the African National Congress signified a major turning point in the struggle against apartheid. For the first time, a meaningful dialogue ensued between the protagonists, and the prominence of the participants gave legitimacy to the feasibility of a democratic nonracial society in South Africa. In some sense, this event is analogous to the secret contacts between Israeli and PLO emissaries preparing the ground for the Oslo Accords. The Institute for a Democratic Alternative for South Africa (Idasa), one of the most prominent P/CROs in South Africa, initiated and organized the meeting. The South African Report quotes several participants in the event: Theuns Eloff stated, "I think Dakar will yet be seen as the water-shed in the negotiation process";[22] Kader Asmal declared, "On a very personal level it had an extraordinary effect, at a personal level. And the personal should never be excluded, you see, in the political. So from that point of view Dakar was a turning point";[23] Alex Boraine made the point that "half the Cabinet [of today] were at Dakar . . . we showed that Africa is open to South Africans, black and white, who have abandoned apartheid and are genuinely searching for a non-racial democracy . . . [it] point[s] towards the possibility of a negoti-ated settlement."[24] While several P/CROs also participated in the implementa-tion of the National Peace accord, the signal role of Idasa in organizing the Dakar meeting stands out as one of the P/CROs' most significant contributions to the events leading to the dismantling of the apartheid regime.

Impact on the Political Process

To assess the impact that the P/CROs might have had on the political pro-cesses to achieve peace or resolution of the conflict, we first examined the degree to which these organizations had access to the various political groups involved in the processes. Of all three regions, only Israel had a representa-tive democracy at the time of the study; therefore, the Israeli P/CROs had the greatest potential for gaining access to the political parties. In Palestine, few P/CROs existed prior to the Intifada, and most of the nongovernmental orga-nizations (NGOs) were formed as an extension of the PLO. Following the Oslo Accords and the formation of the Palestinian Authority, the emerging P/CROs faced a nascent political entity to which access had yet to be institutionalized. Therefore, it was unclear whether the P/CROs could find any effective chan-nels to influence the Authority. In Northern Ireland, the nature of the con-flict itself, coupled with the British government's direct rule, preempted the importance of conventional political groups. Paramilitary groups filled the void, and we did not expect the P/CROs to have any significant contact with them. South Africa operated under an apartheid regime; nonetheless, the tricameral parliament structure and the existence of formal political parties provided some limited access opportunities for the white-led P/CROs. Mostly, however, access had to be informal. In the case of the ANC, of course, it had to be clandestine.

In sum, the findings indicate that in both Israel and South Africa certain P/CROs did have access to important political parties, but these contacts were mostly either informal or clandestine in nature. In Palestine, after the Oslo Accords, the relations between the P/CROs and the Palestinian Authority became quite strained. In Northern Ireland the P/CROs had no access to significant political parties.

As expected, therefore, the Israeli P/CROs were best able to gain access to some of the political parties. In particular, there was a close alliance between Peace Now and Bat Shalom with the Meretz Party. Indeed, the Meretz Party became an effective political lobby on behalf of the movement, especially during the years in which the Party served in the Labor coalition government (1992–1996) and adopted the goals of Peace Now in its political platform. In addition, a number of key activists, again mostly from Peace Now, had personal relations with important figures in the Labor Party. However, the P/CROs had limited capacity to influence the Labor Party's decision-making processes. Despite having attained several access points, the P/CROs were not able to engage the Labor Party decision makers when they were in power, particularly because the Party was concerned that the public not perceive it as being influenced or "captured" by the peace movement. Thus, when the Meretz Party was part of the Labor coalition, Prime Minister Rabin accused it of being too close to the peace movement. In other words, the potent party rivalries and tenuous governing coalitions that characterize Israeli electoral politics made it difficult for the peace movement to use its political access to influence the national policies about the peace process.

In Palestine the P/CROs faced a paradoxical situation after the Oslo Accords. Prior to the Accords, it was difficult to distinguish between the P/CROs and other organizational entities that the PLO developed and sponsored. The P/CROs were very much an instrument of the PLO in the struggle to gain recognition for the Palestinians' right to self-determination. In particular, they were an important voice against the human rights abuses of the Israeli occupation. After the Accords, the P/CROs distanced themselves from the Palestinian Authority since it too became a target for human rights violations. Contact with the Authority became quite problematic and fraught with apprehension for fear of retaliation. Thus, although some individual members of the P/CROs had personal contact with Authority officials, access became exceedingly limited.

As noted earlier, the Northern Ireland P/CROs had no appreciable access to any of the main political players. Although some organizations, such as Quaker House, provided a discrete forum where opposing political leaders could meet, most of the P/CROs did not pursue access to political leaders. Organizations such as Families Against Intimidation and Terror (FAIT) actually demonstrated against the political parties of both sides (i.e., Sinn Féin and the Progressive Unionist Party). The P/CROs that focused their efforts on intra- or inter-community level activities, such as the Ulster People's College, Clogher Valley Rural Development, and Springfield Inter-Community Development Project, pursued access to or cultivated local community leaders with some degree of success.

In South Africa, the core P/CROs established various degrees of contact with mass-based movements (e.g., ANC, United Democratic Front or UDF), and political parties (e.g., National Party or NP, Inkatha), despite the apartheid regime. Of course, these relations were either informal or clandestine. For example, Idasa had contact with the ANC, the UDF, the unions, the National Party, and the Progressive Federal Party/Democratic Party. Black Sash had close ties to and shared similar objectives with the UDF and the unions. It also had contacts with the NP, but these focused on registering its opposition to the NP's policies. The End Conscription Campaign (ECC) had very close ties to the UDF.[25] Several P/CROs attempted to establish contact with both sides of the conflict in order to initiate some form of dialogue. As noted earlier, these included Idasa, with the Dakar meeting, and the Centre for Intergroup Studies—in the person of H. W. van der Merwe—which tried to initiate dialogue between the National Party and the ANC in the early 1980s. The ANC also engaged in some individual contacts with several P/CROs, mostly to gather political intelligence and influence their strategies.[26]

As expected, the differential access that the P/CROs had in each of the three regions was manifested in their abilities to influence the respective political processes. In Israel, the peace movement—particularly Peace Now—established itself as an important political force whose demands the political elite could not ignore. Doug Stuck, an external observer of the peace movement, offered the following assessments in the Israeli Report: "It has painstakingly helped turn the question of returning land to the Palestinians from one of 'whether' to one of 'how much,'" and "It shamed the Israeli government into pulling its troops back from Beirut after the invasion of Lebanon."[27] Other informants were less enthusiastic but acknowledged that the peace movement had had some impact on the political process. They recounted such specific political events as pressuring Prime Minister Menachem Begin into making peace with Egypt, and the fact that during the years that the Labor Party was in power (1992–1996), the government's peace agenda resembled that of the peace movement. Of course, the assassination of Prime Minister Rabin and the subsequent change in government a few months later greatly diminished the peace movement's influence.

In addition to the dominant influence among the P/CROs of Peace Now on the political process, it is worth noting the impact of There is a Limit. By advocating for the refusal of soldiers to serve in the Occupied Territories, it triggered a serious concern among the military and the political establishment of the possibility that reserve soldiers' motivation to serve could massively decline. The Israeli Report notes that, "It also encouraged a wave of 'gray' disobedience, that is, a massive number of reserve soldiers who asked to be exempt from service for feigned medical or economic reasons."[28]

In Palestine, as noted earlier, the P/CROs worked very closely and in concert with the PLO to influence international public opinion prior to the Oslo Accords. The aim was to generate pressure on the Israeli government to stop human rights abuses and to acknowledge the national aspirations of the Palestinians. There was a consensus among the informants that these efforts also served as a check on the Israeli authorities. While they did not eliminate abuses, they certainly prevented their escalation. A number of organizations rejected the Oslo Accords as a "bad" deal for the Palestinians and thus were denied any influence on the Palestinian Authority after the Accords were passed. Others who became concerned with and spoke out against the authoritarian style of the Authority and its own human rights abuses also found themselves excluded from any access or significant political influence. Although a number of organizations raised this issue, even under the threat of imprisonment, the assessment of such advocates as Dr. Nusseibeh was that the effect was minimal.[29]

In Northern Ireland, there was a consensus among the informants that the P/CROs had no overt influence on the political process. According to one informant, the demonstrations, such as the Peace People's rallies, "signalled that there was a considerable section of the community totally opposed to violence, and there was always a rein on terrorism and on those who went for the violent option."[30] However, other observers argued that the large-scale movements, which tried to mobilize mass opinion through public demonstrations, marches, and vigils, actually gave "peace" a bad name by "peddling . . . soft and trite messages by a self-appointed middle-class elite."[31]

On the other hand, there was greater consensus that the P/CROs, especially those doing community and development work, did lay the groundwork for the emergence of important locality-based political institutions that could influence the peace process. By attracting and enabling people from the contesting communities to mobilize and work together on shared problems, the P/CROs also showed how a political agreement might be forged. In other words, the P/CROs contributed to a gradual grassroots mobilization of people for community-based political action. In the process, they cultivated community leaders within both loyalist and republican communities who could play a crucial linking role between the traditional political process and their communities. To quote one informant, "There is no way that the old-style politicians could have brokered a deal which would have been sold to those communities, because those communities would not have been part of it if their community leaders had not been part of the talks, and the NGO sector has probably been instrumental in helping that forward."[32] This view, therefore, sees the efficacy of the P/CRO sector in terms of producing new leaders and activists within the local communities who, over a period of time, had a significant effect on the political process and the level of politically motivated violence in Northern Ireland. These pressures from below to reduce violence and increase dialogue enabled the main political antagonists to legitimate their own efforts in finding a political settlement to the conflict.

In South Africa, the P/CROs used their informal and clandestine contacts with the political parties and mass movements to influence the political process. However, they met with various degrees of success. The South African Institute of Race Relations' databases and annual surveys of race relations were particularly influential in the formulation and justification of the ANC's policy statements and positions. Idasa used its contacts with the ANC to obtain its blessing for the Dakar meeting. Black Sash and the South African Institute of Race Relations (SAIRR) had regular contacts with government officials—mostly to protest against their actions—but they had little success.

In general, the Afrikaner-controlled state institutions were impervious to the P/CROs' efforts. One notable exception was the the Rikhoto case, in which Black Sash, the Legal Resources Centre, and the Transvaal Rural Action Committee (TRAC) waged a successful legal battle to give urban residence rights to "black" South Africans with an unbroken employment record of ten years in a city.[33] Similarly, the ECC's activities against military conscription, which resulted in the group's banning, nonetheless led the apartheid regime to reassess its military capability to wage war against its neighbors (Angola and Namibia). The South Africa Report quotes Willem de Klerk as saying, "ECC had a considerable influence also on Afrikaner students who were getting sick of the so-called war against communism."[34]

Summary: Impact on Politics

Reviewing our findings thus far regarding the P/CROs' relative effectiveness in shaping events and influencing the political processes in the three regions, a key factor stands out: the political context in each region. The structure of the political institutions, the makeup of the political elites, the stability of and changes in political alignments, and the state's capacity and willingness to repress dissent all played a major role in the P/CROs' ability to facilitate policy changes in their respective countries.[35]

In Israel, the P/CROs were more successful because they operated in a political environment characterized by a representative democracy, a heterogeneous political elite, coalition governments in which small parties had considerable influence, and a regime that was reluctant to repress dissent, coupled with a free press. Although this political structure provided several access points for the P/CROs, it also moderated their political influence because of the regime's dependence on frail coalitions to maintain power.

At the other extreme we find the Northern Ireland P/CROs, which had no appreciable impact because they operated in a political vacuum that was taken over by the paramilitaries. The British government's direct rule preempted local political institutions and greatly diminished the role of conventional political parties. The political elites, so to speak, were taken over by their military arms—the IRA, the Ulster Volunteer Force, and the Ulster Defence Association. By using violence and intimidation they could readily suppress dissent, despite the existence of an open press. It is not surprising that in such an environment several P/CROs opted to work at the local community level, helping to develop intercommunity institutions and leadership. In doing so, they attempted to influence micro-level political institutions with the hope that these would exert counterpressure from below against the paramilitaries.

During the apartheid years, South Africa's political context was characterized by a pseudo-representative democracy open only to whites, a moderately free press, a monolithic political elite, and a regime with a high capacity and willingness to repress dissent. Yet, in the 1980s—the years during which the P/CROs were most active—there were also visible signs of unstable political alignments, in large measure due to the black uprising that forced the government to adopt several political and economic liberalization measures. These included, for example, legalizing black trade unions, allowing the political participation of coloreds and Indians, and accepting such broad-based political organizations as the United Democratic Front and the National Forum. In this environment, the P/CROs found political allies and had greater access to the major political players, including both the ANC and the National Party. At the same time, the apartheid regime's enormous consolidation of power enhanced its repressive capacities, limiting greatly the P/CROs' ability to influence the political process. However, in such a centralized regime, singular political events had signal effects on the process, as evidenced by the Dakar meeting and the campaign to end conscription.

Finally, the Palestinian P/CROs found themselves operating in a political context that was undergoing rapid changes, especially with the emergence of the Palestinian Authority. Prior to the Oslo Accords, the political target had been external—the Israeli occupation. After the Accords, the P/CROs faced a nascent regime that was authoritarian, repressive, and controlled by a small and powerful political elite. In such a context, the P/CROs lacked both access and influence.

Achieving Cultural Change

Probably the most important achievement of the P/CROs in all three regions was their ability to create cultural images and symbols that provided new and novel frames for the definition and resolution of the conflicts. Once these new frames were accepted more broadly into public discourse, they provided powerful alternative models on how to think about, respond to, and resolve the conflict. In other words, the P/CROs were most successful at enriching the cultural toolkit available for public debates and discussions by offering novel ways to advance the cause of peace and conflict resolution. Still, as Gamson cautions, "It is quite possible to win the battle of public discourse without being able to convert this into new advantages that flow from actually changing public policy."[36] As we saw earlier, this was particularly the case in Northern Ireland, and to some extent in Israel.

In all three regions the P/CROs were very active and quite successful in promoting new frames. In Israel, the peace movement's most significant accomplishment was its ability to influence public opinion by offering two alternative themes that had not been hitherto visible in the mass media. The first was the notion that the occupation was a political, financial, and moral liability rather than a strategic asset. Indeed, the occupation had been framed as a threat to the long-term security and the "Jewish" identity of the state. Second, and equally important, was the idea that the Palestinians had justifiable aspirations for a national identity and a right to self-determination, and that the Intifada was a legitimate Palestinian national struggle. Both of these themes gradually gained greater currency in public discourse. This was one of the greatest accomplishments of Peace Now. Over time there was a clear shift in public opinion so that by the mid-1990s the majority of the Israeli public accepted the Palestinians' right to a state. One of the reasons that Peace Now was successful in changing public discourse was that it cast its position within the dominant Zionist ideology and maintained a strong allegiance to the state.[37]

Legitimizing contact and dialogue between Israelis and Palestinians was another important contribution of the Israeli peace movement. In doing so, the P/CROs broke a major taboo in Israeli society. Organizations such as Bat Shalom showed that joint Israeli-Palestinian peace activity was a feasible option. To quote from the Israeli Report, "The belief in feminism and the desire to raise one's family in a nonviolent environment shared by a number of Palestinian and Israeli women seem to serve as a fairly stable bridge over the various gaps between the two peoples."[38] Similarly, Rapprochement— although its supporters were never able to expand their dialogue group— nonetheless presented an important cultural symbol that sustained itself even at times of serious intercommunity violence. One indication of how contact and dialogue between Israelis and Palestinians became a regular staple in the cultural toolkit was the rise of hundreds of Israeli-Palestinian dialogue groups during the 1980s.[39]

Prior to the Oslo Accords, the Palestinian P/CROs were very active in trying to draw international attention to the Palestinian plight and the human rights violations they suffered. As noted earlier, their target was the international media. There is no doubt that the P/CROs, in concert with the PLO, were successful at introducing a different image of the Palestinians—that of being victims of oppression, thereby countering the oft image of the Palestinians as terrorists. At the same time they were also instrumental in changing the portrayal of the Israelis from beleaguered defenders to ruthless occupiers. After the Oslo Accords, the P/CROs continued their efforts to shape the media discourse about the Israeli occupation's human rights violations, and also tried very gingerly to bring the Palestinian Authority's violations to both the local and international media's attention. At the local level they were less than successful because the Authority controlled the media and maintained heavy-handed censorship.

In Northern Ireland, the engagement of several P/CROs in intercommunity projects and the cultivation of community activists helped to introduce new cultural symbols, a different language in which to address the conflict, and alternative images of peaceful intercommunity relations. In particular, the P/CROs were able to present a new vocabulary that emphasized peaceful coexistence, economic development, social justice, and community harmony. The main political factions then appropriated this vocabulary. To quote one informant in the Northern Ireland Report, "What the NGO sector has been able to do is to stand back a bit and try and articulate what the values should be of a deal, and in as far as that's been there, that has been crucial, and I think we do now have the basic language to put the architecture together."[40] That the major parties to the conflict incorporated this vocabulary into public statements and policy declarations should not, however, be construed as evidence of substantive changes in their ideologies, a point several informants forcefully made.

In South Africa, the P/CROs were particularly effective in promoting the view that the conflict was not simply racial but rather linked to human rights, social justice, and the need for a democratic society. The P/CROs advanced the vision of an alternative social order based on social justice, democratization, responsive social institutions—such as law, education and welfare—and nonviolent conflict resolution. The South African Report quotes Charles Nupen of IMSSA as saying that the aim of the organization was "to present . . . credible alternatives to systems that the apartheid state offered. And . . . that gave people an increasing faith in processes of negotiation and mediation."[41]

The South African P/CROs played a key role in challenging the officially sanctioned conceptions of racial and ethnic identities. They offered instead a nonracialist vision. According to Laurie Nathan, the former director of ECC, it "was a matter of ideology and idealism, it was a matter of analysis, in other words we've misunderstood, we've misdiagnosed, the nature of the problem if you see this as 'white' versus 'black.' And it was also a matter of revolutionary strategy."[42] A major and effective strategy the P/CROs used to break down racialist conceptions was to develop contacts and relations between black and white communities. As Bishop Paul Verryn, a church activist living in Soweto, stated in the South African Report, "And what was good about them [the network] was that there was an interaction between black and white, and both blacks and whites struggled with racism in these organizations, and people had to be educated as to exactly what the issues were. In fact, a lot of these organizations were places of empowerment and places for clarifying the thinking processes for many people, both black and white. They were a forum in which black people could express themselves without fear."[43] In other words, through their various activities the P/CROs successfully challenged the cultural symbols and vocabulary that emanated from and justified the apartheid regime. They offered instead an alternative vocabulary and competing symbols and images to describe and promote a nonracialist society, and in doing so helped to undermine the cultural and moral legitimacy of the regime.

In all three regions the P/CROs were also instrumental in introducing new social action tactics into the dominant cultural toolkit. These included public demonstrations, educational events, dialogue groups, and services to the victims of the conflict. In Israel, Peace Now's mass demonstrations and Women in Black's weekly vigils were new modes of protest that other groups—both for and against the peace process—rapidly adopted. The P/CROs were quite effective in staging public events that drew media attention. Gush Shalom frequently published ads in one of the daily national newspapers to protest the government's policies regarding the peace process. Alternative Information Center (AIC) developed numerous publications on the conflict and was a major source of information for the foreign press. Such organizations as AIC, Bat Shalom, and Rapprochement initiated dialogue as a peace strategy. Several organizations, such as Physicians for Human Rights and Bet Tzelem, provided medical and legal assistance to Palestinians. These were especially important cultural innovations because they promoted a radically different view of the Palestinians as victims while offering an alternative role model for the Israelis.

In Palestine, the P/CROs endorsed and promoted the Intifada—although they did not initiate it—as a legitimate form of protest, especially in the international media. A few organizations, such as the Jerusalem Center for Women and the Palestinian Center for Rapprochement, also initiated dialogue between Palestinians and Israelis, but these efforts were not considered terribly successful, certainly much less so than their Israeli counterparts. Since NGOs were already very active in the provision of services prior to the establishment of the Palestinian Authority, the P/CROs were followers rather than innovators in this area.

In Northern Ireland, such organizations as Peace Train and Women Together for Peace introduced public demonstrations. These, in turn, provided an alternative image of a society opposed to violence and searching for a way to end it. Dialogue groups, such as Quaker House, Ulster's People's College, and Women Together for Peace, were particularly important cultural innovations in a climate of increasing sectarian violence. They were able to demonstrate that inter-community, nonviolent communications and joint activities were possible. Several P/CROs also engaged in inter- and intra-community work, helping the local communities to organize and tackle common economic problems (e.g., Springfield Inter-Community Development Project). By doing so, they offered an alternative model to hostile inter-community encounters and the feeling of impotence against communal violence.

In South Africa, Black Sash's silent vigils and the South African Catholic Bishops' Conference's (SACBC) candlelight vigils were innovative forms of social protest. Several P/CROs, including ECC, SACBC (Justice and Peace Commission (J&P)), Black Sash, and SAIRR, developed educational materials and media events to promote peace and used these as tools to change public discourse. ECC was particularly effective at launching dramatic and spectacular media events that successfully undermined the legitimacy of conscripting young men to the military for the purpose of suppressing apartheid opposition. Several of the P/CROs also jointly sponsored ads in the daily press that called for releasing detainees, lifting the state of emergency, releasing Nelson Mandela, getting troops out of the townships, and initiating negotiations. The use of dialogue groups to build bridges between blacks and whites was a potent tool because the groups attempted to shatter officially sanctioned barriers as well as prevailing stereotypes between the two communities. It is important to remember that participation in such dialogue groups often meant that the participants were potentially exposed to considerable risk. Several organizations also organized visits and events that promoted contact between blacks and whites, such as Koinonia's "Encounter" groups. The provision of social services to the victims of apartheid was a prominent activity in such organizations as Black Sash. J&P offered support to detainees, and the Centre for the Study of Violence and Reconciliation (CSVR) provided a trauma clinic. While modest in scope, these services had important symbolic value in terms of demonstrating both the evil effects of apartheid and the moral responsibility of whites to combat it.

Finally, an important measure of success was the ability of the P/CROs, in all three regions, to attain media coverage and thus gain acceptance in public discourse. Media recognition and acceptance—if not adoption—of the peace movement's vocabulary, images, and symbols were indispensable to their ability to bring about cultural change. In Israel, organizations such as Peace Now were particularly effective at mobilizing the mass media on their behalf, especially in the early days of the movement. As noted in the Israeli Report, "The use of the media was particularly effective in influencing public opinion to accept the Palestinians' right for self-determination and, thus, for a state. A salient example of an initially dissident view that later became fairly widespread was the peace movement's reading of the Intifada as a legitimate Palestinian national struggle of liberation."[44] Similarly, AIC became a very important source of information and data for the foreign press, and European journalists regularly published reports on the conflict based on the perspective that organization provided.

As noted earlier, the Palestinian P/CROs were very effective at getting the international media to publicize their views on human rights violations and abuses by the Israeli authorities. This was especially true during the Intifada. It represented a major shift in the international press, which hitherto had ignored much of the Palestinian perspective on the conflict. In contrast, the P/CROs were less successful in gaining media access to publicize human rights abuses by the Palestinian Authority, due in part to the harassment journalists and reporters experienced when they attempted to provide such coverage.

In Northern Ireland, media coverage was also extensive, to the point where some felt that it had led to overexposure. The Northern Ireland Report quotes one informant as saying, "'I think the media does over-emphasise their importance and they get a fair amount of space from the media. . . . I doubt if there is any organisation that has become involved in one way or another that can reasonably complain about lack of attention from the media."[45] Yet, despite the ability of many of the P/CROs to effectively publicize their cause in the mass media, several informants felt that such exposure came with a price. They portrayed the media as seeking sensationalism and presenting the conflict in simplistic terms. As one informant put it, "I do think that I'm not at all positive in broad terms about the role of media. Until recently, I think the media has always tried to simplify and fascinate and therefore the more photogenic opportunities have got [greater attention]."[46] There were also suggestions that the P/CROs' access to the media was mostly directed toward the middle class at the expense of the working classes. Similar criticisms were voiced about the Israeli press, as well as the Israeli P/CROs' inability to reach the working classes, who by and large supported the Likud Party. It is also important to note that several Northern Ireland P/CROs, such as Quaker House, avoided media attention in order to maintain their neutral image.

In South Africa, the English-speaking press was a very important instrument that the P/CROs used to influence public discourse. As one informant put it, "There were ways in which those newspapers (i.e., the *Rand Daily Mail*, and the *Star*) took the stuff we gave them, and they ran big exposures. . . . I think that if we hadn't been there, the newspapers wouldn't have had half of the things they did expose. Nobody else knew about, nobody else ever thought about the Pass Laws. . . . So the Black Sash was the source of information about what was going on."[47] Moreover, the P/CROs' ability to publicize, in the mainstream newspapers, security force abuses had a deterrent effect on them, not dissimilar to the effect the international press had on restraining the Israeli authorities' actions against the Palestinians.

Summary: Impact on Cultural Change

Reviewing the impact that the P/CROs had on the cultural norms that framed the conflict in each region, there is little doubt that they succeeded in introducing and institutionalizing alternative conceptions, symbols, and vocabularies to address the conflict. These alternative frames enabled both the public and political interest groups to address the intractable conflicts in novel ways and to push for peaceful solutions. In all three regions, the P/CROs were instrumental in formulating and demonstrating innovative formulae for the conflict that were not previously available or visible in the cultural toolkit of each country. They did so through their public demonstrations and media events, educational and research activities, efforts at initiating dialogue, and the provision of services. The cumulative effect of these activities was to chip away at and challenge dominantly held cultural beliefs, symbols, and vocabularies that reinforced the conflict. A prerequisite to the P/CROs' success in changing the culture surrounding the conflict was their access to the mass media. Media acceptance and the incorporation of new vocabularies and symbols to describe the conflict and its solution were essential to the organizations' ability to reach the public, mobilize mass support, and influence policy decision makers.

Of course, the degree of success varied by region and country. Most notably, the P/CROs in Israel and South Africa were particularly effective in achieving such cultural changes. In Northern Ireland, the change was much more limited, and in Palestine, for obvious reasons, the influence was mostly external (i.e., the international press and foreign government) rather than internal. To some extent, the differential impact can be explained by the P/CROs' ability to link their new symbols to deeply held cultural belief systems in each country. In Israel, for example, organizations such as Peace Now sought legitimacy for their ideologies by appealing both to the Zionist dream of a "Jewish" state and the principles of a democratic society, without challenging the importance of national security. In South Africa, the P/CROs drew upon the international condemnation of apartheid as immoral, and they appealed to the principles espoused by the South African churches of a nonracialist and socially just society. These powerful cultural forces were instrumental in giving legitimacy to the ideologies and actions of the P/CROs.

In contrast, in Northern Ireland, the great cultural, religious, political, and economic divides between the two communities made it difficult for the P/CROs to appeal to commonly held cultural norms, except for the amorphous desire to end the violence. Those P/CROs that focused on intra- and inter-community empowerment drew normative strength from the commitment of both Catholics and Protestants to community self-help. In Palestine, the P/CROs could only embrace the overwhelming public fervor for a national identity and statehood, and had to couch their own ideologies in these terms. Doing so, however, greatly limited the range of cultural tools available to them to address the conflict.

Conclusion

We started this chapter by raising the question of whether the three regions would have fared worse without the P/CROs. The evidence amply indicates that the answer is a strong affirmative. It is fair to say that in each region the P/CROs individually and collectively were able to at least slow the course of violence, if not hasten the process of peace and the resolution of the conflict. In each region they were able to present alternative models toward the resolution of the conflict that, at the very least, offered the public and political actors viable options to exit the vicious cycle of violence. Producing new cultural symbols, vocabularies, and tools to address the conflict was vital to "unfreeze" ingrained conceptions of the conflict and challenge its seeming intractability. These novel symbols enabled the P/CROs to mobilize new constituencies—including individuals, groups, and organizations—in support of the resolution of the conflict, which, in turn, forced the political elites to respond to them. Of course, the response varied in each region, and the P/CROs' efficacy was dependent on the particular constellation of political forces in each country. Even though ultimately progress was made because of powerful political and economic forces that pushed the parties toward a resolution, the P/CROs were crucial in laying the groundwork that enabled the contesting parties to consider alternatives to violence.

Notes

1. Thomas D'Aunno, "The Effectiveness of Human Service Organizations: A Comparative of Models," in *Human Services as Complex Organizations*, ed. Yeheskel Hasenfeld (Newbury Park, Calif.: Sage Publications, 1992), pp. 341–361.

2. Chor-fai Au, "Rethinking Organizational Effectiveness: Theoretical and Methodological Issues in the Study of Organizational Effectiveness for Social Welfare Organizations," *Administration in Social Work* 20 (1996): 1–21.

3. Lester M. Salamon, *Partners in Public Service* (Baltimore: The John Hopkins University Press, 1995); Steven Rathgeb Smith and Michael Lipsky, *Nonprofits for Hire: The Welfare State in the Age of Contracting* (Cambridge, Mass.: Harvard University Press, 1993).

4. For example, see Sheri Berman, "Civil Society and Political Institutionalization. (Social Capital, Civil Society and Contemporary Democracy)," *American Behavioral Scientist* 40 (1997): 562–575; Robert D. Putnam, Robert Leonardi, and

Raffaella Nanetti, *Making Democracy Work: Civic Traditions in Modern Italy* (Princeton, N.J.: Princeton University Press, 1993).

5. For example, see Helmut K. Anheier, "The Logic of Evil: The Social Origins of the Nazi Party, 1925-1933," *Social Forces* 77 (1998): 394–397.

6. For example, see Marco Giugni, Doug McAdam, and Charles Tilly, eds., *How Social Movements Matter* (Minneapolis: University of Minnesota Press, 1999).

7. Bert Klandermans, *The Social Psychology of Protest* (Oxford: Blackwell, 1997), p. 186.

8. Kenneth T. Andrews, "Impacts of Social Movements on the Political Process: The Civil Rights Movement and Black Electoral Politics in Mississippi," *American Sociological Review* 62 (1997): 800–819.

9. For example, see Paul Burstein, April Eaton, and Adria Scharf, "Why Do Social Movement Organizations, Interest Groups, and Political Parties Seem to Have So Little Impact on Public Policy" (Paper presented at the American Sociological Association Annual Conference, Toronto, Canada, 1997).

10. Tamar Hermann, Final Country Report, Israel, 1998, p. 141.

11. Edwin Amenta and Michael P. Young, "Making an Impact: Conceptual and Methodological Implications of the Collective Goods Criterion," in *How Social Movements Matter*, ed. Marco Giugni, Doug McAdam, and Charles Tilly (Minneapolis: University of Minnesota Press, 1999), pp. 22–41.

12. Bruce Kent, "Protest and Survival," *History Today* (1999): 14–16.

13. William A Gamson, *The Strategy of Social Protest* (Homewood, Ill.: Dorsey Press, 1975).

14. Ann Swidler, "Culture in Action: Symbols and Strategies," *American Sociological Review* 51 (1986): 273.

15. William A. Gamson, "Social Movements and Cultural Change," in *From Contention to Democracy*, ed. M. G. Giugni, D. McAdam, and C. Tilly (Lanham, Md.: Rowman & Littlefield Publishers, 1998), pp. 57–77.

16. Ibid., p. 68.

17. See Chapter 4.

18. See Hanspeter Kriese, Ruud Koopmans, Jan Willem Dyvendak, and Marco G. Giugni, *New Social Movements in Western Europe: A Comparative Analysis* (Minneapolis: University of Minnesota Press, 1995).

19. Hermann, Final Country Report, p. 152.

20. Reuven Kaminer, *The Politics of Protest* (Sussex: Polity Press, 1996), p. 216. Cited in Hermann, Final Country Report.

21. Feargal Cochrane and Seamus Dunn, Final Country Report, Northern Ireland, 1998, p. 217.

22. Rupert Taylor, Final Country Report, South Africa, 1998, p. 151.

23. Ibid.

24. Ibid., pp. 151, 179.

25. Ibid., Fig. 4.1, p. 140.

26. Based on an interview with Mac Marahaj, the secretary of the ANC underground from 1977, as reported by the South African research team.

27. Doug Struck, "'Peace Now' Movement Still Wonders, 'When?'" *Washington Post*, April 15, 1998, p. A01. Cited in Hermann, Final Country Report.

28. Hermann, Final Country Report, p. 211.

29. Manuel Hassassian, Final Country Report, Palestine, 1998, p. 47.

30. Cochrane and Dunn, Final Country Report, p. 214.

31. Ibid., p. 225.

32. Ibid., p. 224.

33. Richard L Abel, *Politics by Other Means: Law in the Struggle Against Apartheid, 1980-1994* (New York: Routledge, 1995), chapter 3. Cited in Taylor, Final Country Report.

34. Taylor, Final Country Report, p. 158.

35. Doug McAdam, "Political Opportunities: Conceptual Origins, Current Problems, Future Directions," in *Comparative Perspectives on Social Movements*, ed. D. McAdam, J. D. McCarthy, and M. N. Zald (New York: Cambridge University Press, 1996), pp. 23–40.

36. Gamson, "Social Movements and Cultural Change," p. 64.

37. Hermann, Final Country Report, p. 60.

38. Ibid., p. 167.

39. Ibid., p. 34.

40. Cochrane and Dunn, Final Country Report, p. 241.

41. Taylor, Final Country Report, p. 170.

42. Ibid., p. 171.

43. Ibid., pp. 173–174.

44. Hermann, Final Country Report, p. 158.

45. Cochrane and Dunn, Final Country Report, p. 229.

46. Ibid., p. 229.

47. Taylor, Final Country Report, p. 153.

CONCLUSION

We began the research project on which this book is based in an effort to undertake a cross-national empirical study of nongovernmental organizations (NGOs) dedicated to the promotion of peace in three regions beset by protracted conflicts. Our initial interest was exclusively in the structure and performance of these organizations. We assumed that in all three regions, these organizations served a similar function and, therefore, could justifiably be grouped into the same category. However, once we identified "peace" organizations as a category, we immediately had to confront several conceptual and methodological issues: (1) we had to formulate an operational definition of "peace/conflict resolution organizations" (P/CROs) that could encompass the great variations we found in the three regions; (2) since we wanted to focus on a phenomenon that intersects the domain of both social movements and the third sector, we had to use theoretical formulations from both of these areas; (3) we had to devise methodological means to obtain data that were both relevant and valid for a national analysis, as well as an international comparative analysis; and (4) finally, in interpreting the findings of this study, we wanted to identify and understand the general attributes of this category of organizations while, at the same time, appreciate the differences among them resulting from the environments in which they operated.

We initiated this study because we were interested in the phenomenon of NGOs serving as peace organizations across countries and cultures in the context of the breakthroughs that occurred in the three major international conflicts during the early 1990s. We soon discovered that the phenomenon we were interested in was more complex than we had imagined. This is because of the myriad ways organizations and individuals perceive the concept of peace and the strategies for achieving it. This, in turn, impacts the organizational domain of citizens' peace groups. As a result, in all of the countries studied, we found a great variety of such organizations, each with a different perception of what peace means and how to achieve it. In addition, the organizations varied in the major strategies they adopted to promote peace, ranging from advocacy to dialogue and the delivery of services. This complexity compelled us to enlarge the term "peace organizations" to include the concept of conflict resolution, because many of the organizations also undertook strategies aimed at bridging and mediating between the contesting parties.

Hence, the resulting concept we used to depict the domain studied, "peace and conflict-resolution organizations," identifies a phenomenon that is substantially broader than the one commonly used in the literature on "peace movement organizations" (PMOs). These so-called new social movements—that is, PMOs—arose mostly in Europe and the United States in protest against the nuclear arms race, and in the United States against the war in Vietnam.[1] In contrast, the organizations we studied primarily focused on protracted internal social conflicts fueled by national, ethnic, religious, and class animosities. Indeed, the P/CROs were more akin to the civil rights organizations, which several of the P/CROs in Northern Ireland and South Africa used as a model.

In adopting P/CROs as a category of nongovernmental organizations, we also were following a line of inquiry used in other studies on the third sector.[2] Studies in this tradition characteristically begin by developing a taxonomy of NGOs that classifies them on the basis of their fields of activity, such as health, education, culture, and so on. Once such a category has been identified and defined, it is possible to map this entire group of nonprofit organizations within a certain locale. Such an approach provides a census of the organizations within a sphere of activity, the specific and differing roles they assume (e.g., service delivery, advocacy), and the "division of labor" among them.[3] Such a map also enables researchers to do comparative international studies in order to study the factors that shape the size and attributes of the NGOs in a given category.

Of course, no such category of peace and conflict-resolution organizations existed in third-sector studies prior to our research. In other words, we have introduced into the field a new category of organizations, which, as this study has shown, play a critical role in the development of civil societies. In particular, these organizations, which mostly operate in the polity arena, make significant contributions to the development and the strengthening of democratic political institutions.

P/CROs, as a category of organizations, share several common characteristics. First and foremost, they have an explicit mission to address and resolve through peaceful means the intractable social conflicts in their respective countries. In particular, their missions are based on a worldview that respects the human and citizenship rights of the contesting parties. In doing so, they frame the conflict and its solutions in ways that are radically different from those that are dominant in their societies.

Second, the P/CROs take substantial risks, which threaten both their members and the organizations themselves. As we have seen, these risks can be very significant for certain individuals and organizations, resulting in danger to individuals' lives (and actual deaths) and/or the banning of the organization. Yet risk (or activities that "produce" risk) is often what makes these organizations tick and brings them to the forefront of the public's attention; so at least some of the groups use it consciously and plan their strategies around it. In these cases the activists can be considered "fighters for peace," putting their lives on the line in order to further their ideals and convictions. In so doing they are likely to clash with official law enforcement agents or members of countermovements. In addition to the personal and organizational risks, however, there is a third risk, namely the mobilization of counterorganizations. There is always a danger that major and dramatic activities by P/CROs will spark counteractivities and create a backlash to the peace process.

Third, to survive, these organizations must find effective ways to recruit members who buy into the organization's worldview and once recruited to maintain their ongoing commitment. For those P/CROs committed to collective action, such as public protests and demonstrations, this is a particularly daunting challenge.[4] We found that the P/CROs responded to these issues in two very different ways. Some P/CROs made mass public appeals, hoping that those sympathetic to their message would join them in some capacity. Others appealed to a particular audience distinguished by a unique ascriptive attribute, such as religious affiliation, gender, or professional occupation. These P/CROs can be said to be identity-based associations.

Using ascriptive affiliations to recruit and retain members poses some interesting questions: do these groups pursue peace as an expression of their particular identity or ideology (i.e., peace as an extension of one's religious convictions)? Or are the founders of these groups committed to peace, in general, and by forming identity-based groups, are they in fact expressing a preference to pursue peace with other individuals to whom they can relate more easily? Our findings suggest, on the basis of the analysis of these identity-based groups' respective programs, that they seem to frame their ideologies and choose their activities so as to fit their particular identities. For example, religious organizations use religious texts as a base for their activities; women's organizations use feminist arguments to object to war. By doing so they actually are sending a dual message: an internal message to other members of their group and an external one to the rest of the world. In the internal message, they are enlarging the definition of their respective identities to include the issue of peace/conflict resolution. In the external message, they are using the moral foundation of their particular identity (e.g., physicians' commitment to the preservation of life) to convince the public of the necessity of peace.

In this study we set out to understand the forces that give rise to P/CROs, examine their approaches to peace making, identify their organizational attributes and how they may change over time, and assess their impact on peace-making. We used three intersecting theoretical perspectives to guide us in answering these questions. Viewing P/CROs as social-movement organizations helped us to explore how the political context influenced their formation, what structures they developed to mobilize resources, how they framed the nature of the conflict and its resolution, the tactics they used, and what impact they had on their respective societies. The third-sector perspective provided us with the analytic tools that, for the first time, enabled us to map the P/CROs in the three regions, identify the organizational patterns they assumed (e.g., funding, leadership, structure, personnel, activities), and examine their place and relations with other NGOs. Finally, the institutional theory of organizations enabled us to understand the changes that these organizations experienced over time and how they negotiated their relations with the external environment.

In undertaking this study, there were some important methodological issues that we had to address, as well. Our main challenge was how to deal effectively with both the *local* and *comparative* foci of the study—specifically the need to present the particular local reality and at the same time enable meaningful cross-country comparisons. Although we did not intend to use highly standardized research tools across the three local conflicts, neither were we prepared for each team to pursue its research independently, thus undermining the comparative aspect of the study. Therefore we developed a research strategy based on (1) a continuous dialogue among the entire research group (the local teams and the comparative researchers); and (2) the collection of data in three stages, each based on the analysis of data from the previous one. We believe that this approach was crucial to our ability to conduct a meaningful comparative analysis, identifying the general/universal attributes of the phenomenon studied along with the particular/local findings for each of the three conflicts in their national contexts.

In the comparative analysis phase, we had to devise a method for analyzing the large amounts of data that the several teams collected in their individual settings, which of course were not uniform. In order to make sense of those specific data collected we needed to devise a coding scheme, informed both by our theoretical framework and the data themselves. This entailed an iterative process whereby we organized the data in accordance with our framework, but at the same time we allowed the data "to speak" so that we could modify and refine the framework to account for what we actually found.

Moreover, each team was asked to review the actual coding of their data to ensure that their findings were not distorted in the process. In other words, we used a grounded-theory approach of moving back and forth between the data and the theory development until we were satisfied that our theoretical framework provided a meaningful way to code and analyze the data without distorting their meaning as understood and reported by each research team.[5]

Turning to the comparative part of the study, we would like to highlight four major findings that, in our judgment, have important theoretical and practical implications:

1. *The centrality of foreign funding for these organizations.* This finding was particularly evident in South Africa and Israel, where almost all of the organizations studied received overseas funding; however, if one considers the United Kingdom to be "foreign" in Northern Ireland, then such funding was evident there, as well. Moreover, foreign funding often came close to providing the organizations' total funding. This was the case for South African organizations such as the Institute for a Democratic Alternative for South Africa (Idasa) and the Independent Mediation Service of South Africa (IMSSA)—97 percent and 85 percent of whose funding came from foreign sources, respectively—the Center for Conflict Resolution (CCR), the Centre for the Study of Violence and Reconciliation (CSVR), Koinonia, the South African Catholic Bishops' Conference (SACBC), and the End Conscription Campaign (ECC). A similar picture was found in Israel, where various foreign sources significantly supported the Alternative Information Center (AIC), Bat Shalom, Council for Peace and Security, Oz Ve'Shalom, Physicians for Human Rights, and Peace Now. This finding belies the commonly held notion that P/CROs, as grassroots organizations, rely on their members for financial support.

In the cases of South Africa and Israel, this foreign funding could be perceived as undermining official government policy and thus raises the question of "intervention by foreign powers in a sovereign country's domestic affairs." What is most interesting about these foreign "interventions" are the funding sources themselves: depending on the conflict and the type of organization, we discovered the primary sources of P/CRO funding to be foreign governments, foundations, and religious organizations. Also interesting are the specific countries involved: Scandinavian and other European countries, the United States, and Canada. What are the motivations of these respective sources in supporting P/CROs? Whose interests do they serve and how? Obviously these questions are not limited to foreign funders of P/CROs; they also apply to foreign funders of NGOs, in general.

On another level, these patterns reflect not only foreign intervention in these conflicts but also the needs of the P/CROs themselves. The citizens' organizations in all three conflicts had no practical opportunities to find local sources of funding for their operations during times of open violence, when government policy and the public mood tended toward force as the best means for solving the conflict. When the P/CROs turned to international sources, often it was out of necessity. On the surface, it seems that these sources of funding came with few strings attached, with the exception of Northern Ireland. Less clear, however, are the long-term ramifications of dependence on foreign funding, and whether and when the P/CROs can develop locally based funding sources. Will the P/CROs lose their grassroots orientation as a consequence? Will they be constrained in their choices of tactics as a result of such dependence? Will their local legitimacy erode? There is some limited evidence in the country reports that in the long run dependence on foreign funding may exact some costs to the organizations, especially in terms of their legitimacy and choice of tactics.

2. *The importance of charismatic leadership.* The oppositional nature of P/CROs, the major struggles in which they engage, and the risks they take mean that special types of individuals are needed to found such groups. These individuals (or small groups) must have strong convictions regarding the objectives of the organization that is to be founded, and they also must manifest leadership abilities that enable them to attract followers. We found such attributes among the leaders in the organizations studied in all three locales, but especially in South Africa, where almost all of the organizations studied emphasized the critical role of the organization's founder and his or her charismatic characteristics. Thus, for example, Ruth Foley of Black Sash was described in the South African Final Report as a "forceful personality and well versed in issues of white politics, she is credited with being the League's mainstay during its embryonic phase."[6] The report adds: "Leaders were so strong in the Black Sash that without them the organization would not have survived its infancy and metamorphosis into an anti-apartheid organization in the late fifties, or its political isolation during the sixties, or the threat of radicalism in the eighties."[7] Similar leading roles were played by individuals such as H. W. van der Merve in CCR; Loet Douwes Dekker, who was described as "the founding father of IMSSA";[8] Nico Smith at Koinonia; Rommel Roberts at the Quaker Peace Centre; and Rheinhalt Jones at the South African Institute of Race Relations (SAIRR). Such charismatic leadership also was noted in the organizations in the other two conflicts, but especially was stressed in the Alternative Information Center and Physicians for Human Rights in Israel, and in the Ulster People's College in Northern Ireland. While such qualities are important for almost any new NGO, our findings suggest that they are especially salient for P/CROs since they must operate in a hostile and risky environment. In this sense the P/CROs are similar to other social movement organizations that depend on the availability of leadership to mobilize members.[9]

3. *The formalization and professionalization of P/CROs.* We discovered that, like other organizations, for P/CROs to survive and grow they have to formalize and professionalize their organizational structure. Many P/CROs start off as spontaneous, voluntary, and informal associations characterized by a very

fluid internal structure that lacks hierarchy or formal division of labor. Over time, however, the P/CROs undergo a process of formalization of structure and professionalization of their staff. This is particularly apparent for those P/CROs that grow, expand, and increase their resource base. For example, in Israel, the AIC expansion was accompanied by a change in structure, which meant less autonomy for the different projects' teams. In Bat Shalom, the leadership discovered that their changed organizational structure created a situation in which the organization would soon lose its grassroots nature. At Peace Now, the hiring of professionals in the mid-1980s necessitated a restructuring of the organization. Similar processes were apparent among the South African P/CROs. While the first director of the Quaker Peace Centre ran the organization practically by himself, the director replacing him had to formalize the organization—she developed a constitution for the Centre, as well as conditions of service for the staff. In Northern Ireland, the processes of formalization at the Ulster People's College were linked to the need to develop an appropriate system of finances.

Formalization of structure and professionalization of staff are clear indicators of an institutionalization process in which the P/CROs adopt organizational forms that can ensure their survival and success. This transformation is common to many successful social movement organizations.[10] Indeed, as part of this institutionalization process the P/CROs may augment their mission to include additional activities. For example, P/CROs that begin as protest movements may add a service or educational function. Others that may have emphasized research and dissemination of information may include mediation and dialogue to their mission.[11] We believe that the institutionalization process that P/CROs undergo reflects what Meyer and Rowan, and DiMaggio and Powell call "structural isomorphism."[12] That is, in order to survive and succeed these organizations must conform to the dominant organizational forms in their environment.

Still, the institutionalization of a formal structure is not inevitable. Six organizations in our study rejected formalization and professionalization. Three Israeli organizations never obtained office space, hired paid staff, recognized formal leaders, or established formal decision-making procedures, depending solely on volunteer efforts at the time of our data collection. Three other organizations, all in Northern Ireland, were only minimally formalized in that they had small unchanging budgets, minimal office space, and just one or two paid staff. The ideology of these six organizations, each of which had a collectivist orientation and a single-issue focus, provides at least a partial explanation for why they did not grow in size and formalize.

The price of maintaining these informal structures was the willingness to operate with very limited resources. All three Israeli organizations never systematically looked for or received core funding, while two of the Northern Irish groups were committed to keeping their budgets small. The third Northern

Irish group was simply unable to obtain additional funds; their "political" image prevented them from obtaining charitable status.

4. *Impact of P/CROs.* One of the most important questions we had hoped to address was what impact these organizations had on the respective peace processes in each region. This obviously is not only a very important question, but is also the most difficult to answer, as was discussed in detail in chapter 9. The methodological difficulties involved are well known to scholars who have tried to assess the achievements of social movements and advocacy organizations. On the other hand, it is important to stress that despite all of these difficulties, the four research teams identified very similar contributions that the P/CROs made to the three respective peace processes. While they could not identify specific *direct* contributions, the research teams practically reached a consensus that the P/CROs studied played an important *indirect* role in the promotion of the peace processes. This role can be summarized as preparing the public for a new reality of peace by demonstrating the unsatisfactory character of the current political situation (and by showing that alternatives are possible), and as creating and legitimizing a new language of peace.

This is well described in the research teams' Final Reports. The Israeli researcher writes:

> The introduction of innovative ideas into the public discourse over security matters—even though they were not immediately "saleable"—is indeed considered by many within the peace movement as one of its greatest successes. . . . [The peace movement] challenged the mainstream perception regarding the inevitability of the conflict. . . . On the practical level it established itself as a strong political voice in the public discourse, and as a capable political body whose demands cannot be ignored by the decision-makers without risking a significant negative reaction in the shape of massive protest.[13]

The South Africa researchers identified, in particular, two contributions their peace organizations made—namely, "projecting a vision of an alternative social order,"[14] and "promoting alternative identities."[15] The Northern Irish team made a similar point, contending that while they could not show that individually the P/CROs studied made a measurable difference, cumulatively and longitudinally the organizations had a "major impact on 'civil society' in Northern Ireland."[16] They introduced concepts such as "inclusive dialogue" and created a new "tier" of community activists, and "such individuals within both loyalist and republican communities played a crucial intermediate role between the traditional political process and their communities."[17] The Palestinian researcher stressed the contribution of P/CROs not only in upholding human rights but also in serving as a means of communication both externally and internally, presenting the Palestinian narrative to overseas audiences and demonstrating to other Palestinians different facets of Israel and Israelis, and differentiating among them.

The importance of such roles for P/CROs should not be overlooked. In democratic countries they are the basis on which future settlements or peace agreement are "sold" to the population; without their input the public may perceive the agreements as being imposed. In other words, in cases where political agreements between contending parties are reached without preparing the population for a settlement, especially when foreign powers are involved, the public perception is likely to be one of a forced settlement, with all of the implications that entails. If at least part of the population desires such an outcome, the settlement may be perceived as fitting within the nation's self-interest. When viewed from this angle, the P/CROs' contribution individually, and even more so collectively, can be considered the sort of major contribution to the peace process that only an authentic expression of civil society can perform.

Looking ahead, this study suggests several new research avenues. It has shown that P/CROs, as a category of NGOs, play an important role in the development of a civil society and in the promotion of peace and conflict resolution. Third-sector studies generally have failed to account for these organizations and their contributions. Yet, with the rise of ethnic, religious, and national conflicts in different parts of the world, it is essential that these organizations receive more prominent attention. When thinking about the roles citizens' organizations play in changing the course of protracted conflicts in their respective societies, one cannot refrain from comparing the three conflicts we studied to other contemporary ones, such as those in Bosnia, Kosovo, Chechnya, and Rwanda. Citizens' organizations involved in the promotion of peace hardly have been observed in these conflicts. Therefore, it is important that we understand the macro social and political conditions that are the prerequisites to the formation of such organizations. We suspect that in order for P/CROs to emerge, a foundation of democratic institutions must exist already, including elements of a civil society. Yet, we urgently need to understand these conditions. Moreover, we need to pay closer attention—much more than we have done in this study—to the social processes that lead citizens to organize for peace and conflict resolution. For example, we need to appreciate the circumstances that lead individuals to take the initiative to form such associations, the organizational skills they require, and the strategies that lead to successful organizing within the particular political context and the nature of the conflict they encounter.

In order to address these issues a better interface is needed between studies of social-movement organizations and research on the third sector. We have benefited from integrating theoretical conceptions and methodological tools from both fields. Studies of social movement organizations, while paying close attention to the political opportunity structure, generally ignore the role of the third sector. As our study points out, a key factor that enabled the P/CROs to rise and survive was the existence of a fairly developed third sector in their respective countries. Both in Israel and Northern Ireland, for example, the surge in the formation of P/CROs occurred in a period of expansion of the third sector. In Palestine, on the other hand, where the third sector was highly constrained, it was difficult for P/CROs to emerge. It is clear that a developed third sector can offer the organizational expertise, experiences, and network relations that are necessary for P/CROs to arise. In other words, theories of social movements will be enriched if they pay much closer attention to the structure of the third sector, its organizational features, and relations to the state.[18]

Third-sector researchers also could benefit by incorporating theories and research on social-movement organizations—their formation, structure, and outcomes—into their studies.[19] Indeed, classical third-sector theories mostly ignore the third sector's role in advocating for social change in society.[20] Third-sector research is preoccupied with measuring the scope and size of the third sector, mapping the organizational attributes of its constituent organizations, and articulating their relations (mostly fiscal and service delivery) to the state; the research tends to ignore organizations that challenge the state. Moreover, a significant number of third-sector organizations, as our study has shown, combine several different functions—advocacy, service, and research—in the arsenal of tools they use to bring about social change. That is, the organizations themselves combine features of social movements and service organizations.[21] Hence, research on third-sector organizations needs to identify those associations that can be categorized as being related to social-movement organizations in order to better understand them and their impact on the state and civil society. Indeed, a more dynamic perspective on the third sector will recognize that organizations may begin as social movement organizations and over time become institutionalized members of the third sector. In our own study, several P/CROs, especially in South Africa, changed their focus once a reduction or resolution of the conflict occurred. They undertook to promote social justice, offer mediation services, and provide access to educational resources. In other words, they sought for themselves a new role in the third sector, building on their legacy as social movement organizations.

Finally, we want to dedicate this volume to the peace workers all over the world. We hope that our study has made a modest contribution by giving them a better insight into the organizations they have formed, and a greater understanding of how they can make their organizations stronger and more effective. If this book encourages the formation of P/CROs in various parts of the world, all of us who participated in this research endeavor will feel greatly rewarded.

Notes

1. See, for example, B. Klandermans, "The Peace Movement and Social Movement Theory," *International Social Movement Research* 3 (1991): 1–39; M. Zald and J. McCarthy, "Social Movement Industries: Competition and Cooperation among SMOs," in *Social Movements in an Organizational Society*, ed. M. Zald and J. McCarthy (New Brunswick, N.J.: Transaction Books, 1987), pp. 161–180.

2. L. Salamon and H. Anheier, *Defining the Nonprofit Sector: A Cross National Analysis* (Manchester: Manchester University Press, 1997).

3. See, for example, K. Gronbjerg, "Developing a Universe of Nonprofit Organizations: Methodological Considerations," *Nonprofit and Voluntary Sector Quarterly* 18 (1989): 63–80; W. Bielefeld, J. C. Murduch, and P. Waddell, "The Influence of Demographics and Distance on Nonprofit Location," *Nonprofit and Voluntary Sector Quarterly* 26 (1997): 207–225.

4. B. Klandermans, *The Social Psychology of Protest* (Oxford: Blackwell, 1997).

5. See, for example, Ian Dey, *Grounding Grounded Theory: Guidelines for Qualitative Inquiry* (San Diego: Academic Press, 1999); Barney G. Glaser and Anselm L. Strauss, *The Discovery of Grounded Theory: Strategies for Qualitative Research* (Chicago: Aldine Publishing Company, 1967).

6. M. Rogers, *The Black Sash: The Story of the South African Women's Defence of the Constitution League* (Johannesburg: Rotonews, 1956), quoted in C. Taylor, Black Sash case report for ISPO study, 1998, p. 7.

7. C. Taylor, Black Sash case report for ISPO study, 1998, p. 33.

8. C. Taylor, IMMSA case report for ISPO study, 1998, p. 3.

9. J. Lofland, *Social Movement Organizations* (New York: Aldine de Gruyter, 1996).

10. W. A. Gamson, *The Strategy of Social Protest* (Homewood, Ill.: Dorsey Press, 1975).

11. See also D. C. Minkoff, *Organizing for Equality: The Evolution of Women's and Racial-Ethnic Organizations in America, 1955-1985* (New Brunswick, N.J.: Rutgers University Press, 1995).

12. J. W. Meyer and B. Rowan. "Institutionalized Organizations: Formal Structure as Myth and Ceremony," *American Journal of Sociology* 83 (1977): 340–363; P. D. DiMaggio and W. W. Powell, "The Iron Cage Revisited: Institutional Isomorphism and Collective Rationality in Organizational Fields," *American Sociological Review* 48 (1983): 147–160.

13. T. Hermann, Final Country Report, Israel, 1998, p. 124.

14. R. Taylor, Final Country Report, South Africa, 1998, p. 18.

15. Ibid.

16. F. Cochrane and S. Dunn, Final Country Report (first draft), Northern Ireland, 1998, p.190.

17. Ibid., pp. 166–167.

18. For research on social movement organizations that incorporates this dimension, see D. C. Minkoff, *Organizing for Equality*.

19. L. Salamon and H. Anheier, "Social Origins of Civil Society: Explaining the Nonprofit Sector Cross-Nationally," *Voluntas* 9 (1998): 213–248.

20. W. W. Powell, *The Nonprofit Sector* (New Haven, Conn.: Yale University Press, 1987).

21. This has been a common strategy for many feminist organizations. See, for example, C. Hyde, "The Ideational System of Social Movement Agencies: An Examination of Feminist Health Centers," in *Human Services as Formal Organizations*, ed. Y. Hasenfeld (Newbury Park, Calif.: Sage Publications, 1992), pp. 121–144.

APPENDIX A: PRELIMINARY QUESTIONNAIRE FOR THE INTERNATIONAL STUDY OF PEACE/CONFLICT-RESOLUTION ORGANIZATIONS

During the first phase of its operation, the International Study of Peace/Conflict-Resolution Organizations (ISPO) used a version of this draft questionnaire to gather preliminary organizational profile data.

A. Internal Organizational Variables

1. Establishment and Formation

1.1. In what year was the organization founded? _____

1.2. Who initiated the organization's establishment?
    a. Individual
    b. Small group
    c. Large group
    d. Split from another group
    e. Other _____
    Please specify briefly _____
    _____

1.3. What triggered the organization's establishment?
    a. A specific event _____
    b. Prolonged process _____
    Please specify briefly _____
    _____

1.4. Where was the organization established?
    a. Abroad b. Within the conflict area
    Please specify briefly _____
_____

2. Participation

2.1. Estimate the number of people in each of the following categories.
    a. Participants _____
    b. Supporters _____
    c. Members _____
    d. Staff _____
    e. Other _____

2.2. Is the organization based on some category of participants, on the basis of gender, ethnic/ racial/ national affiliation, profession etc.? Yes _____ No _____
    If yes, what is it? _____

2.3. What is the ratio of total participation from each party of the conflict? Please mark percentage of total participation:
    a. 1st party _____—_____ %
    b. 2nd party _____—_____ %

3. Organizational Structure

3.1. What is the organization's legal status? (Please use the legal term applied in your country.) _____

3.2. What is the organization's structure?
    a. Single center _____
    b. Center + branches _____
    c. Multiple independent centers _____
    d. Roof organization _____
    e. Other _____

3.3. Please mark all operating bodies which exist in the organization. What is the operating pattern of these bodies? For each body in the list below mark yes/no for existence in the organization, mark yes/no for operation regularity, and specify the body's meeting frequency in the organization according to the following key: (1) weekly, (2) monthly, (3) annual, or (4) specify other.

Body	Existence	Regularity	Frequency
Board			
Permanent committees			
Ad hoc committees			
Informal bodies			
General membership			
Other _____			

4. Leadership

4.1. Who leads the organization?
   a. A single person _____
   b. A group _____
   c. Leaderless organization _____
   d. Other____ _____

4.2. To which conflict party do(es) the leader(s) belong?
   a. 1st party_____
   b. 2nd party_____
   c. mixed _____

5. Decision-Making Patterns

5.1. Who mostly makes the decisions in the organization?
   a. A single leader _____
   b. A forum/committee _____
   c. The organization's assembly____ _____
   d. Other _____

5.2. How are decisions taken?
   a. By consensus _____
   b. By majority vote _____
   c. Other _____

5.3. Decisions are usually taken:
   a. Upon previous planning _____
   b. Ad-hoc _____

6. Funding

6.1. Does the organization have an annual budget? _____

If yes, what is the organization's current annual budget? (in U.S. dollars) _____

6.2. Mark percentage from total funding for each funding source. Specify local (L) or foreign (F).
   a. Private donations L_____ F _____
   b. Foundations L _____ F _____
   c. Government L _____ F _____
   d. Fees for services L _____F _____
   e. Membership fees L _____ F _____
   f. Specify other _____ L ____ F ____

6.3. Estimate the current organization's expenditures (annual, in % of total budget).
   a. Compensation of employees _____
   b. Purchases of goods and services _____
   c. Other _____

6.4. Does the organization receive tax benefits?
   a. Tax exemptions for the organization _____
   b. Tax breaks for donors _____

7. Ideology

7.1. What is the organization's explicit ideology? (Mark as many as apply.)
   a. Peace _____
   b. Social justice _____
   c. Equality _____
   d. Coexistence _____
   e. Religious and ethnic tolerance _____
   f. Pacifism _____
   g. Nonviolence _____
   h. Other—specify briefly _____
   _____
   _____

7.2. Evaluate* the organization's ideological position within its peace/
conflict-resolution environment (compared to others in the domain) from
radical* to moderate* (circle a number):
*Researcher's evaluation and definition:

radical					moderate				
1	2	3	4	5	6	7	8	9	10

8. Goals

8.1. What are the organization's explicit goals?
   a. Education _____
   b. Changing public opinion _____
   c. Changing government policy _____
   d. Other _____
   Please specify briefly_____
   _____
   _____

9. Activities

9.1. What are the organization's activities?

For each activity mark approximate number in the past year, mark yes\no in
the appropriate places to state if the activity is based on planning or as a
reaction to an event. Specify also the activity's frequency according to the following key: (1) weekly, (2) monthly, (3) annual, or (4) specify other.

	Approximate number in past year	Planned yes\no	Reactive yes\no	Frequency
Protest (demonstrations, petitions)				
Counseling and advice or assistance				
Educating (courses, seminars, workshops)				
Information or publication				
Other _____				

9.2.   Mark all audiences toward which the organization addresses its activities:

    a. General public_____
    b. Specific group(s) within the public _____
       Please specify briefly _____
    c. Politicians _____
    d. Journalists _____
    e. Opposition_____
    f. Government _____
    g. Economic elite(s) _____
    h. Other _____

10. Evaluation

10.1. Are there organizational mechanisms engaged in evaluation of activities and organizational processes? Yes _____ No _____
      If yes, what are they? _____

11. Organizational Change

Organizations change over time. The changes may be in the structure, the funding sources, the ideology, the strategies, the activities, etc. Sometimes changes in one element bring about changes in the others. The changes may be moderate or full; they may be slow and incremental (over a long period), or it may be swift or revolutionary.

11.1. To what extent has the organization changed in the past 10 years? (circle a number):

not at all	to a moderate extent	to a good extent	fully
I	2 3	4 5	6

11.2. If there has been organizational change, can it be defined as incremental (slow, partial, moderate change) or revolutionary (basic, fast, full-scale)? (Place the organization on the scale below):
      incremental change I 2 3 4 5 revolutionary change

B. External Relations Variables

12.1. For each category in the list below, estimate the number of organizations
or individuals with which the organization has/had relations* over the years:

    a. Similar peace/conflict-resolution organizations _____

    b. Opposition** organizations _____

    c. Funding organizations (foundations) _____

    d. Government ministers _____.

    e. Government officials _____

    f. Opposition** leaders _____

    g. "Enemy"*** peace/conflict-resolution organizations _____

    h. "Enemy"*** personalities _____

    i. Journalists (specific) _____

    j. Universities _____

    k. Support groups _____

    l. Lawyers _____

    m. Consultants _____

    n. Other _____

*By "relations" we mean both cooperative relations (e.g., joint planning, coordination) and contest relations (over the same resources), both sustained and short-lived.

**"Opposition"—entities within the society opposing peace or reconciliation as advocated by the organization.

***"Enemy"—entities on the other side of the conflict.

APPENDIX B: COMPREHENSIVE QUESTIONNAIRE FOR THE INTERNATIONAL STUDY OF PEACE/CONFLICT-RESOLUTION ORGANIZATIONS

During the second phase of its operation, the International Study of Peace/Conflict-Resolution Organizations (ISPO) used the following questionnaire outline to gather comprehensive data.

1. Formation

a. What was the general context that brought about the formation of the organization (e.g., violation of human rights, occupation, terror)?

b. What were the specific events that brought about the formation of the organization (e.g., war, declaration of peace, parades)?

c. What was the main issue and focus of the organization during formation (e.g., medical services, education for coexistence)?

d. What was the original organizational raison d'être?

e. Who was involved (e.g., roles, characteristics)? Here, special attention should be paid to religion, class, age, race, and geographic region.

f. What role did gender play in the formation process?

g. Formation process. Debates and weighing of options around the following during the critical phase of formation:

—Ideological considerations

—Personal considerations (e.g., who should join, who should lead?)

—Target of intervention (e.g., the public at large, policymakers, specific groups)

—Interorganizational considerations (e.g., are there already other organizations which have a similar mission? Did the organization view itself as "mirroring" another organization, perhaps from the "other side"?)

—Legal considerations. Should the organization be a formal or informal entity?

—Funding considerations. Were funding issues taken into account from the outset? Were there identified funding sources?

—Contextual. General—relating to the overall social/political circumstances prevailing at the time; and/or specific—related more to the prevailing "NGO culture" with implications for funding, voluntary action, etc.

2. Organizational Raison d'être

How an organization conceives of its reason for being, the belief system or ideology shared by most or some of its members, the rationale underlying the organization's activities—these are often important components in understanding peace/conflict-resolution organizations. We are interested to learn about the raison d'être of the organization as it relates to the conflict and the conflict resolution. Is it anchored in some broader ideological framework (socialism, religion, feminism)? Is the conflict resolution seen within that context? Are there arguments and debates about these issues? If so please specify the major parameters of these debates.

a. Perception of the conflict: What is the organization's perception of the nature of the conflict, what is it about, what are its sources, who is it between, and who opposes resolution?

b. Perception of the conflict resolution: How does the organization perceive a resolution of the conflict? How is it related to a broader concept of society and social order (if at all)? How does the organization view the ultimate relations between the two feuding parties?

c. Support for that raison d'être:

—How much consensus is there in the organization for each of those two components? It is a condition to join the organization?

—Around which ideological issues have there been debate, disagreement, if at all?

d. What organizational raison d'être influenced, in any way, by funding imperatives? If so, how?

Time Dimension: How has the organizational raison d'être changed over time?

3. Goals

Organizations formulate goals to achieve their mission. We are interested to find out what are the organization's goals, as well as the process of formation of these goals, the dilemmas involved, and the support for these goals throughout the organization.

  a. List all the organizational goals as stated. Differentiate among *general* goals pertaining to the conflict (e.g., "bringing peace and reconciliation") and *operative* goals related to the organization's mission ("creating a dialogue between youth on both sides of the conflict"). Why and how were these goals chosen? Elaborate in terms of ideology and events/situation.
  b. List the organization's goals in order of priority.

Time Dimension: How have the organizational goals changed over time?

4. Strategy, Programs, Activities, and Campaigns

This refers to the process through which the organization's raison d'être and goals are translated into organizational outputs. Programs are generally understood as the routine actions in which the organization engages (weekly seminar, monthly newsletter, weekly vigil), while activities are the nonroutine actions (rallies, lobbying against a specific issue, etc.). We are interested in all these forms of organizational output undertaken to achieve its goals. In discussing these, we are interested in the organizational mechanisms employed in their planning, implementation, and evaluation (if pertinent). (See: group interview)

Description

  a. List (1) all the programs, (2) all the activities, and (3) the campaigns the organization engaged in during a certain year.
  b. Importance. Have the respondent attempt to rank each list according to its importance for the accomplishment of the organization's goals.
  c. For each program or activity indicate who in the organization (person, committee) is responsible for its implementation.
  d. Effort. Have the respondent attempt to rank according to the organizational effort required in terms of funding and staff/participants' time.

e. Distinguish between those conducted secretly/clandestinely and those not.

f. Risk. Rank each list according to (1) the organizational risk, and (2) the risk to the participants involved.

Process

Mechanisms of conducting activities. In two types of activity, routine and nonroutine, we are interested in (1) the process (internal to the organization) of carrying out an activity, from the stage of idea formation, to its implementation and through its aftermath (i.e., Did activities and programs undertaken meet organizational goals? If not, what was done?); and (2) in the patterns of interaction with other organizations and individuals in conducting that activity.

Perhaps the best manner in which to illustrate this "process" is to have respondent(s) describe in detail an example or two of such an activity, program, or campaign, and analyze it according to both the internal mechanisms at work, and the environmental actors involved.

Nature of the Fit between Organizational Goals and Outputs

We are also interested in exploring the relationship between goals and programs/activities. In so doing, we will be probing, albeit in an inductive fashion, the conceptual link between the two, namely, organizational strategy.

Time Dimension: How have the activities, programs, and organizational strategy changed over time?

5. People Involved in Organization

In these questions we are interested to find out about the types of people associated with the organization—rank-and-file participants as well as leaders; their patterns of participation, their backgrounds, their motives, etc., and also in the organizational practices dealing with recruitment of new members, assuring continued commitment of members, etc.

a. Divide the people into different categories of participation relevant to the organization: e.g., dues paying members—supporters; volunteers—paid staff; inner-core (active); outer-core (less active). How many participants are there in each group?

b. What are the characteristics of the typical rank-and-file person involved? Relate to the following dimensions: *Demographic* (e.g., gender, age, ethnicity); *socioeconomic* (e.g., education, status, occupation); *political affiliation or identification* (e.g., liberal, conservative, radical); *background in similar organizations*; and *degree of social/political involvement*. What might explain the characterization provided?

c. Recruitment: How do most people become involved in the organization? Is there any "initiation" or "socialization" process?

d. Retention: Why do they tend to remain involved in the organization (incentives, motivations, both collective and personal)? Why do they leave (e.g., ideological debates, disagreement with activities, burnout)?

e. What is expected of those involved in the organization (e.g., attendance, commitment, breaking the law, participation in activity)?

f. Multiple affiliation: To what extent do people involved belong to organizations other than this one? If so, which ones or what type?

Time Dimension: How have the patterns of recruitment, retention, and participation changed over time?

6. Leadership

a. Leadership structure. Is there a leadership structure? How would it be characterized (one leader, a group, other)? To what degree is it formal or informal?

b. Leadership background. What are the leaders' socio-demographic characteristics (who is/are he/she/they, what is his/her/their former background)?

c. Leaders' selection. How was/were he/she/they elected, nominated or otherwise selected for this job? Is there a rotation system?

d. Leaders' style. How does/do the leader(s) make major decisions in the organization (consulting with people [whom], authoritarian, other)?

e. Support for leaders. How much support does/do the leader(s) have in the organization? Is/are he/she/they often challenged on their decisions and actions?

f. Leaders' influence. How much influence or say do(es) the leader(s) have in determining the organization's policies?

Time Dimension: How has organizational leadership changed over time?

7. Structure

    a. Operating bodies. List the organization's operating and/or governing bodies (board, committees) and describe their roles, how frequently each convenes, and the relations among them.

    b. Positions. Are there any designated positions? List all positions in the organizations (e.g., chairs of committees, PR officer, organizer); for each position indicate whether paid (full/part-time) or not and how many people occupied it in the past two years.

Time Dimension: How has the structure of the organization changed over time?

8. Decision Making

The process of decision making is central in any organization. Organizations differ in the patterns they make decisions. In some cases one person or a small group makes all the decisions; in others, a division of labor exists, and some decisions are made by some persons or bodies, others are made by different persons and bodies. In this question we are interested in the process(es) of decision making regarding different types of decisions used in the organization: the methods by which they are made, the people involved.

    a. Decision-making pattern. Indicate the process(es) and the individuals/bodies involved in making decisions around the following: (1) selection of goals for the organization; (2) program/activity; and (3) budget (see group interview) and salary policies.

    b. Accountability. Describe the patterns of responsibility of leaders to members.

    c. Is there reason to suspect that the actual decision-making processes in the organization differ from those reported? If so, who really has power in this organization?

Time Dimension: How have organizational decision-making patterns changed over time?

9. Funding

Funding issues can be crucial for organizations. We are interested in the funding sources, the fund-raising processes and procedures, and the relationships between the funders and the organization.

a. Budget size and funding sources (in %). Elaborate on nature of funding source: breakdown between external and internal; % of state funding; % of third-party funding (or undisclosed sources and/or through conduits)
b. Stability. How stable is each source (can the organization count on it beyond the short term)?
c. Preferred funding sources. Are any of the sources preferred over others? Why?
d. "Forbidden" sources. Any sources offering to fund the organization that were refused?
e. Relations with funders. Indicate the level of involvement of each funder in the organization's policies, program. Modes of reporting and maintaining accountability. Have some attempted to influence the organization's ideology, activities?
f. Fund-raising strategies. Indicate all the strategies the organization uses to raise its funds (domestically and abroad): dues from members, appeals to specific donors, the general public, grant writing, etc. Indicate which has been especially successful.
g. Budget expenses. How do the exigencies of funding relate to budgetary expenditures?

Time Dimension: How have the organizational budget, funding considerations, and expenses changed over time?

10. The Organizational Environment

In order to accomplish their mission, organizations forge relations with various entities in their environment. In this set of questions we are interested in identifying the specific environment of your organization and the type of relations it forms(ed) with different entities.

a. List those entities in the organization's environment that impact (in one way or another) its work. Include international as well as local actors. Attempt to classify the organizational entities listed according to a few primary categories.
b. Try to describe the mode of relations (e.g., exchanging information and resources, consultation, joint planning, coalition building, etc.) and their nature and frequency. (In exploring this particular question, we strongly recommend the use of a chart on which the respondents will

be able to graphically situate and characterize their organization's interorganizational relations. The group interview should also provide illustrations of those relations.)

    c. Identify the most important of these environmental entities (approx. five).

Time Dimension: How has the organizational environment changed over time?

11. Risks

Peace/conflict-resolution organizations often operate in a hostile, or at least unstable, environment. As such, they are sometimes subject to an element of risk (collectively and individually) in the pursuit of their mission. In this question we are interested in the risk(s) confronting the organization as a whole and/or the people involved therein.

    a. Opposition/hostile entities. List the entities in your environment that can be seen as hostile to the organization's mission (e.g., government, paramilitary groups, organizations on the other side of the conflict, army, police).

    b. Organizational risk. What risks is the organization subject to by each of those entities (e.g., threats, limitations, restrictions of all kinds, prohibited activities, prevention of funds, sanctions, delegitimization, attacks of any kind etc.)?

    c. Handling organizational risk. How did/does the organization deal with these risks (i.e., change or accommodate the structure, goals, tactics, interorganizational relations)?

    d. Participants' risk. What risks are the leaders and participants facing (e.g., harassment, arrests, detentions, physical attacks, murder etc.)?

    e. Handling participants' risk. How did/does the organization deal with these risks?

Time Dimension: How has the element of risk confronting the organization changed over time?

12. Major Events

When analyzing peace/conflict-resolution organizations, it is important to take into consideration external events concerning the conflict that might have had an impact on the organization, its mission, and its operation. We are interested in the following:

a. Listed events impacting the organization. Which of the following events impacted the organization and in what ways?
b. Other events. Which other events, not listed, had impacted the organization and in what ways?
c. Events the organization had impacted. Which events, listed or not listed, the organization believes it had (directly or indirectly) impacted. In what ways? (A list of events by dates will accompany this question.)

APPENDIX C: EFFICACY PROTOCOL FOR THE INTERNATIONAL STUDY OF PEACE/CONFLICT- RESOLUTION ORGANIZATIONS

On the basis of the input from all the teams and our own thoughts and reflections we have developed the following protocol to measure efficacy in each country. It is important to keep in mind that our purpose is to provide for a design that will enable us to do a comparative analysis of the efficacy of P/CROs across countries. Therefore, it is very important that each team adhere to it as much as possible. However, beyond these basic data-collection requirements, each team should feel free to add whatever other measures, questions, and interviewees it wishes. In fact, we encourage each team to do so, since we are fully aware that the particular context of each country might call for additional measures of efficacy and strategies to obtain them, above and beyond those we ask for. Still, these should not be made at the expense of the protocol we have provided.

Who to Interview

Representatives of the mass media (i.e., newspapers, radio, and television) who have covered the conflict. Political leaders (formal and informal) who are identified with the conflict and who represent the various factions involved in the conflict.

Government officials (i.e., civil servants, state security) responsible for the management and handling of the conflict.

Academics and intellectuals who have studied and written about the conflict.

Recognized leaders of the P/CROs.

Representatives of international organizations, such as foundations, NGOs, or religious organizations, who have followed the conflict, and possibly contributed resources to P/CROs.

We would like each team to select, when possible, at least 4–5 interviewees in each category.

Topics to Cover

We recognize that it would be next to impossible to attribute causality to any of the P/CROs we are studying for specific developments toward the resolution of the conflict. Therefore, we are more interested in the extent to which the P/CROs as a movement or as a social institution have facilitated social, political, and cultural changes with regard to the conflict. In other words, we want to assess the effects of the peace movement as a whole. Still, in such an assessment, we would like you also to ask the interviewees whether they could single out one or more of the organizations we have studies that played a pivotal role in promoting the effect.

A. Impact on Peace/Conflict Resolution

Looking at the conflict from [the critical years], can you identify key events or developments that have contributed to the resolution of the conflict? [List each event and provide a brief description of it.]

To what extent did the peace movement play a role or contributed toward each of these events or developments?

If yes how? If not, why not?

If yes, can you identify any particular P/CROs or P/CRO activities that were especially important? [Provide a list of the 10 P/CROs to the interviewees.]

Are you aware of any decisions or discussions by the key decision makers in the conflict (i.e., leaders of the factions in the conflict, state officials, leaders of political parties) that might have been initiated or influenced because of the activities of the peace movement?

If yes, list the decisions or discussions and indicate which P/CRO activities influenced them?

B. Impact on the Peace-Making/ Conflict-Resolution Process

How much recognition of importance did the peace movement gain in the following?
a) mass media
b) the parties to the conflict
c) government officials

If recognized in importance, did some P/CROs gain greater recognition than others? [Provide a list of the 10 P/CROs to the interviewees.]

Over time, was the peace movement able to develop any access or links (formal or informal) to any of the main factions in the conflict (these may include political parties or factions, mass-based movements, and state officials)?

If yes, describe the nature of the access (e.g., informal consultation, lobbying, participation in formulating positions or policy statements).

If yes, did certain P/CROs have greater access than others? [Provide a list of the 10 P/CROs to the interviewees.]

What about access or links to government officials?

If yes, describe the nature of the access (e.g., informal consultation, lobbying, participation in formulating positions or policy statements).

If yes, did certain P/CROs have greater access than others? [Provide a list of the ten P/CROs to the interviewees.]

Did the peace movement bring about any changes in the political process (e.g., rise of new political parties, changes in political coalitions, changes in governmental procedures) that have contributed toward the peace/conflict resolution?

If yes, describe these changes.

If yes, did some P/CROs play a greater role in bringing about such changes than others? [Provide a list of the ten P/CROs to the interviewees.]

Did the peace movement serve as a catalyst for other organizations (i.e., business associations, religious organizations, professional associations, international organizations) to mobilize and participate in the peace process?

If yes, describe how.

If yes, did some P/CROs play a greater role than others? [Provide a list of the ten P/CROs to the interviewees.]

C. Impact in Defining the Conflict and Its Resolution

Did the peace movement bring about any changes in public perceptions about the following?
   a) the nature and reasons for the conflict
   b) how the conflict should be resolved

If yes, what were the nature of these changes?

If yes, to what extent were these ideas about the nature and resolution of the conflict picked up by political leaders and/or government officials?

If yes, did some P/CROs play a greater role than others? [Provide a list of the 10 P/CROs to the interviewees.]

Did the peace movement create any new ways (or new vocabulary) to define and describe the conflict, including the parties to the conflict, that were not used before?

If yes, how often were they expressed and conveyed in the mass media?

To what extent did the peace movement mobilize public support and/or raised the public sense of urgency for resolving the conflict?

To what extent did the peace movements introduce new norms of conduct or relations between people representing the various factions in the conflict (e.g., new images of the people involved in the conflict, new modes of dialogue)?

If yes, which P/CROs were particularly influential in introducing these new norms?

Did the peace movement link its ideas about peace/conflict resolution to other values such as democracy, human rights, social justice, and the like?

If yes, what other values were promoted?

If yes, to what extent were public perceptions toward the conflict also linked to these other values?

Did the peace movement develop a new set of strategies or activities (e.g., public demonstrations, dialogue groups, educational material, media events) to promote peace/conflict resolution that others not directly involved in the movement have adopted?

If yes, describe them.

Finally, looking at the country/region over the past twenty years of so, what do you think would have happened to the conflict and its resolution without the work of the P/CROs?

APPENDIX D: ORGANIZATIONS STUDIED IN THE INTERNATIONAL STUDY OF PEACE/CONFLICT-RESOLUTION ORGANIZATIONS

Phase I

South Africa

ACCORD
Azanian People's Organization (AZAPO)
Black Consciousness Movement
Black Sash
Call of Islam
Centre for Applied Legal Studies
Centre for Intergroup Studies/Centre for Conflict Resolution (CCR)
Centre for Policy Studies (CPS)
Centre for the Study of Violence and Reconciliation (CSVR)
Christian Institute of Southern Africa
Committee of Ten (Soweto Civic Association)
Community Agency for Social Enquiry (CASE)
Community Dispute Resolution Trust
Congress of South African Students (COSAS)
Congress of South African Trade Union, COSATU
Consultative Business Management
Conscientious Objectors' Support Group (COSG)
Detainees' Parents Support Committee (DPSC)
Diakonia
Ecumenical Monitors for Peace in South Africa (EMPSA)
End Conscription Campaign (ECC)
Five Freedoms Forum
Heuwssa Trust

Human Awareness Programme
Human Rights Commission (now Human Rights Committee)
Independent Mediation Service of South Africa (IMSSA)
Inkatha Institute
Institute for Black Research (IBR)
Institute for Contextual Theology
Institute for Defense Policy (IDP)
Institute for a Democratic Alternative for South Africa (Idasa)
Institute for Multi-Party Democracy
Johannesburg Democratic Action Committee (JODAC)
Kagiso Trust
Koinonia—Southern Africa
Kontac
Lawyers for Human Rights
Legal Resources Centre
Military Research Group
National Council of Trade Unions (NACTU)
National Council of Women
National Medical and Dental Association (Namda)
National Peace Accord Structures
National Union of South African Students/South African Students Congress
New Era Schools Trust (NEST)
Organization for Appropriate Social Services of South Africa (Oasssa)
Peace Action
Peace Vision
PLANACT
Promat
Quaker Peace Centre (QPC)
Reforum
South African Association for Conflict Resolution
South African Catholic Bishops Conference—Justice and Peace Commission
Justice and Peace Committee for Higher Education Trust (Sached)
South African Council of Churches (SACC)
South African Council on Sport (SACOS)
South African Freedom Foundation
South African Institute of Race Relations (SAIRR)
South African National Civic Organization (SANCO)
Surplus Peoples Project
Transvaal Rural Action Committee (TRAC)
Trust for Christian Outreach and Education
United Democratic Front (UDF)
Urban Foundation
Urban Monitoring and Awareness Committee

Vuleka Trust
Women for Peace (WFP)
Women's National Council
Young Christian Students (YCS)

Israel

Alternative Information Center (AIC)
Bat Shalom (Jerusalem link)
Clergy for Peace
Committee for Israeli-Palestinian Dialogue
Council for Peace and Security
East for Peace
International Center for Peace in the Middle East (ICPME)
Israeli Council for Israeli-Palestinian Peace (ICIPP)
Jewish-Arab Center/Givat Haviva
Mental Health Workers for the Advancement of Peace/IMUT
Movement for Peace and Security
New Outlook
Oasis for Peace/Neve Shalom
Oz Ve'shalom
Palestinians and Israelis for Non-Violence
Peace Generation/Dor Shalom
Peace Movement Coordinating Committee in Haifa and the North
Peace Now
Physicians for Human Rights
Rapprochement
Truman Institute for the Advancement of Peace in the Middle East
Wolfson Community Project—Akko
Women in Black
Workers' Hotline
Yesh Gvul

Northern Ireland

Ballynafeigh Community Development Centre
Clogher Valley Rural Development Centre (CVRDC)
Columbanus Centre of Reconciliation
Committee on the Administration of Justice (CAJ)
Community Relations Council (CRC)
Co-operation North
Corrymeela
Counteract

Dove House Resource Centre
Enniskillen Together
Evangelical Contribution on Northern Ireland (ECONI)
Holiday Projects West (HPW)
Initiative '92
Irish School of Ecumenics
Mediation Network Northern Ireland
National Union of Students/Union of Students in Ireland (NAS/USI)
North Belfast Community Development Centre
Northern Ireland Association for the Care and Resettlement of Offenders
    (NIACRO)
Northern Ireland Council for Integrated Education (NICIE)
Northern Ireland Voluntary Trust (NIVT)
Parents and Kids Together (PAKT)
Pat Finucane Centre
Peace and Reconciliation in Derry
Peace People
Peace Train
Protestant and Catholic Encounter (PACE)
Quaker House
Springfield Inter-Community Development Project (SICDP)
Ulster Community Action Network (UCAN)
Ulster Peoples College (UPC)
ULTACH Trust
Widows Against Violence Empower (WAVE)
Women Together for Peace
Women's Information Group (WIG)

Palestine

Due to the circumstances described in the Palestine Chapter, the Palestinian
team was not able to develop a formal list of NGOs for the first phase of the
research.

Phase II

South Africa

Black Sash
Centre for Applied Legals Studies
Centre for Intergroup Studies/Centre for Conflict Resolution (CCR)
Centre for Policy Studies (CPS)

Centre for the Study of Violence and Reconciliation (CSVR)
Christian Institute of Southern Africa
Congress of South African Trade Union, COSATU
Consultative Business Management
End Conscription Campaign (ECC)
Five Freedoms Forum
Heuwssa Trust
Human Rights Commission (now Human Rights Committee)
Independent Mediation Service of South Africa (IMSSA)
Inkatha Institute
Institute for Defense Policy (IDP)
Institute for a Democratic Alternative for South Africa (Idasa)
Institute for Multi-Party Democracy
Koinonia—Southern Africa
Lawyers for Human Rights
Military Research Group
National Council of Women
National Medical and Dental Association (Namda)
National Peace Accord Structures
National Union of South African Students/South African Students Congress
Organization for Appropriate Social Services of South Africa (Oasssa)
Quaker Peace Centre (QPC)
South African Catholic Bishops Conference—Justice and Peace Commission
Justice and Peace Committee for Higher Education Trust (Sached)
South African Council of Churches (SACC)
South African Institute of Race Relations (SAIRR)
South African National Civic Organization (SANCO)
Transvaal Rural Action Committee (TRAC)
United Democratic Front (UDF)
Women's National Council

Israel (same organizations studied in Phase I)

Alternative Information Center (AIC)
Bat Shalom (Jerusalem link)
Clergy for Peace
Committee for Israeli-Palestinian Dialogue
Council for Peace and Security
East for Peace
International Center for Peace in the Middle East (ICPME)
Israeli Council for Israeli-Palestinian Peace (ICIPP)
Jewish-Arab Center/Givat Haviva

Mental Health Workers for the Advancement of Peace/IMUT
Movement for Peace and Security
New Outlook
Oasis for Peace/Neve Shalom
Oz Ve'shalom
Palestinians and Israelis for Non-Violence
Peace Generation/Dor Shalom
Peace Movement Coordinating Committee in Haifa and the North
Peace Now
Physicians for Human Rights
Rapprochement
Truman Institute for the Advancement of Peace in the Middle East
Wolfson Community Project—Akko
Women in Black
Workers' Hotline
Yesh Gvul

Northern Ireland

This sample was actually larger than that of Phase I and included FAIT and
NIMMA.

Ballynafeigh Community Development Centre
Clogher Valley Rural Development Centre (CVRDC)
Columbanus Centre of Reconciliation
Committee on the Administration of Justice (CAJ)
Community Relations Council (CRC)
Co-operation North
Corrymeela
Counteract
Dove House Resource Centre
Enniskillen Together
Evangelical Contribution on Northern Ireland (ECONI)
Families Against Intimidation and Terror (FAIT)
Holiday Projects West (HPW)
Initiative '92
Irish School of Ecumenics
Mediation Network Northern Ireland
National Union of Students/Union of Students in Ireland (NAS/USI)
North Belfast Community Development Centre
Northern Ireland Association for the Care and Resettlement of Offenders
    (NIACRO)
Northern Ireland Council for Integrated Education (NICIE)

Northern Ireland Mixed Marriages Association (NIMMA)
Northern Ireland Voluntary Trust (NIVT)
Parents and Kids Together (PAKT)
Pat Finucane Centre
Peace and Reconciliation in Derry
Peace People
Peace Train
Protestant and Catholic Encounter (PACE)
Quaker House
Springfield Inter-Community Development Project (SICDP)
Ulster Community Action Network (UCAN)
Ulster Peoples College (UPC)
ULTACH Trust
Widows Against Violence Empower (WAVE)
Women Together for Peace
Women's Information Group (WIG)

Palestine

Al Haq
Bisan
Sabeel Liberation Theology Centre, Jerusalem
Muwatin—The Palestinian Insitute for the Study of Democracy
PCDE
IHRE
Maan Development Centre
PCG
Al Liqa'
CARE
WI'AM
Palestinian Academic Society for the Study of International Affairs (PASSIA)
Center for Palestine Research and Studies (CPRS)
Gaza Community Mental Health Programme

Phase III

South Africa

Black Sash
Koinonia—Sourthern Africa
Quaker Peace Centre
Justice and Peace Commission

End Conscription Campaign (ECC)
Centre for Intergroup Studies/Centre for Conflict Resolution (CCR)
Institute for a Democratic Alternative for South Africa (Idasa)
South African Institute of Race Relations (SAIRR)
Independent Mediation Service of South Africa (IMSSA)
Centre for the Study of Violence and Reconciliation (CSVR)

Israel

Alternative Information Center (AIC)
Bat Shalom (Jerusalem link)
Council for Peace and Security
Oz Ve'shalom
Peace Now
Physicians for Human Rights
Rapprochement
Women in Black
Yesh Gvul

Northern Ireland

Clogher Valley Rural Development Centre (CVRDC)
Committee on the Administration of Justice (CAJ)
Families Against Intimidation and Terror (FAIT)
Peace Train
Quaker House
Springfield Inter-Community Development Project (SICDP)
Ulster Peoples College (UPC)
Women Together for Peace

Palestine

Children of Abraham*
Rapprochement—Beit Sahour
Alternative Information Center (AIC)
Palestinian Center for Human Rights (PCHR)*
Committee for Dialogue of Peace Forces*
Jerusalem Center for Women (Jerusalem link)

* Not included in the international comparison

APPENDIX E: TEAMS AND ASSISTANTS FOR THE INTERNATIONAL STUDY OF PEACE/CONFLICT-RESOLUTION

Principal Investigators

Benjamin Gidron, Ben Gurion University
Stan Katz, Princeton University

Research Teams

South Africa

Rupert Taylor, University of Witzwatersrand
Anthony Egan, University of Witzwatersrand
Mark Shaw, Institute for Defense Policy
Adam Habib, Dept. of Policial Science, UD-W
Simon Stacey, Princeton University
Aubrey Lekwane
Jacklyn Cock, University of Witzwatersrand
Joanfie Van Wyk

Northern Ireland

Seamus Dunn, University of Ulster
Feargal Cochrane, Lancaster University
Ed Cairns, University of Ulster
Deirdre Heenan, University of Ulster
Sally McClean, University of Ulster

Palestine

Manuel Hassassian, Bethlehem University
George Sahhar, Bethlehem University

Israel

Tamar Hermann, Tel Aviv and Open University
Yuval Lebel, Open University
Peter Lemish, Bet Berl Teachers College

International Team

Yeheskel Hasenfeld, UCLA
Raviv Schwartz, Ben Gurion University
Megan Meyers, UCLA
Jonathan Crane, Hebrew Union College

Board of Advisors

Wilmot James (South Africa)
Adrian Guelke (Northern Ireland)
Quintin Oliver (Northern Ireland)
Galia Golan (Israel)
Musa Buedeiri (Palestine)
Virginia Hodgkinson (United States)
Helmut Anheier (United States)
Alan Abramson, Aspen Institute
Dirk Rumberg, Bertelsmann Foundation

SELECTED REFERENCES

Acker, J. "Feminist Goals and Organizing Process." In *Feminist Organizations*, ed. M. Feree and P. Y. Martin. Philadelphia: Temple University Press, 1995, pp. 137–144.

Blain, M. "Power and Practice in Peace Movement Discourse." *Research in Social Movements: Conflicts and Change* 2 (1989): 197–218.

Brown, M., ed. *The International Dimensions of Internal Conflict*. Cambridge: MIT Press, 1996.

Cable, S. "Professionalization in Social Movement Organization: A Case Study of Pennsylvanians for Biblical Morality." *Sociological Focus* 17 (1984): 287–304.

Carroll, W., and Ratner, R. S. "Master Framing and Cross-Movement Networking in Contemporary Social Movements." *Sociological Quarterly* 37 (1996): 601–625.

Chatfield, C. *The American Peace Movement*. New York: Twayne Publishers, 1991.

Chatfield, C. and van den Dungen, P. *Peace Movements and Political Culture*. Knoxville: University of Tennessee Press, 1989.

Cochrane, F. and Dunn, S. Final Country Report, Northern Ireland, 1998.

Cress, D. and Snow, D. "Mobilization at the Margins: Resources, Benefactors and the Viability of Homeless Social Movement Organizations." *American Sociological Review* 61 (1996): 1089–1109.

Dalton, R. *The Green Rainbow*. New Haven: Yale University Press, 1994.

Downton, J. and Wehr, P. "Peace Movements: The Role of Commitment and Community in Sustaining Member Participation." *Research in Social Movements, Conflicts and Change* 13 (1991): 113–134.

Edwards, B. and Marullo, S. "Organizational Mortality in a Declining Social Movement: Demise of Peace Movement Organizations in the End of the Cold War Era." *American Sociological Review* 60 (1995): 908–927.

Elias, R. and Turpin, J. eds. *Rethinking Peace*. Boulder: Lynne Rienner Publishers, 1994.

Ennis, J. "Fields of Action: Structure in Movements' Tactical Repertoires." *Sociological Forum* 2, no. 3 (1987): 520–533.

Feree, M. M. *Controversy and Coalition: New Feminist Movement*. New York: Maxwell Macmillan International, 1994.

Gamson, W. *The Strategy of Social Protest*. Homewood, Ill.: Dorsey Press, 1975.

Giliomee, H. "Introduction." In *The Elusive Search for Peace*, ed. H. Giliomee and J. Gagiano. South Africa: Oxford University Press, 1990.

Giugni, M., McAdam, D. and Tilly, C. *From Contention to Democracy*. Lanham, Md.: Rowman & Littlefield Publishers, 1998.

Hunt, S. and Benford, R. "Identity Talk in the Peace and Justice Movement." *Journal of Contemporary Ethnography* 22 (1994): 488–517.

Hyde, C. "Feminist Social Movement Organizations Survive the New Right." In *Feminist Organization*, ed. M. M. Ferree and P. Y. Martin. Philadelphia: Temple University Press, 1995, pp. 306–322.

James, E. "The Nonprofit Sector in Comparative Perspective.' In *The Nonprofit Sector*, ed. W. W. Powell. New Haven: Yale University Press, 1987, pp. 397–415.

Jenkins, C. and Klandermans, B. *The Politics of Social Protest*. Minneapolis: Minnesota University Press, 1995.

Jurgen, G. and Rucht, D. "Mesomobilization: Organizing and Framing Two Protest Campaigns." *American Journal of Sociology* 98 (1992): 555–596.

Katzenstein, M. F. and Mueller, C. M. *The Women's Movements of the United States and Western Europe*. Philadelphia: Temple University Press, 1987.

Kendrick, R. "Meaning and Participation: Perspectives of Peace Movement Participants." *Research in Social Movements, Conflicts and Change* 13 (1991): 91–III.

Kodama, K. and Vesa, U. *Towards a Comparative Analysis of Peace Movements*. Hants: Dartmouth, 1990.

Kriesberg, L. *International Conflict Resolution*. New Haven: Yale University Press, 1992.

Kriesi, H. "The Organizational Structure of New Social Movements in a Political Context." In *Comparative Perspectives on Social Movements*, ed. D. McAdam, J. McCarthy, and M. Zald. New York: Cambridge University Press, 1996, pp. 152–184.

Lipset, S. "The Social Requisites of Democracy Revisited." *American Sociological Review* 59 (1994): 1–22.

Lipsky, M. and Smith, S. R. "Nonprofit Organizations, Government and the Welfare State." *Political Science Quarterly* 104 (1989): 625–648.

Lofland, J. *Social Movement Organizations: Guide to Research on Insurgent Realities*. New York: Aldine de Gruyter, 1996.

Lofland, J. and Marullo, S. *Peace Movements in the 1980's: Social Science Perspectives*. New Brunswick, N.J.: Rutgers University Press, 1990.

Lund, M. *Preventing Violent Conflicts*. Washington, D.C.: United States Institute of Peace, 1996.

Macdonald, M. "The Dominant Communities and the Costs of Legitimacy." In *The Elusive Search for Peace*, ed. H. Giliomee and J. Gagiano. South Africa: Oxford University Press, 1989.

Maguire, D. "When the Streets Begin to Empty: The Demobilization of the British Peace Movement after 1983." *West European Politics* 15 (1994): 75–94.

Marwell, G. and Oliver, P. "Collective Action Theory and Social Movement Research." *Research in Social Movements, Conflict and Change* 7 (1984): 1–27.

Mattausch, J. "The Peace Movement: Some Answers Concerning its Social Nature and Structure." *International Sociology* 4 (1989): 217–225.

McAdam, D. "Tactical Innovation and the Pace of Insurgency." *American Sociological Review* 48 (1983): 735–754.

McAdam, D. "Conceptual Origins, Current Problems, Future Directions." In *Comparative Perspectives on Social Movements*, ed. D. McAdam, J. McCarthy, and M. Zald. New York: Cambridge University Press, 1996, pp. 23–40.

McAdam, D., McCarthy, J. and Zald, M. "Introduction: Opportunities, Mobilizing Structures, and Framing Processes—Toward a Synthetic, Comparative Perspective on Social Movements." In *Comparative Perspectives on Social Movements*, ed. D. McAdam, J. McCarthy, and M. Zald. New York: Cambridge University Press, 1996, pp. 1–20.

McAdam, D., McCarthy, J. D. and Zald, M. eds. *Comparative Perspectives on Social Movements*. New York: Cambridge University Press, 1996.

McCarthy, J. D. and Zald, M. *The Trend of Social Movements in America: Professionalization and Resource Mobilization*. Morristown, N.J.: General Learning Press, 1973.

McCarthy, K., Hodgkinson, V., Sumariwalla, R. and Associates. *The Nonprofit Sector in the Global Community*. San Francisco: Jossey-Bass, 1992.

Mertig, A. G. and Dunlap, R. E. "Public Approval of Environmental Protection and Other New Social Movement Goals in Western Europe and the United States." *International Journal of Public Opinion Research* 7 (1995): 145–156.

Minkoff, D. *Organizing for Equality: The Evolution of Women's and Racial-Ethnic Organizations in America 1955–1985*. New Brunswick, N.J.: Rutgers University Press, 1995.

Oskamp, S., Bodin, J. and Edwards, T. "Background Experiences and Attitudes of Peace Activists." *Journal of Psychology* 126 (1992): 49–61.

Ostrander, S. *Money for Change*. Philadelphia: Temple University Press, 1995.

Powell, W. ed., *The Nonprofit Sector*. New Haven: Yale University Press, 1987.

Ragin, C. *The Comparative Method*. Berkeley: University of California Press, 1987.

Rapaport, A. *Peace: An Idea Whose Time Has Come*. Ann Arbor: University of Michigan Press, 1992.

Rothschild-Whitt, J. "The Collectivist Organization: An Alternative to Rational Bureaucratic Models." *American Sociological Review* 44 (1979): 509–527.

Sarup, G. "A Reference Group Theory of Social Movements and Identity." *Social Science* 50 (1975): 219–226.

Schmitt, R. "Organizational Interlocks between New Social Movements and Traditional Elites: The Case of the West German Peace Movement." *European Journal of Political Research* 17 (1989): 583–598.

Seibel, W. "Government/Third Sector Relations in a Comparative Perspective: The Cases of France and West Germany." *Voluntas* 5 (1990): 42–61.

Snow, D. and Benford, R. "Ideology, Frame Resonance, and Participant Mobilization." *International Social Movement Research* 1 (1988): 197–217.

Snow, D. and Benford, R. "Master Frames and Cycles of Protest." In *Frontiers in Social Movement Theory*, ed. A. Morris and C. M. Mueller. New Haven: Yale University Press, 1992, pp. 133–155.

Salamon, L. M. and Anheier, H. K. "Social Origins of Civil Society: Explaining the Nonprofit Sector Cross-Nationally." *Voluntas* 9 (1998): 213–248.

Sussman, G. and B. Steel. "Support for Protest Methods and Political Strategies among Peace Movement Activists: Comparing the US, Great Britain, and the Federal Republic of Germany." *Western Political Quarterly* 44 (1991): 519–40.

Tilly, C. *From Mobilization to Revolution.* Reading, Pa.: Addison-Wesley, 1978.

Van den Dungen, P. ed. *West European Pacifism and the Strategy for Peace.* New York: St. Martin's, 1985.

Weiss, T. "Nongovernmental Organizations and Internal Conflict." In *The International Dimensions of Internal Conflict*, ed. M. Brown. Cambridge: MIT Press, 1996, pp. 435–460.

Zald, M. and Garner, R. A. "Social Movement Organizations: Growth, Decay, and Change." In *Social Movements in an Organizational Society*, ed. M. Zald and J. McCarthy. New Brunswick, N.J.: Transaction Books, 1987, pp. 121–141.

Zald, M. and McCarthy, J. "Social Movement Industries: Competition and Conflict among SMOs." In *Social Movements in an Organizational Society*, ed. M. Zald and J. McCarthy. New Brunswick, N.J.: Transaction Books, 1987, pp. 161–180.

INDEX

cultural symbols/tools, 19, 20, 214, 215–217, 219, 221

CVRDC (Northern Ireland). *See* Clogher Valley Rural Development Centre

Dakar Conference (1987), 4, 8, 20, 76, 82, 177, 208–209, 211, 213

death squads, 79

Declaration of Principles of 1993 (Washington, D.C.), 61, 207

Degenaar, Johan, 87

Deir Yasin massacre, 56

Dekker, Loet Douwes, 230

de Klerk, F. W., 8, 46–47, 213

Delmas treason trial (1988), 80

democratic institutions
British Irish policies and, 189
comparative P/CROs study and, 24
fundamental freedoms of, 11
Israelis and, 107, 115, 190, 209, 213, 218
NGO functions and, 9, 10–12
Palestinian development of, 133, 139, 140, 203
Palestinian resistance to, 132
P/CRO functioning and, 6
P/CRO goals and, 15, 19
population preparation for, 8
South African achievements, 3, 8, 47, 76, 87
South African goal of nonracial, 46–47, 85, 86, 87, 191, 203, 209
as South African P/CROs' focus, 19, 190–191, 192, 214
See also elections

demography. *See* socio-demographic features

demonstrations, 10, 217, 227
Israel, 59, 103, 112, 194
Northern Ireland, 49, 51, 153, 210, 217–218
by Palestinians. *See* Intifada
P/CRO comparisons, 180, 181, 182, 194, 197
South Africa, 41–42, 46, 70, 218

Derry marches/countermarches, 51

development organizations, 9

dialogue development, 15, 20, 181, 182, 183, 217
Israeli-Palestinian, 59, 60, 100, 103, 112–113, 121–122, 207, 215, 217
in Northern Ireland, 153, 154, 156, 158, 160, 189, 203, 208, 218
in South Africa, 75, 76, 177, 208–209, 211, 218

dialogue organizations, 25, 26

Diamond, L., 16

DiMaggio, P. D., 231

Disclosure of Foreign Funding Act of 1989 (South Africa), 80

dispute resolution. *See* conflict resolution

diversity recognition, 189, 191

dominant strategy of action, 181–182

Dove House Resource Centre (Northern Ireland), 154, 160, 166–167, 168

Downing Street Declaration (1993), 53, 168, 189

draft. *See* conscription

Dublin, 4, 47, 48

Duncan, Sheena, 77, 81

Durban labor strikes (1973), 70

Easter Rising of 1916 (Ireland), 48

East for Peace (Ha'mizrach Le'shalom) (Israel), 102, 115

East Jerusalem (Israel), 61

ECC (South Africa). *See* End Conscription Campaign

economic boycott, 8, 46, 63, 70

economic conditions
apartheid effects, 40, 43
Israeli, 56–57
Israeli/Palestinian disparities, 109
Northern Ireland community development, 19, 159
Northern Ireland downturn, 52
Northern Ireland grievances, 153
Palestinian peace moves and, 133
South African apartheid effects, 8, 40, 41–44, 46, 191
Zionist vs. non-Zionist Israeli peace groups and, 108
See also service organizations; welfare programs

education
advocacy groups, 5
anti-apartheid NGOs and, 79
Israeli NGOs and, 59
Northern Ireland and, 196, 49
Palestinian NGOs and, 138–139
Palestinian political ideology and, 132
South African apartheid and, 69, 79
South African nonracial policies and, 85–86
See also consciousness-raising; student protests; universities

Education Act of 1947 (Northern Ireland), 49

educational level
P/CRO leaders, 177, 72
P/CRO members, 98, 115, 116, 127n.33, 178

Education Policy Units (South Africa), 86

effectiveness of P/CROs, 202–222
definition problems, 202
theoretical perspective, 205–206

egalitarianism, 187, 197

Egypt
Arab League reinstatement, 60
Arab peace movement, 97, 123–124, 125n.12
Israeli accords (1979), 4, 58, 59, 101, 107, 125n.12, 211
Israeli conflicts, 56, 57–58

Einstein, Albert, 74, 85

elections, 8
apartheid restrictions, 69
first democratic South African, 3, 8, 47, 87
Irish, 48
Israeli, 61, 62, 101, 119, 121, 122
Northern Irish, 207

elites
alignment stability vs. instability and, 18
Israeli peace movement, 98, 115–116, 117, 128n.39, 178, 182
Israeli political establishment, 110, 126n.20, 213
Palestinian human rights advocates, 144
Palestinian NGOs, 130
Palestinian refugees, 56
as P/CRO allies, 18, 72

South African peace process and, 47
Zionist immigration and, 55
See also educational level; elites; universities
inter-community groups. *See* community
development
International Fund for Ireland, 165–166
international funding. *See* foreign funding
international relations
apartheid condemnations and, 41, 69–70, 220
economic boycott of South Africa and, 8, 46, 63, 70
Israeli peace groups and, 107–108
Northern Irish P/CROs and, 219
Palestinian consciousness-raising and, 137, 142, 143–144, 145–147, 208, 212, 215–216, 219
regional conflicts and, 62–63
See also foreign funding
interpersonal prejudice, 19
interpersonal skills, 20
interracial contact, 75
Intifada, 60–61, 62, 102, 103, 112–113, 114, 122–123, 133, 134
consciousness-raising by, 147–149, 219
human rights abuse awareness and, 143
Israeli peace movement's reading of, 219
Oslo Accords and, 146
Palestinian P/CRO development prior to and after, 139–140, 146, 190, 208, 209, 217
intractable conflicts, characteristics of, 7
IRA (Irish Republican Army), 4, 48, 49, 51–54, 154, 156, 187, 214
cease-fire, 3, 53, 54, 207, 208
Maze Prison hunger strike, 52–53
resurgence of, 51, 52
Iraq, 56, 60
Ireland
economic conditions, 50
history, 47–54
partition of, 48–49
unionism and, 156
See also Northern Ireland
Irish Americans, 193
Irish Free State, 48
Irish Parliamentary Party, 48
Irish Republican Army. *See* IRA
Isaac, Rael, 125n.11
Islamic radicals, 61–62
Islamic Resistance Movement (Hamas), 61, 144
Israel, 94–124
advocacy groups, 5
civil society growth in, 17
comparative view of conflict, 62
critical events in peace process, 207–208
Egyptian accords (1979), 4, 58, 59, 101, 107, 125n.12, 211
framing of conflict, 19, 190
historical background, 54–62
human rights violations and, 144–145
"magic moment" for, 4
meaning of "peace" in, 12, 25, 203
neutral third party and, 20
Palestinian accord (1993). *See* Oslo Accords

Palestinian consciousness-raising in, 147–149
peace movement status. *See* Israeli P/CROs
political/cultural contexts, 188–189
security ethos of, 59, 106–107, 121, 179, 215, 220
social movements and, 21
statehood declaration (1948), 56, 99, 130
U.S. loans, 193
See also Arab-Israeli conflict; Occupied Territories
Israeli-Arab War (1967), 10
Israeli Committee against the Demolition of Homes, 104
Israeli Council for Israeli-Palestinian Peace
(Ha'moetza Ha'yisraelit Le'shalom) (Israel-Palestine), 101, 112
Israeli Defense Force (IDF), 4, 56, 57, 59, 60, 61, 62, 113
Israeli Final Country Report (Hermann), 204, 207
Israeli Final Report, 211–212, 215, 218–219, 232
Israeli P/CROs, 3, 9, 10, 19, 94–124
achievements of, 123–124
backlashes to, 204
collectives, 186–187
critics of, 109–110
cultural change effects, 220
cultural symbols and, 215
decentralization of, 96
efficacy assessment, 95, 118–124, 203, 206, 207
foreign vs. domestic funding sources, 114, 179, 192–193, 204
formalization/professionalization of, 231
framing by, 190
goals of, 12, 15, 19, 142–143
heyday of, 101–102, 104
historical development of, 59, 60–61, 62, 95, 97–104, 178, 234
ideological diversity within, 107
ideological nuances of, 96
Israeli security concerns and, 179
joint Palestinian organizations, 10, 108, 113, 135, 148
leadership, 177
lists of, 261, 263–264, 266
media recognition/acceptance of, 218–219
number of groups/organizations, 97
obstacles to, 95
official disregard of, 94–95
organizational structure and dynamics, 110–115
organizations studied, 25
Palestinian consciousness-raising and, 147–149
Palestinian P/CRO relationship, 142–143
political access of, 209, 210, 213
political agenda of, 95, 106–110
political force of, 211–212
political naïveté charges against, 98, 117
public opinion influence of, 215
radical groups, 113–114
secular nature of, 118
socio-demographic features, 98, 115–118, 178
sophisticated slogans and publications, 116
study methodology, 96–97
study questionnaire translation, 31

peaceful protest. *See* nonviolence

peace-keeping, 8–9

peace-making, 4, 8

  P/CROs' indirect impact on, 207–209, 232–233

  theories of, 19–20

Peace Mizrachi (Israel) groups, 102, 107

peace movement organizations (PMOs), P/CROs

  contrasted with, 226

Peace Now (Israel), 3, 103, 114, 116, 117, 121, 126n.20

  achievements of, 215

  appeals by, 220

  challenges to, 102

  emergence of, 4, 59, 101–102

  funding sources, 229

  media use by, 218–219

  "Officers' Letter," 4, 107

  Oslo Accords signing and, 207

  political alliance and impact of, 210, 211–212

  professionalization of, 231

  protest measures, 217

Peace People (Northern Ireland), 3, 10

Peace Train (Northern Ireland), 4–5

  focus of, 187

  founding date and purpose, 154, 155–156

  funding sources, 163

  members and leaders, 159, 160–161

  risk and, 168

  tactics, 217

People's Democracy (Northern Ireland), 51

Peres, Shimon, 61, 103, 114, 120–121, 122, 124

Peres Center for Peace (Israel), 103–104

person-oriented frame, 188–189, 195

Peters, Rommel, 72

philanthropy, *See* charitable organizations

Physicians for Human Rights (Israel), 5, 113, 114, 177, 181, 217

  funding sources, 229

Plantation of Ulster, 47

PLO. *See* Palestine Liberation Organization

PMOs. *See* peace movement organizations

political action, 16

  Israeli peace movement and, 96, 99, 106–110

  Palestinian organization and, 57, 132, 214

political opportunity structures (POS), 17–18

political prisoners

  Israeli-Palestinian negotiations, 62

  Palestinians as, 132, 143, 144

  South African anti-apartheid, 78–79, 80, 218

  South African release of, 46

political system

  comparative P/CROs studies and, 187–188, 228

  Israeli extra-parliamentary activity and, 110–111, 113–114

  Israeli peace movement and, 95, 106–110, 119–122, 125n.12, 148, 179, 190, 204, 208, 209, 210, 211–212, 213, 217

  lobbying of, 180, 181, 194, 195–196

  Northern Ireland and, 8, 54, 153

  Northern Ireland P/CROs and, 159–160, 213–214

  open vs. repressive, 18

Palestinian development of, 133–134, 214

Palestinian P/CROs vs. Palestinian Authority, 147, 148, 211–212

  P/CROs' impact on, 209–214

  P/CROs' lobbying of, 195–96

  South African exclusions. *See* apartheid

  South African P/CROs and, 179, 190, 209, 210, 211, 213, 214

  See also democratic institutions; elections; left-wing politics; right-wing politics

Port Elizabeth Black Civic Organization, 81

POS. *See* political opportunity structures

poverty, 40, 52

Powell, W. W., 231

pragmatic collectives, 186–187

press. *See* media

professionalization, 5, 18, 230–232

  formal memberships vs., 183–184

  within Israeli peace movement, 114

  of Northern Ireland P/CROs, 164–165

  South African NGOs, 44

Professors for Political Strength (Israel), 127n.33

Progressive Federal Party (South Africa), 177, 211

Progressive Unionist Party (Northern Ireland), 161, 210

Project for the Study of Violence (PSV) (South Africa)

  founding date, 72

  name change, 88n.11

  work of, 74, 75

Protestants (Northern Ireland)

  Catholic coexistence goal, 15, 51, 216

  cease-fire and, 3, 53, 54, 207, 208

  community self-help and, 221

  historical background, 47–50

  P/CRO membership, 178

  social organizations, 52

  unionist perspective, 152

protests. *See* demonstrations

PSV (South Africa). *See* Project for the Study of Violence

public education. *See* consciousness-raising; education

public opinion

  Israeli-Palestinian conflict, 122–123, 212, 215, 218–219

  P/CROs' influence on, 182, 197–198, 215, 218–219

  See also media

QPC (South Africa). *See* Quaker Peace Centre

Quaker House (Northern Ireland), 20, 210

  cultural changes by, 218

  formation date and purpose, 154, 158

  funding source, 164

  international Quaker auspices of, 177, 179

  laissez-faire self-regulation of, 161

  neutral image of, 183, 195, 219

  risk and, 168

  target audience, 162

Quaker Peace Centre (QPC) (South Africa)

  charismatic leadership, 230

  formalization, 231